**The Party and Agricultural
Crisis Management in the USSR**

STUDIES IN SOVIET HISTORY AND SOCIETY

edited by Joseph S. Berliner, Seweryn Bialer, *and* Sheila Fitzpatrick

Research Guide to the Russian and Soviet Censuses
  edited by Ralph S. Clem

*The Party and Agricultural Crisis Management in
  the USSR* by Cynthia S. Kaplan

*Will the Non-Russians Rebel? State, Ethnicity,
  and Stability in the USSR* by Alexander J. Motyl

Revolution on the Volga: 1917 in Saratov
  by Donald J. Raleigh

The Party and Agricultural Crisis Management in the USSR

CYNTHIA S. KAPLAN

CORNELL UNIVERSITY PRESS

Ithaca and London

First published 1987 by Cornell University Press.

International Standard Book Number 0-8014-2021-0
Library of Congress Catalog Card Number 86-32223
Printed in the United States of America
Librarians: Library of Congress cataloging information
appears on the last page of the book.

The paper in this book is acid-free and meets the guidelines for permanence and durability of the Committee on Production Guidelines for Book Longevity of the Council on Library Resources.

In honor of my parents,
Harold Kaplan and Ann Goodman Kaplan,
and my sister,
Sharon T. Kaplan

Contents

Tables

Acknowledgments

This book had its beginnings almost a decade ago. In retrospect, many of its theoretical interests originated even earlier, when I first encountered the study of comparative politics and the Soviet Union at the University of Chicago. Since then I have greatly benefited from the hospitality of many institutions, teachers, and colleagues, but those first years opened a world of excitement for which I am particularly grateful. Through hours of conversation and courses Jeremy Azrael sparked an interest in the USSR which continues to grow. I am greatly indebted to him.

I was also particularly fortunate in my graduate advisers at Columbia University, Zbigniew Brzezinski and Seweryn Bialer. During my early years at Columbia, Professor Brzezinski carefully monitored my progress and supported my studies. Seweryn Bialer, whose erudition pushed me ever further toward an unattainable model of perfection, provided invaluable assistance throughout my graduate work. At a later stage, Thomas Bernstein's comments on an early version of this work were vital to its successful completion.

Other scholars have generously assisted my work. I have been greatly influenced by the scholarship of Jerry Hough, whose suggestions at an IREX (International Research and Exchanges Board) interview led me to add Rostov Oblast and agriculture to my research agenda. Vera Dunham provided valuable advice and was most gracious in sharing her unpublished work with me. Barbara Ann Chotiner and Blair Ruble have offered advice and support. I thank them.

Many institutions have supported my research on the role of local party organizations in Soviet agriculture. Columbia University and the then Russian Institute were most generous in providing President's fellowships and National Defense Foreign Language fellowships. IREX awarded me a preparatory fellowship for special language study before I embarked on research in the Soviet Union. When I returned to the United States, the Russian Institute supported me through its Junior Fellows Program and later, as the W. Averell Harriman Institute for the Advanced Study of the Soviet Union, allowed me to visit for a year as a postdoctoral Mellon fellow. I particularly thank Marshall Shulman, whose leadership of the Harriman Institute has been instrumental in training the next generation of Soviet scholars.

This book could not have been written without the support of the International Research and Exchanges Board. My participation in the Junior and Young Faculty Exchange during 1976–77 not only enabled me to conduct essential research but afforded me the privilege of living in Soviet society and meeting Soviet citizens. The importance of this experience cannot be overestimated. While on the IREX exchange, I enjoyed the hospitality of Leningrad State University and Moscow State University, and an assignment to Rostov-on-the-Don permitted me to consult with scholars there. I am grateful to all these Soviet institutions and to my Soviet colleagues and friends for their innumerable kindnesses and valuable assistance.

Several institutions at which I have taught also deserve thanks. Kalamazoo College provided funds at an early stage of my work. The University of Michigan and its Center for Russian and East European Studies provided library facilities and a hospitable environment in which to teach and write. Tulane University was most gracious in granting me a leave of absence for further work on the manuscript. Among my many debts to the University of Chicago, I owe thanks for the support of the Department of Political Science through the use of its computers. I particularly thank my colleague Lutz Erbring for his patience in introducing me to the world of microcomputing and for his assistance in reading and commenting on a manuscript far removed from the area of his own research.

This book owes a great deal to libraries in both the Soviet Union and the United States. I thank the Saltykov-Shchedrin Library (Leningrad), the Leningrad State University Library, the Lenin Library (Moscow), the library of the Institute of Scientific Information in the Social Sciences (Moscow), and especially the library of Leningrad's Academy of Science, where I read local newspapers. In the United States, the Library of Congress has on numerous occasions provided hospitality in the form of a private study. I have also benefited from the assistance of Nina Lencek and the late Vaclav Laska, respectively the Slavic bibliographers of Columbia University and the University of Chicago.

Material from my article "The Communist Party of the Soviet Union and Local Policy Implementation," *Journal of Politics* 45 (February 1983): 2–27, and my chapter "The Impact of World War II on the Party," in *The Impact of World War II on the Soviet Union*, edited by Susan J. Linz (Totowa, N.J.: Rowman & Allanheld, 1985), pp. 157–87, appear in this book. I thank the journal and Rowman & Allanheld for permission to use them.

CYNTHIA S. KAPLAN

Chicago, Illinois

Glossary

aikom	party committee of an administrative unit based on nationality
CPSU	Communist Party of the Soviet Union
gorkom	city committee of the Communist Party
kolkhoz	collective farm
kolkhozniki	workers on collective farms
krai	territory
kraikom	territorial committee of the Communist Party
MTS	machine tractor station
nomenklatura	roster of persons appointed to positions of responsibility in the Communist Party
obkom	provincial committee of the Communist Party
oblast	administrative subdivision of a republic
okrug	administrative district based on nationality
okruzhkom	party committee of an okrug
PPO	primary party organization
raiispolkom	district executive committee
raiispolkom soviet	executive committee of a district council
raikom	district or borough committee of the Communist Party
raion	district
raisoviet	district council (of workers' deputies)
rai'zemotdel	district land department

RAPO	district agroindustrial association
RSFSR	Russian Soviet Federated Socialist Republic
sel'soviet	village council
sovkhoz	state farm
sovkhozniki	workers on state farms
tolkach'	"pusher"; expeditor
zampolit	assistant director for political affairs

The Party and Agricultural
Crisis Management in the USSR

CHAPTER 1

Introduction: Party Unity and Soviet Development

Western scholars have traditionally described the Communist Party of the Soviet Union as a monolithic organization involved primarily in policy-making and ideological activities. This image reflects the focus of Western scholarship, which has concentrated on central party organs, such as the Politburo and the Central Committee, and on middle-level party activities in the industrial sector. Until recently, relatively few researchers have studied the role of local party organizations in the implementation of policy. This situation can be traced in part to the difficulty of obtaining evidence about party behavior. A more important factor, perhaps, is the preoccupation of Western analysts with general models of Soviet politics, which has led them to neglect research on informal institutional ties and on the functions of local organizations. In addition, the Soviet Union's own historical emphasis on ideology and heavy industry has no doubt helped to shape the concerns of Western research.

The evolution of the Soviet economy and the political/state system, which has managed to muddle through in a period of broad economic and social change, now obligates Western analysts to adopt a more sophisticated approach. In the last decade we have seen a shift in interest from model building to a concern with middle-level theory. At the same time, research has begun to focus on the actual behavior of the party and of other formal and informal groups and organizations.

Of course, even as we shift to the middle level of analysis, the party continues to occupy a prominent place on our agenda. Researchers have grown increasingly interested in party leaders' responses to the effects of economic change. The fundamental issue is whether the party is more threatened by economic development and technological change or by the negative consequences of their absence.

Some scholars argue that the party's legitimacy—and therefore its power—is threatened by economic development. In their view, a party whose authority is based on its political skills and ideology is a competitor of those managers (read experts) who seek authority on the basis of their technical or professional skills. In this scenario, the political nature of party authority is questioned and the party ultimately attempts to thwart technological development because it makes the party redundant at best and irrelevant at worst. This argument fails to consider, however, how an alternative basis of legitimacy might affect party behavior. Revolutionary parties that rely on ideology for their legitimation find it increasingly difficult to maintain the allegiance or compliance of their citizens as they turn to the task of creating a new state system and pursuing economic development. Political rhetoric declines in efficacy as citizens increasingly focus on their own economic well-being. The regime may seek to meet these economic expectations, but if it fails to do so or chooses to ignore them, its legitimate authority disintegrates. Ultimately, the regime is forced to turn to coercion.

In fact, of course, all regimes rely on a mix of ideology, economic performance, and coercion (broadly understood) to ensure the compliance of their populations. The nature of the mix, however, varies with the tasks of state building, and so do the costs and consequences of relying on each of its elements. In the case of the Soviet Union, we could argue that during the initial period of industrialization, when the economy was less complex than it has since become, the unintended consequences of coercion on the work force were less detrimental to the economy than they are now. Today coercion invites economic stagnation since it lowers worker productivity and undermines managers' willingness to take risks. In brief, the more mature the regime, the more it must rely on material rather than normative incentives, and the more complex the economy, the higher the price of coercion in terms of economic performance. Severe economic problems can eventually undermine political stability.

Against this background, then, we must consider an alternative pattern of party behavior. In this scenario, party legitimacy, no longer based primarily on ideology, relies increasingly on economic performance. Thus technological development and expertise become crucial for the regime's ultimate stability. Rather than being threatened by experts, the party seeks to increase its own level of expertise in order to improve economic performance, foster development, and, of course, supervise the experts. If we can assume that party leaders are aware of these contingencies, we may expect them to make choices accordingly. Indeed, it appears that the Brezhnev regime, in attempting to create a socialist welfare state, began to adopt this alternative pattern of behavior.

In any case, the issue of party legitimacy requires further study. The complexity of the issue also clearly requires that we analyze party behavior so that we can test our deductions while beginning to work empirically. To the extent that party behavior has been examined at all, these efforts thus far have been restricted primarily to policy making. Relatively little research has actually focused on policy implementation, despite the fact that political scientists have long recognized that policy is often effectively made in the process of its implementation. This research focus becomes even more important as societies and economies grow increasingly complex as a result of the multiplication of factors that affect policy and of the layers of organization responsible for carrying it out. In short, research on policy implementation is crucial if we are to understand how and why the party responds to economic development and technological change.

To the limited extent that political scientists and others who focus on the Soviet Union have examined the party's role in local administration, they have assumed that the party reacts to economic complexities in a uniform manner. Such unified responses are thought to be inherent in the party's hierarchical structure. Western scientists, whether they understand the party as an ideological instrument, a rational-technical organization, a system of prefectoral administration, or a corporate bureaucracy, have continued to treat it as a unified organization.[1] When one analyzes the party's actual role in policy implementation, however, this supposed unity quickly disappears, as some descriptive work on rural party organizations has suggested.[2] Increasingly, then, we must view the party as a complex organization whose functioning reflects the influence of diverse factors. If these factors vary by policy arena, we should expect organizational responses and patterns of behavior to vary as well.

This book seeks to understand the role that local party organizations play in the implementation of agricultural policy and how this role evolved after World War II. Agriculture is a vital policy arena in the Soviet Union, a country that has only recently become urbanized. It not only affects the well-being of the Soviet domestic economy but increasingly influences Soviet foreign policy and trade. In analyzing the party's role in agriculture, I will not examine policy making or evaluate agricultural policy, although both subjects merit study. Rather, I hope to throw light on the distinctive behavior of local party leaders in the implementation of agricultural policy.

Local party organs in rural areas could not replicate the party's role in industry and hope to succeed in implementing agricultural policy, for reasons that will become clear as we examine the factors that affect policy implementation—plan targets, the characteristics of party and farm personnel, and the policy environment. Agricultural administration required rural party leaders to adopt a mode of behavior unlike that of their comrades in the urban in-

1. See, for example, Merle Fainsod, *How Russia Is Ruled*, rev. and enl. ed. (Cambridge: Harvard University Press, 1967); Zbigniew Brzezinski and Samuel Huntington, *Political Power USA/USSR* (New York: Viking, 1965); Barrington Moore, Jr., *Terror and Progress USSR* (New York: Harper Torchbooks, 1954); George Fischer, *The Soviet System and Modern Society* (New York: Atherton, 1968); Jerry F. Hough, *The Soviet Prefects* (Cambridge: Harvard University Press, 1969); Alfred Meyer, *The Soviet Political System* (New York: Random House, 1965).

2. See Merle Fainsod, *Smolensk under Soviet Rule* (New York: Vintage, 1958); Robert F. Miller, *100,000 Tractors* (Cambridge: Harvard University Press, 1970). For a more theoretical perspective, see John A. Armstrong, "Party Bifurcation and Elite Interests," *Soviet Studies* 17 (April 1966): 417–30; T. H. Rigby, "Politics in the Mono-Organizational Society," in *Authoritarian Politics in Communist Europe*, ed. Andrew C. Janos (Berkeley: Institute of International Studies, University of California, 1976), pp. 31–80.

dustrial sector, and thereby to create a distinctive role for themselves in the administrative system. When we examine the crucial postwar years during which this distinctive behavior arose and was solidified into a pattern of administration, we begin to understand what lies behind party behavior and why it varies by policy arena. The differentiated behavior of local party organizations belies the purportedly uniform structure of the party. In place of a unified party we glimpse a segmented organizational structure in which both the cadres and their behavior are specific to particular policy arenas.

In our efforts to understand the roots of local party behavior, we must ask why the party has resisted particular adaptations in its own role despite radical changes in economic and social conditions, and to what extent resistance to change may actually be the result of nondecisions, that is, to what extent it results from the multitude of constraints that affect organizational behavior. The better our understanding of the sources of continuity—some might say lethargy—within the Soviet political system, the more sophisticated our assessment of the difficulties that Soviet leaders encounter when they do in fact decide to adapt to new conditions.

As we explore the party's role in the implementation of agricultural policy, with particular attention to the way it differs from its role in the more familiar industrial realm, the real difficulty of modifying party behavior becomes more comprehensible. At the same time, it becomes clear that the regime's attempts to transform administrative and institutional relations, which often hinge on the roles played by experts and local party leaders, did not emerge *de novo* at the beginning of the 1970s, but rather were part of a long history of complex organizational relations that evolved after World War II.

The Antecedents of Local Party Behavior

The roots of the postwar administrative system are found in the experiences of the 1930s and World War II. The party had to adjust to the new tasks chosen by its leaders and to a changing environment. Its informal behavior, like that of any complex organization, was influenced by both the conditions it had created and those it could not control. Before World War II the regime had been preoc-

cupied by its revolutionary task of transforming society and developing the economy; when it took on the task of postwar
recovery and the consolidation of the Soviet administrative system, the patterns of party behavior in the industrial and agricultural sectors began to diverge.

During industrialization and collectivization, the party acted
upon the rest of society as an external force, mobilizing the masses,
attacking the "remnants" of the past, and constructing new Soviet
institutions. It played an instrumental role in both industry and
agriculture. As Stalin turned from the task of transforming Soviet
society to the challenges of administering it, however, the party's
role began to change. Now, Seweryn Bialer has pointed out, the
"prime function of the [party] apparatus . . . [was] to participate in
the administration of the state. Its 'clients' were not the party itself,
but primarily other bureaucracies."[3] The way the party apparatus
participated in state administration defined both the scope and
the nature of the party's function in the Soviet system. The party's
administrative role in industry clearly differed from the role it
played in agriculture.

The nature of party and state elites of course helped to shape
the administrative role of the party. Stalin's cultural revolution of
the 1930s created a new technical intelligentsia that was ready to
occupy the vast majority of state and party positions. In industry,
the presence of these cadres facilitated the removal of both the
prerevolutionary experts and to some extent the red directors, and
led to an expansion of the industrial managers' professional autonomy.[4] This trend was intensified by the purges. By the end of
the 1930s, cooperation between the new technical intelligentsia
and local political leaders had increased.[5] It can be argued that
the common educational backgrounds of many local industrial
and party leaders contributed to their greater capacity to share
authority in an increasingly interdependent relationship. The
sharing of authority, to the extent that it occurred, paved the way
for what Jerry Hough has characterized as a prefectoral system of
administration, in which first obkom secretaries provided coor-

3. Seweryn Bialer, *Stalin's Successors: Leadership, Stability, and Change in
the Soviet Union* (New York: Cambridge University Press, 1980), p. 16.

4. Kendall E. Bailes, *Technology and Society under Lenin and Stalin* (Princeton:
Princeton University Press, 1978), pp. 287–93, 324–28.

5. Ibid., pp. 295, 333–35.

dinating functions.[6] The emergence of a politically reliable, technically competent industrial elite facilitated the party's with-
drawal from day-to-day administration in the industrial sector.

No comparable agricultural intelligentsia existed. Stalin's cultural revolution had failed to increase the number of agricultural
experts substantially. From 1928 to 1941, the proportion of new
agricultural specialists who had graduated from a university or
institute of higher learning fell from 12 percent to 7.7 percent.[7]
This decline reflected the greater importance that Stalin accorded
to industry. Without a technically competent, politically reliable
agricultural intelligentsia to take charge of production, the party
acted through its own special representatives and through the
heads of machine tractor stations.[8]

The Great Purge provided the opportunity for—indeed, necessitated—the emergence of a new generation of leaders. The purge
struck the leading members of the party apparatus with great force.
These losses, along with wartime casualties, left a vacuum to be
filled by the inexperienced political generation that emerged in
1938–41.[9] The absence of experienced party cadres broke the phys-
ical link by which past behavior could be directly replicated.

To the degree that this new generation of party and state leaders
had any professional experience, it was gained during prewar
mobilization and the war. This background shaped their future
roles in policy implementation. The emergency conditions of
those years required industrial and agricultural production at any
cost, and this situation naturally tended to concentrate political
authority in the hands of the local party organizations. Before the
war, the Soviet administrative system had been an amalgam of
local chaos and attempts at overt central control. The decimation
of the party by the purges had left it at a disadvantage vis-à-vis
state and police organs. Only in the extraordinary conditions pro-

6. Hough, *Soviet Prefects.*
7. *Vysshee obrazovanie v SSSR Stat. sb.* (Moscow: Gosstatizdat TsSU SSSR,
1961), p. 52. Percentages are calculated in Bailes, *Technology and Society*, p. 219
(see also p. 220).
8. For the mid- to late 1930s, see Miller, *100,000 Tractors*, chap. 9, esp. pp.
256–60. Also see I. I. Vinogradov, *Politotdely MTS i sovkhozov v gody Velikoi
Otechestvennoi voiny (1941–1943 gg.)* (Leningrad: Izdatel'stvo Leningradskogo
Universiteta, 1976).
9. Bialer, *Stalin's Successors*, p. 60.

duced by the war did the local party emerge with renewed authority as a center for decision making. The fact that this new role developed while local party organizations were often relieved of direct supervision by central party representatives was to have important consequences for postwar party behavior.[10]

After the war, the regime repudiated the local party's direct intervention in economic decision making and policy implementation. In the industrial sector, local party leaders had become accustomed to issuing directives to be carried out by state economic cadres. Now these line functions gradually reverted to economic leaders. This change reflected Moscow's political preference for less direct interference in matters of daily economic administration and more attention to political issues, such as indoctrination and mobilization. It responded as well to the fact that industrial leaders were often better qualified for management functions than the party leaders who had been exercising them. In any event, the cumulative effect of postwar economic conditions fostered an interdependent relationship between local party and state leaders in the industrial sector. In fact, even during the war, secretaries of obkoms—provincial party committees—had frequently enjoyed cooperative relationships with industrial managers.

In the agricultural sector, in contrast, wartime conditions served to enlarge the role played by raion (district) party organizations in production.[11] Thus an important precedent was established for postwar behavior. The factors that transformed the local party's direct role in industry into a more coordinative, supervisory role after the war were either weak or absent altogether in the agricultural sector.

The Institutionalization of Local Party Relations

The years from 1945 to 1953 served as a crucible in which the party's new role was refined. The end of World War II marked the emergence of the mature Stalinist system. Although the Stalinist revolution had ended in the 1930s, the purges and the war delayed

10. N. S. Patolichev, *Ispytanie na zrelost'* (Moscow: Politizdat, 1977), pp. 281–82.
    11. Ibid., p. 272.

the institutionalization of the new, conservative Soviet system. The characteristics of this system were to structure the conditions in which members of the postpurge generation gained their first experience as administrators and full-time party officials in a non-crisis atmosphere. As the Soviet regime became increasingly concerned with the maintenance of the status quo, it came to be characterized by

- the system of mass terror;
- the extinction of the party as a movement;
- the shapelessness of the macro-political organization;
- an extreme mobilizational model of economic growth, tied to goals of achieving military power, and the political consequences thereof;
- a heterogeneous value system which favored economic, status, and power stratification, fostered extraordinary cultural uniformity, and was tied to extreme nationalism;
- the end of the revolutionary impulse to change society and the persistence of a conservative status quo attitude toward existing institutions;
- the system of personal dictatorship.[12]

The primary goal of the postwar regime was to conserve the institutions established in the 1930s. If those institutions were to survive intact, the postwar administration had to redefine the relationship between state and party organs which had emerged during the war. Previously, as the "movement model" suggests, the party had encouraged systematic change.[13] What was the appropriate role for the party in an increasingly conservative system?

The party's new postwar role represented a dilemma for Soviet leaders. As the political elite increasingly focused on administering established institutions, the depth of party involvement in routine matters of administration became controversial, especially in relation to the economy. Indeed, the proper division of the

12. Bialer, Stalin's Successors, p. 10.
13. See Robert C. Tucker, "On Revolutionary Mass-Movement Regimes," in The Soviet Political Mind, ed. Tucker, rev. ed. (New York: Norton, 1971), pp. 3–19.

party's attention and activities between the economic and political spheres was itself at issue.[14]

The political activities of local party organs were clearly to be strengthened, although party organizations were simultaneously urged to supervise the work of economic organizations. The leading party journal, *Partiinaia zhizn'*, declared in 1946, "The main direction of party work in the immediate period must be the *strengthening of our local party organs, which will be judged by what our party organs do* through [their] ability to establish actual supervision [*kontrol'*] over the activity of state and economic organs at the local level, to criticize, to eliminate defects in their work, and to fulfill their political and organizational *role among the masses.*" In order to perform these duties, the party was to maintain its independence from economic organizations and thus was no longer to be involved in daily economic matters. "The Bolshevik method of directing the economy consists of systematic aid to economic organs, their strengthening, not their displacement; it directs the economy not in spite of economic organs but through them."[15] As one Western scholar has observed, "involvement of local party organs in the administrative process has, indeed, prevented a precise definition of the authority and responsibilities of every official and the establishment of clear lines of authority."[16]

On the one hand, the party's direct involvement in economic details for supervisory purposes carried with it the danger of interfering with and possibly supplanting economic officials. On the other hand, if the party disengaged itself from economic details in order to devote itself entirely to political issues, it might well lack the basic economic knowledge needed for effective supervision. Some scholars have argued, however, that this dilemma is more apparent than real. State economic officials, rather than being displaced by local party leaders, might form a management team with them in order to deal with the ambiguities produced by official policies. Jerry Hough, the main proponent of this view, maintains that the

14. L. Slepov, "Stalinskaia programma pod'ema partiino-politicheskoi raboty," *Bol'shevik*, no. 3 (February 1952), pp. 25–26. Slepov discusses the February–March 1947 Plenum of the Central Committee.

15. "Peredovaia-zadacha partiinoi raboty v sovremenykh usloviiakh," *Partiinaia zhizn'*, no. 1 (November 1946), pp. 18–20; italics in original.

16. Hough, *Soviet Prefects*, p. 3.

party's exercise of kontrol' was not synonymous with direct intervention in economic administration. Consequently, the concept of
edinonachalie, one-man management, permitted economic leaders to direct policy implementation while party leaders supervised and coordinated such activities.[17] As we shall see, this development reflects the conditions and policies associated with the
industrial sector. The same ambiguity that arose from the new official party role led to quite a different outcome in agriculture: agricultural leaders were indeed often displaced by local party cadres.

Thus, the ambiguity engendered by the formal demands made
on the party led local organizations to respond in their own ways,
according to their policy arena. Party behavior was shaped by the
particularities of plan goals, investment priorities, background
characteristics of state and party personnel, and the policy environment. Ultimately the party's actual role not only differed from
its official definition but varied widely by sector. Thus the party's
behavior in regard to agriculture differed from that associated with
the pervasive image of the party in Western scholarship, an image
based primarily on the party's industrial activities. The murky
division of responsibility between state and party cadres in agriculture permitted local rural party leaders to assume both line
and staff administrative functions. As a result, the displacement
of agricultural leaders by local party representatives became a
central feature of the system of agricultural crisis management in
the Soviet Union.

Crisis Management in Agriculture

Structural Origins

The factors that shape the party's organizational behavior—the
nature of the economy, the characteristics of personnel, and the
policy environment—form an integrated whole. Briefly stated, the
highly centralized nature of the Soviet economy produces a system
of crisis management. Central planning produces a taut economic
plan with extraordinarily difficult targets. With little flexibility on
the input side of production, management is under constant pres-

---

17. Jerry F. Hough, "The Soviet Concept of the Relationship between the Lower
Party Organs and the State Administration," *Slavic Review* 24 (June 1965): 222.

sure to fulfill plan targets. Inadequate coordination between production units associated with different hierarchies contributes to managerial crises. One way to alleviate such difficulties would be to delegate authority from the center to local authorities through a system of either decentralization or deconcentration.[18] Despite the economic rationality of such an approach, the postwar Stalinist system remained formally centralized.

Although the general characteristics of crisis management pertain to the entire Soviet system, the crisis management associated with industry and with agriculture had distinctive features. The ability of industrial managers to adjust the assortment and quality of the goods they produced, to obtain assistance from central ministries, and to use informal, quasi-legal means to obtain supplies, such as reliance on a *tolkach*—an expediter who works as a supply agent at a factory[19]—enhanced their authority. These practices were encouraged by a natural tendency toward deconcentration in standardized production, industry's high priority within the USSR, and the managers' own expertise and experience.[20] During industrial crises, therefore, managers increased their professional autonomy. In agriculture, by contrast, crisis management produced an informal pattern of administrative behavior in which the local rural party apparatus supplanted agricultural leaders.

Several factors peculiar to agriculture explain this phenomenon. First, leadership at the collective farm tended to be inexpert and politically unreliable. These characteristics limited the autonomy enjoyed by rural leaders, and their position was further weakened by the fact that local party organs exercised control over their appointment and dismissal. Second, as agricultural production was by its very nature highly uncertain, it required greater flexibility than industrial production. The central plan prevented such flexibility without resort to extraordinary measures—that is, party

18. "By 'deconcentration' is meant the devolution of authority *within* the hierarchy of the state administration, usually from a central administration to the field. The devolution of authority from the central government to legally distinct minor units of government, such as provinces and communes, . . . [is] referred to as 'decentralization' " (Robert Fried, *The Italian Prefects: A Study in Administrative Politics* [New Haven: Yale University Press, 1963], p. 17).

19. Fainsod, *How Russia Is Ruled*, p. 508.

20. Peter M. Blau, "Decentralization in Bureaucracies," in *Power in Organizations*, ed. Mayer N. Zald (Nashville: Vanderbilt University Press, 1970), pp. 150–74.

intervention.[21] Third, agriculture's low priority, along with the nature of agrarian production, made the substitution of materials in the production process infeasible and prevented the gross alteration of plan targets. Under the cumulative weight of these factors, farm managers could achieve the increases in production stipulated by the plan only by increasing labor productivity. The labor force had to be mobilized. The party's authority to launch such campaigns far exceeded that of local economic and state leaders, who might sympathize with the peasants' plight. Thus it was rural local party secretaries and their representatives who became crisis managers, thereby assuming direct control over policy implementation.

Postwar Evolution

Postwar party behavior evolved under the diverse conditions of crisis management. As the industrialization process neared completion, the party developed a more purely political role at the workplace and a coordinative staff role at the provincial level. The party bureaucracy supervised and verified the work of industrial managers. Urban local party organs were also involved in the political education and mobilization of workers. Yet the urban party only rarely managed a factory or established the structure of the workplace itself. Given the nature of the industrial environment, the party had to remove itself from day-to-day decision making and policy implementation in order to avoid duplicating the roles of state cadres. As a result, local party leaders assumed staff positions from which they could pressure or assist industrial managers. Industrial leaders remained in charge of policy implementation.

The party played a very different role in the agrarian sector. It remained an active participant in the transformation of agriculture after the war. The demands placed upon local party leaders fostered their active involvement in line administration, particularly in the resolution of day-to-day problems. As the distinction be-

21. Roy D. Laird, "The Politics of Soviet Agriculture," in *Soviet Agriculture and Peasant Affairs*, ed. Laird (Lawrence: University of Kansas Press, 1963), p. 326; James R. Millar, "Post-Stalin Agriculture and Its Future," in *The Soviet Union since Stalin*, ed. Stephen F. Cohen, Alexander Rabinowitch, and Robert Sharlet (Bloomington: Indiana University Press, 1980), p. 149.

tween line and staff personnel grew obscure, some state agricultural personnel were actually supplanted by party leaders. The party's sporadic undermining of rural leaders' authority prevented the institutionalization of agricultural administration in the Soviet Union. This circumstance has important consequences for the system's ability to reform itself.

The patterns of behavior associated with agricultural crisis management have enjoyed considerable longevity. Their persistence is rooted in at least two major sources. First, many of the factors that gave rise to postwar party behavior continued in existence through the 1970s. Second, just as the presence of a new postwar generation was critical in expediting the emergence of a new role for the party, so the long-time stability of cadres after the war served to perpetuate party behavior. Postpurge and wartime leaders, members of the Brezhnev generation, began to relinquish their hold on power only in the mid- to late 1970s. Their replication of behavioral patterns hindered attempts to alter local authority relations. These relations had to change if local agricultural leaders were to exercise greater authority in the implementation of policy. The resultant expansion of agricultural leaders' authority could in principle stabilize agricultural administration—indeed, institutionalize it. It can be argued that greater certainty in administration would contribute to a more rational and therefore more effective system of agricultural production.

The party's segmentation has also had significant unintended results. It continues to affect party–state relations, finding particular reflection in the issue of professional autonomy. The "red" versus "expert" debate over the nature of state leaders' qualifications evolved quite differently in the agricultural sector than it did in industry.

The segmentation of the party seen in behavior patterns, cadre qualifications, and career ladders also affects policy making as younger local cadres begin to enjoy upward mobility and assume decision-making positions. These leaders, long associated with sectoral interests, may find it more difficult to reach compromises than the generalists of the Brezhnev era did. As party leaders increasingly specialize in policy areas and enjoy the same qualifications as experts, they may form informal networks with state and expert cadres on the basis of policy sectors. Such arrangements would alter the policy-making process and affect the regime's ability to reform and delegate administrative authority. Party leaders who view policy from the same perspective as the experts may no longer see policy reform and the delegation of authority as undermining the party's legitimacy; indeed, the potentially positive results of reform may seem to enhance their own and the regime's legitimacy. Thus the evolution from the Brezhnev to the Gorbachev generation will be profoundly influenced by the segmented nature of the party.

In examining the thesis that rural party leaders assumed a direct economic role in agricultural crisis management after the war, the following chapters first analyze independent variables that affect organizational behavior. Our focus then shifts to the dependent variable—the party's actual behavior in agricultural policy implementation—with special attention to two case studies: Leningrad Oblast, an industrial and urban province, and Rostov Oblast, a predominantly agricultural province. The distinctive patterns of party behavior in agriculture are then compared with those in industry to demonstrate the segmentation of the party. We conclude by examining the reasons for the persistence of party behavior and the consequences that arise from it.

The major questions posed in each chapter and the kind of evidence examined may be summarized briefly. Chapter 2 examines the policy environment, defined as the nature of the Soviet economy, the work force, and the political penetration of the countryside. Special attention is devoted to the effects of World War II on these factors, which serve as the givens in our quest for independent variables that shape party behavior. Our object here is to assess the degree of difficulty produced by the policy environment for agricultural policy implementation. Chapter 3 expands these themes by examining Soviet postwar agricultural policy in detail with the explicit purpose of assessing its contribution to the crisis of agricultural policy implementation. Its central theme is how particular features of the plan exert pressure on agricultural leaders.

Chapter 4 focuses on the agricultural leaders of the postwar era—who they were, where they came from, and what type of qualifications they had—so that we may assess the thesis that the regime initially sought leaders who could control agricultural production rather than experts. The educational qualifications of agricultural leaders, their job tenure, their geographic origins, and their political credentials were the critical factors in their ability or inability to carry out agricultural policy. Chapter 5 explores the same factors in the case of party leaders and pursues the issue of party segmentation through a comparison of rural and urban party leaders' qualifications. Both chapters are concerned with the effects of such characteristics on the functioning of local leaders in policy implementation. These chapters argue not that these background characteristics actually determine behavior but rather that in the agricultural context they contribute to a leader's ability to carry out the plan. Unless the policy environment and the degree of difficulty posed by plan targets are accounted for, personnel characteristics are meaningless; indeed, their use would constitute a methodological error.

The party's role in agricultural crisis management, the dependent variable, is examined in detail in chapter 6 and compared with the behavior of party organizations in industry in chapter 7. Chapter 6 examines who exercises authority and on what basis. Particular attention is devoted to the distribution of authority both within the party hierarchy and in party–state relations. These chapters seek to demonstrate that fundamental differences in party behavior are associated with policy sectors and have their roots in the dynamics of organizational theory.

The final chapter examines informal party behavior after its formative years, post-1953. It highlights those factors that have fostered the persistence of party behavior in spite of economic and social change in the Soviet Union. The focus is on the qualifications of leaders, the issue of professional autonomy for agricultural experts, and the current policy environment in light of the post-1965 agricultural programs. The unintended consequences of party behavior for agricultural reform and state–party relations receive special attention.

CHAPTER 2

The Policy Environment

The implementation of agricultural policy after World War II
was shaped by the characteristics of the Soviet economy, the nature of the postwar work force, and the extent of the party's political penetration of the countryside. These factors structured the
context in which the pressures arising from responsibility for the
implementation of agricultural policy interacted with the characteristics of party and state leaders to define their authority relationship. The outcome of this interaction gave rise to a
distinctive pattern of agricultural crisis management. Local party
leaders' role in agricultural crisis management evolved as a result
of the formal definition of the party's role, the conditions of policy
implementation, the pressure created by difficult policy goals, and
the absence of local leaders who could ensure the successful implementation of policy. Thus a complex array of political, economic, personnel, and demographic factors was instrumental in
the evolution of party behavior at the local level.

The factors that differentiated the rural and urban sectors reflected natural conditions, the consequences of prewar policy preferences, and the disproportionate effects of the war on the rural
sector. In a sense, they set the necessary but not sufficient conditions for the pattern of rural administration which arose after
the war. By specifying objective conditions that made successful

agricultural policy implementation difficult at best and reliance on nonparty personnel risky, they fostered reliance on local party leaders for the implementation of agricultural policy. This reliance, however, was not inevitable. If agricultural policy in the late 1940s and early 1950s had not intensified the difficulties of agricultural production or if agricultural leaders had had greater expertise and the trust of the party, local rural party leaders might not have intruded on their domain. Certainly, central political theoreticians rejected the party's pronounced role in the implementation of economic policy. As earlier studies have demonstrated, urban party leaders conformed more closely to the indirect supervisory role preferred by central party authorities than did their counterparts in rural areas.[1]

The differences associated with the exogenous factors that defined the rural policy environment were relative, not absolute. They reflected the fact that agriculture faced more difficult conditions than industry, in large part because the political preferences and economic priorities of the Soviet regime favored industry. In the long run, the policy environment reinforced behavioral patterns. Ultimately, these patterns impeded the Soviet regime's attempts to alter policy preferences and priorities and to restructure rural administration during the 1960s and 1970s.

When we explore the implications of the regime's economic and political priorities, the consequences of World War II, and the political penetration of the countryside for the implementation of agricultural policy, the fundamental importance of the Soviet regime's economic and political preferences becomes apparent. The urban industrial and rural agricultural sectors have distinctive characteristics, and the regime's ongoing preferences intensified these differences. Whether these distinguishing characteristics can be traced to the material circumstances of the two sectors or to policy preferences, they made policy more difficult to implement in agriculture than in industry. It should be remembered, too, that the regime's own preferences shaped the criteria of success. Thus the differences between the local party's roles in the implemen-

---

1. See Jerry F. Hough, *The Soviet Prefects* (Cambridge: Harvard University Press, 1969); Cynthia S. Kaplan, "The Role of the Communist Party of the Soviet Union in the Implementation of Industrial and Agrarian Policy: Leningrad, 1946–1953." Ph.D. dissertation, Columbia University, 1981.

tation of industrial and agricultural policies arose at least in part as an unintended consequence of the regime's economic and political preferences.

Priorities and Structure of the Soviet Economy

The Soviet economy's fundamental characteristics originated with the Stalinist model of economic development. This growth strategy sought rapid industrialization at the expense of agricultural development.[2] Although the Stalinist model was not inevitable, as Stephen Cohen has argued, it did reflect Marxism's political preference for workers over the potentially reactionary peasants and for industrial over agrarian society as a step toward communism.[3] Forced industrialization also was a means by which comparatively backward Russia could justify its skipping of Marx's historical stages of development under the leadership of the vanguard of the proletariat, the Communist Party. It also may be argued that by the 1930s, the emphasis on heavy industry served military purposes. The Stalinist model's success in industrial production was bought at the price of extraordinary suffering in the rural sector and the stifling of consumer demand. The structure and priorities evidenced by the Soviet economy reflect the regime's economic and political choices.

The two central features of the Stalinist economy, centralized structure and planning and the priority given to heavy industry (A sector) over light industry (B sector) and agriculture have had deep-seated, long-term consequences. These consequences have been more severe for the agricultural sector than for industry. The nature of industrial production itself contributed to the difference in consequences. The process of industrial production permits standardization and routinization, so that uncertainty is minimized and the delegation of authority thus becomes somewhat

2. Whether agriculture actually financed industrialization is now a subject of debate. See James R. Millar, "Mass Collectivization and the Contribution of Soviet Agriculture to the First Five-Year Plan," *Slavic Review* 31 (1974): 750–66; James R. Millar and Alec Nove, "Was Stalin Really Necessary? A Debate on Collectivization," *Problems of Communism* 25 (1976): 49–66.

3. See Stephen F. Cohen, *Bukharin and the Bolshevik Revolution* (New York: Knopf, 1973).

less risky.[4] Although the practice of "storming" associated with monthly or quarterly goals and the political trials and threats against bourgeois experts disrupted industrialization, by the middle of the 1930s Soviet policy began to emphasize the necessity of technical expertise in industrial production.[5] By the end of the 1930s, industrial managers, who were increasingly red and expert, began to enjoy limited autonomy. Minor violations of behavioral norms, such as the use of a tolkach (an expediter) to obtain resources and the manipulation of production in order to reach minimal targets, were overlooked in the name of plan fulfillment. Indeed, central ministries attempted to protect Soviet managers from political interference in economic matters within the factory. Thus, although central planning by no means provided rational goals during the first five-year plans, the nature of industrial production and the regime's growing confidence in industrial managers permitted patterns of informal behavior which mitigated the severest consequences of the plans' irrationalities in the industrial sector.[6]

In sharp contrast to industry, agriculture is in direct conflict with the system of centralized control represented by the Stalinist model.[7] The high degree of uncertainty associated with agricultural production calls for flexibility.[8] To the extent that agricul-

4. See Peter M. Blau, "Decentralization in Bureaucracies," in Power in Organizations, ed. Mayer N. Zald (Nashville: Vanderbilt University Press, 1970).

5. Kendall E. Bailes, Technology and Society under Lenin and Stalin (Princeton: Princeton University Press, 1968); Jeremy R. Azrael, Managerial Power and Soviet Politics (Cambridge: Harvard University Press, 1966).

6. The growing autonomy of industrial managers may not be shared by those in light industry. For an assessment of the rationality of the First, Second, Third, Fourth, and Fifth five-year plans, see Eugene Zaleski, Planning for Economic Growth in the Soviet Union, 1918–1932, trans. and ed. Marie-Christine MacAndrew and G. Warren Nutter (Chapel Hill: University of North Carolina Press, 1971), and Stalinist Planning for Economic Growth, 1933–1952, trans. and ed. Marie-Christine MacAndrew and John H. Moore (Chapel Hill: University of North Carolina Press, 1980).

7. Note that the emphasis in this context is on the degree of local flexibility as reflected in agricultural leaders' autonomy in implementing policy. Logically, this question may be separated from the argument that only a capitalist system that provides individual incentives can make Soviet agriculture efficient.

8. Roy D. Laird, "The Politics of Soviet Agriculture," in Soviet Agricultural and Peasant Affairs, ed. Roy D. Laird (Lawrence: University of Kansas Press, 1968), p. 326; James R. Millar, "Post-Stalin Agriculture and Its Future," in The Soviet Union since Stalin, ed. Stephen F. Cohen, Alexander Rabinowitch, and Robert Sharlet (Bloomington: Indiana University Press, 1980), p. 149.

ture's vulnerability to the vagaries of nature can be limited, as by the use of chemical fertilizers and irrigation, the means require capital investment. And capital investment, as we shall see, was lacking.

These observations speak to the problems of a centrally planned agricultural sector without reference to the rationality of the goals posited. Clearly, the procurement quotas and prices paid for agricultural products during the 1930s, and to a lesser extent later, were dictated by a system focused almost solely on securing agricultural production for the support of the urban work force, even when this goal required the virtual expropriation of agricultural produce.[9] Witness the advent of artificially produced famines during collectivization. Indeed, planning, with its implicit image of set targets, may be a misnomer. Agriculture under Stalin was an arena of constant attack, campaigning, and uncertainty. The sector was transformed through the use of intimidation and direct force. Collectives were organized through campaigns led by outside party and komsomol leaders.[10] These strategies produced an agricultural sector characterized by chronic uncertainty, alienation, and suspicion.

Given the high priority accorded to industry and the special position allotted to workers, Soviet political leaders held agriculture and peasants in low esteem. Indeed, peasants and rural society were viewed as remnants of a past to be overcome, suspect as harborers of an incipient petty-bourgeois mentality. Two additional political factors illustrate agriculture's position in the USSR. Unlike the ministries of the heavy industrial sector, the Ministry of Agriculture wielded little power. It neither appointed nor certified chairmen of *kolkhozy* (collective farms). Though directors of *sovkhozy* (state farms) were at least technically certified by their ministry, agricultural ministries did not function as the protectors of their sector's interests or of its leading cadres. A second factor of considerable significance was the politicization of agronomy. Even if scientific expertise had been recognized as desirable for agricultural leaders, it would have been hard to come

9. Alec Nove, *An Economic History of the USSR* (Baltimore: Penguin, 1969), pp. 299–300.

10. Moshe Lewin, *Russian Peasants and Soviet Power*, trans. Irene Nove and John Biggart (Evanston: Northwestern University Press, 1968).

by after the rise of Lysenkoism shut the door on the study of biology and especially of genetics.[11]

Two additional economic aspects of the Stanlinist plan of development reflect agriculture's disadvantaged position in relation to industry. The premium placed on heavy industrial development led to the neglect of other economic sectors. The allocation of capital investment to heavy industry—the A sector—resulted in the severe undercapitalization of agriculture.[12] In 1937 a plan to increase the capital allocated to agriculture in order to further mechanization was announced, but little came of it. At the start of World War II, agricultural mechanization was still primitive and spotty.[13]

Agricultural production was characterized by extensive cultivation and the intensive use of labor. The kolkhoz sector received limited capital investment from the state and was expected to capitalize itself from "excess" income.[14] As procurement prices often did not cover the actual cost of production, little money remained to invest.[15] Peasants on kolkhozy whose state income was figured on the basis of trudo den' (workday), a system highly dependent on the economic welfare of the kolkhoz, received little monetary income before the war and limited payment in kind. Indeed, they worked at the kolkhoz in order to retain the right to a private plot, from which they both subsisted and earned money through kolkhoz market sales.[16] While the undercapitalization of agriculture was promoting its labor-intensiveness, Soviet labor policies were encouraging peasants to migrate to the cities in order

11. See David Joravsky, The Lysenko Affair (Cambridge: Harvard University Press, 1970); Zhores Medvedev, The Rise and Fall of T. D. Lysenko (New York: Columbia University Press, 1969).

12. Zaleski, Stalinist Planning, pp. 228–59, 403–38, esp. 426.

13. Iu. V. Arutiunian, Mekhanizatory sel'skogo khoziaistva SSSR v 1929–1957 gg. (Moscow: Nauka, 1959); M. A. Vyltsan, Zavershaiushchii etap sozdaniia kolkhoznogo stroia (1935–1937 gg.) (Moscow: Nauka, 1978), esp. pp. 80–98.

14. Zaleski, Stalinist Planning, p. 435; Nove, Economic History, pp. 298, 299.

15. See, for example, Nove, Economic History, pp. 299–300.

16. "In 1939, some 700,000 (out of a total of 19.3 million) households received no grain at all, and distribution to several million others must have been exceedingly small. In 1940, 6.8 percent of collective farms distributed no grain at all as income in kind, while another 42.2 percent issued only less than one kilogram per labor-day worked. During the same year, one-eighth of the farms paid no cash for labor-days worked, while 54.8 percent paid less than 0.60 rubles (of the 1940, old variety)" (ibid., p. 55). Also see Zaleski, Stalinist Planning, pp. 474–76.

to augment the industrial work force. Programs of organized labor recruitment and industrial training schools sought to implement these policies.[17]

Clearly the rationale behind Soviet agricultural policy was non-economic in the sense that it evinced little concern for the welfare of the sector itself. This is not to say that the policy was without rationality altogether. The highly centralized Stalinist model of economic development maximized the regime's ability to pursue its primary goal of developing heavy industry. With industrial development came an ever-increasing urban population, which had to be fed. Agriculture was treated as a sector to be exploited in the pursuit of the regime's primary goal, industrialization. Thus agriculture was subject to both the uncertainties of nature and the extraordinary demands imposed by the Stalinist system. As a consequence, agricultural policy was to be implemented in a highly politicized crisis environment.

The Consequences of World War II

The impact of World War II on the Soviet economy and the demographic structure of Soviet society had different implications for industry and agriculture. The war's effect on agriculture and the rural sector was more extensive and perhaps more enduring than that on industry and urban life. The entire Soviet population paid a tremendous price in human suffering for its victory over Nazi Germany. Yet it can be argued that the rural sector suffered more lasting economic effects because of its initially disadvantaged status and its subordinate role in the recovery effort.[18]

N. A. Voznesensky, in his classic *Soviet Economy during World War II*, highlighted the economic significance of Nazi devastation in occupied territory: "The regions of the USSR which underwent

17. M. Ia. Sonin, *Vosproizvodstvo rabochei sily v SSSR i balans truda* (Moscow: Gosplanizdat, 1959), pp. 178–89.

18. It should be noted that initial pronouncements on economic recovery did not appear to stress heavy industry to the exclusion of other economic sectors. This emphasis emerged in the course of the cold war. See, for example, N. A. Voznesenskii, "Piatiletnii plan vosstanovleniia i razvitiia narodnogo khoziaistva SSSR na 1946–1950 gg.: Doklad na Pervoi Sessii Verkhovnogo Soveta SSSR," *Bol'shevik*, no. 6 (March 1946), pp. 69–92.

a temporary occupation were of considerable relative importance with respect to the whole territory of the USSR: they accounted for 45 percent of the population, 33 percent of the gross output of industry, 47 percent of the sown area, 45 percent of the number of livestock (in terms of cattle), and 55 percent of the length of railroad lines." Voznesensky observed in addition that "in the formerly occupied territory of the USSR the following were completely or partially destroyed or looted: 31,850 plants, factories and other industrial enterprises, exclusive of small enterprises and shops, 1,876 *sovkhozes*, 2,890 machine tractor stations, [and] 98,000 *kolkhozes*."[19] The ultimate impact of this widespread economic destruction on production must be assessed directly in formerly occupied areas, and the assessment must take into account the effect of wartime economic policies on the nation as a whole. Indeed, policies that sought to ameliorate the direct devastation of Nazi occupation warrant particular attention. These wartime policies facilitated future industrial recovery, while analogous agricultural policies portended only minor assistance in the monumental recovery effort that confronted the sector.

Industrial production benefited from the evacuation of productive capacity to the East and high levels of capital investment to facilitate reconstruction in formerly occupied areas. Voznesensky noted:

> After the critical point in the decline of output was passed at the end of 1941, the growth of industrial output in the USSR continued from month to month in the course of all of 1942. Gross output of all branches of industry of the USSR increased more than 1.5 times between January and December 1942. In 1943, output in all the crucial branches of industry, transportation, and of the whole war economy, rose anew. Gross output of industry increased by 17 percent in 1943 as against 1942. . . . The volume of capital construction in the USSR during three years of the Patriotic War (1942, 1943, and 1944) amounted to 79 billion rubles, exclusive of the value of evacuated equipment.[20]

As a result of the evacuation of industry and the construction of new industry during the war, the industrial potential of the USSR

19. Nikolai A. Voznesensky, *The Economy of the USSR during World War II* (Washington, D.C.: Public Affairs Press, 1948), pp. 94–95.
    20. Ibid., p. 26.

in 1945 was only 8 percent below that of 1940, despite the fact
that 70 percent of the productive capacity of the western and
southern areas of the USSR were still not functioning.[21] Although
"the industrial output of the liberated areas in 1945 was only 30
percent of its 1940 level, according to Iurii Prikhod'ko, "by mid-
1945 some two-thirds of the industrial enterprises in those areas
were back in production."[22] The rapid recovery of heavy industry
in the formerly occupied zones was facilitated by the fact that 85
percent of 1.4 billion rubles devoted to industrial recovery in
liberated raions in 1943 was directed toward coal, ferrous metals,
military industry, and energy.[23] It has been argued that the evacuated enterprises did not play the significant role in industrial
recovery usually attributed to them because of the problems of
conversion to civilian production and the lack of labor and raw
materials after the war; all the same, the combined effects of the
evacuated enterprises and the rapid reconstruction of the European industrial base permitted Soviet industry (essentially heavy
industry) to confront the Fourth and Fifth five-year plans from a
position far more advantageous than agriculture's.[24]

Agricultural gross production declined 60 percent during the
war and livestock 87 percent.[25] The effects of wartime destruction
on agriculture were compounded by state policies during and after
the war which failed to ensure the sector sufficient capital investment, mechanization, or labor. Capital investment in agriculture "declined from 19 percent in 1940 to a low of 4 percent in

21. E. Iu. Lokshin, Promyshlennost' SSSR: Ocherk istorii, 1940–1963 (Moscow:
Mysl', 1964), p. 35, cited in M. I. Khlusov, Razvitie sovetskoi industrii, 1946–1948
(Moscow: Nauka, 1977), p. 22. See also Sanford R. Lieberman, "The Evacuation
of Industry in the Soviet Union during World War II, Soviet Studies 35 (January
1983): 90–102.

22. Iu. A. Prikhod'ko, Vosstanovlenie industrii, 1942–50 (Moscow: Mysl', 1973),
p. 181, cited in Timothy Dunmore, The Stalinist Command Economy: The Soviet
State Apparatus and Economic Policy, 1945–53 (New York: St. Martin's Press,
1980), p. 38.

23. Prikhod'ko, Vosstanovlenie industrii, p. 67.

24. Dunmore, Stalinist Command Economy, p. 71. This point is disputed in
A. F. Khavin, "Novyi moguchii pod'em tiazheloi promyshlennosti SSSR v 1946–
1950 gg.," Istoriia SSSR, no. 1 (1963), pp. 25, 26.

25. Istoriia Velikoi Otechestvennoi voiny Sovetskogo Soiuza, 1941–1945, vol. 5
(Moscow: Ministerstva Oborony Soiuza SSR, 1963), pp. 391–92, cited in Bor'ba
partii i rabochego klassa za vosstanovlenie i razvitie narodnogo khoziaistva SSSR
(1943–1950 gg.), ed. A. V. Krasnov et al. (Moscow: Mysl', 1978), pp. 220–21.

1942," James Millar writes.[26] In fact, not only did capital investment fall precipitously, but the regime's financial policies actually sought to absorb the sector's liquidity. Peasants were forced to contribute to the wartime effort through increased taxes and war loans.[27] The effect of these policies was to remove any "excess" liquidity from the rural sector resulting from the sale of produce at peasant markets. In 1943 the state agricultural recovery program was allocated 4.7 billion rubles, according to a party journal; "in 1944 this amount increased to 7 billion rubles and in 1945 to more than 9.2 billion rubles."[28] Because of the sector's absolute need for capital and the allocation of funds primarily to the sovkhoz sector, however (kolkhozy were expected to provide their own capital funds from income), these efforts fell far short of minimum needs.

Other measures aimed at promoting the recovery of agricultural production included the reevacuation of livestock and the reconstruction of machine tractor stations. The reevacuation of livestock was of no substantial aid to formerly occupied areas because the lack of fodder and sheds led to heavy losses.[29] Although the prewar number of machine tractor stations was reached in 1945, the mechanization of agricultural production remained limited. Most of the machinery was antiquated.[30] To the extent that these policies achieved even limited results, their achievements were largely lost during the 1946 drought, which lowered agricultural production below 1945 levels. The gross production of grain, for example, fell

26. James R. Millar, The ABCs of Soviet Socialism (Urbana: University of Illinois Press, 1981), p. 44. State capital investment in agriculture for 1941–46 was 3 billion rubles. During the same period, kolkhozy contributed 14.8 billion rubles. Total capital investment in agriculture constituted 11% of the total capital investment in the economy. See Sel'skoe khoziaistvo SSSR St. sb. (Moscow: Gosstatizdat, 1960), p. 387.

27. Agricultural taxes almost quadrupled on July 3, 1943, over the levels of 1942. The peasants' share of war loans increased "from 17.0 percent in 1940 and 22.7 percent in 1942 to 35.1 percent in 1944"; these outlays enabled the state "to absorb the liquid assets held by the rural population" (K. N. Plotnikov, Biudzet sotsialisticheskogo gosudarstva [Moscow: Gosfinizdat, 1948], pp. 279, 289–91, cited in Zaleski, Stalinist Planning, pp. 321–22).

28. Partiinoe stroitel'stvo, no. 2 (1944), p. 19, cited in Bor'ba partii, ed. Krasnov, p. 221.

29. I. M. Volkov, Trudovoi podvig sovetskogo krest'ianstva v poslevoennye gody: Kolkhozy SSSR v 1946–1950 godakh (Moscow: Mysl', 1972), p. 155.

30. Arutiunian, Mekhanizatory, p. 99.

to approximately 38 percent of that harvested in 1940. By the end of 1946 the state resolved to increase acreage in the nonaffected areas of the East.[31] Thus, despite initial recovery efforts, agriculture not only failed to attain its prewar levels of production but actually fell below those at the end of the war.

The agricultural sector's material losses and its low level of capitalization continued to place a premium on labor and extensive cultivation at a time when the rural labor force was being transformed by the loss of 20 million Soviet citizens during the war and the maiming of countless others. For the first time, agricultural labor was to become a scarce resource. "In 1943 the kolkhoz population was 47.3 million people, or 62 percent of its 1940 level, but the number of those capable of work was 16.6 million people, or 47 percent" according to a Soviet historian.[32] The decline in the size of the kolkhoz population reflected not only wartime losses and the drafting of men into the armed services but also the drafting of rural residents into the industrial work force. The proportion of the peasant population capable of work fell from 47 percent in 1940 to 35 percent in 1944, primarily as a result of the drafting of men into the army.[33] In 1942 the urban population constituted 77.1 percent of those mobilized for work in industry, construction, and transport; they accounted for 41 percent in 1943, 38 percent in 1944. The proportion of the rural population mobilized for work grew from 22.9 percent in 1942 to 61.7 percent in 1944. This increase can be attributed primarily to the cooptation of the population of liberated areas.[34] The structure of the rural population changed, as table 2.1 indicates.[35] In 1944, however, occupied regions of the RSFSR and those behind the front lines showed relatively little variation in the structure of the kolkhoz population over the age of 12 (see table 2.2).

The total number of agricultural workers declined 16.9 percent from 1940 to 1945; those at kolkhozy declined 28.8 percent from

31. Volkov, *Trudovoi podvig*, pp. 128–30.
32. A. V. Mitrofanova, *Rabochii klass SSSR v gody Velikoi Otechestvennoi voiny* (Moscow: Nauka, 1971), p. 424. Data are drawn from Iu. V. Arutiunian, *Sovetskoe krest'ianstvo v gody Velikoi Otechestvennoi voiny*, 2d ed. (Moscow: Nauka, 1970), p. 324.
33. Arutiunian, *Sovetskoe krest'ianstvo*, p. 323.
34. Mitrofanova, *Rabochii klass*, pp. 427–28.
35. See also ibid., p. 329.

TABLE 2.1
Percentage of peasant population capable and incapable of work, 1940 and 1944

	1940	1944
Population capable of work		
Adults	47%	35%
Adolescents	9	10
Population incapable of work	44	55
All population	100%	100%

Source: Based on Iu. V. Arutiunian, *Sovetskoe krest'ianstvo v gody Velikoi Otechestvennoi voiny*, 2d ed. (Moscow: Nauka, 1970), p. 332, table 45.

1941 to 1945.[36] At first, demobilization reversed this trend. As of January 1, 1946, the kolkhoz population had declined 15 percent from the prewar level, but among those capable of work the decline was 32.5 percent. The decline in the number of males capable of work was especially significant at kolkhozy in occupied areas.[37] From 1940 until 1945, the number of males working at kolkhozy declined by nearly a third.[38] Although the demobilization of the army beginning in 1945 initially contributed to the expansion of the rural work force (the number of males capable of work at kolkhozy increased 25 percent in 1946 and 17.6 percent in 1947),

TABLE 2.2
Kolkhoz population capable and incapable of work in occupied and unoccupied regions of the RSFSR, 1944 (percent)

	Unoccupied regions	Occupied regions
Population capable of work		
Men	7%	6%
Women	29	29
Adolescents	10	11
All population capable of work	46%	46%
Population incapable of work	54	54
All population	100%	100%

Source: Iu. V. Ariutunian, *Sovetskoe krest'ianstvo v gody Velikoi Otechestvennoi voiny*, 2d ed. (Moscow: Nauka, 1970), p. 327, table 47.

36. Arutiunian, *Sovetskoe krest'ianstvo*, p. 75. The industrial work force declined by 19% during the war (1940–45) (*Trud v SSSR* [Moscow: Statistika, 1968], p. 124).

37. I. M. Volkov, "Kolkhoznaia derevnia v pervyi poslevoennyi god," *Voprosy istorii*, no. 1 (1966), p. 17.

38. I. M. Volkov et al., eds., *Sovetskaia derevnia v pervye poslevoennye gody, 1946–1950* (Moscow: Nauka, 1978), p. 42.

TABLE 2.3

Number of workers at kolkhozy, sovkhozy, and machine tractor stations (MTS's) and in industry, 1940–1955 (in millions)

	1940	1945	1950	1955
Administrators	3.2	2.7	2.8	2.8
Kolkhozniki	26.1	21.2	25.1	22.5
Sovkhozniki	1.6	2.0	2.2	2.5
MTS workers[a]	0.4	0.2	0.6	2.8
All agricultural workers	31.3	26.1	30.7	30.6
Industrial workers[b]	9.9	8.1	12.2	15.5

[a]Includes workers at tractor repair stations.
[b]Exclusive of white-collar employees.
Source: Trud v SSSR Statisticheskii sbornik (Moscow: Statistika, 1968), pp. 81, 124.

subsequent state labor policies and voluntary rural migration reversed this trend.[39] The effects of the war, labor policies, and individual migration can be seen in table 2.3.

Soviet labor policies sought to recruit rural males into industrial jobs either directly or through training programs.[40] These policies had a particularly pronounced effect on the rural labor force during the initial postwar period; voluntary out-migration was to grow in importance later. In 1948, for example, the organized recruitment of labor for industrial jobs and for seasonal employment and work reserves accounted for the departure of more than 1.5 million adolescent and adult kolkhozniki capable of work.[41] In 1950, kolkhozniki in the RSFSR signed 71 percent of organized recruitment contracts.[42] Labor reserve schools served as another mechanism

39. Volkov, Trudovoi podvig, p. 218; I. M. Volkov, "Kolkhoznoe krest'ianstvo SSSR v pervye poslevoennye gody (1946–1950 gg.)," Voprosy istorii, no. 6 (1970), p. 5.

40. Postanovlenie Soveta Ministrov SSSR, May 21, 1947, "O poriadke provedeniia organizovannogo nabora rabochikh," Reshennia partii i pravitel'stva po khoziaistvennym voprosam (1917–1967 gg.), vol. 3: 1941–1952 gody (Moscow: Politicheskoi Literatury, 1968), pp. 428–32; O. M. Verbitskaia, "Izmeneniia chislennosti sostava kolkhoznogo krest'ianstva RSFSR v pervye poslevoennye gody (1946–1950)," Istoriia SSSR, no. 5 (September/October 1980), p. 127.

41. Volkov, Trudovoi podvig, p. 218.

42. Sheila Fitzpatrick, "Postwar Soviet Society: The 'Return to Normalcy,' 1944–1953," in The Impact of World War II on the Soviet Union, ed. Susan Linz (Totowa, N.J.: Rowman & Allanheld, 1985), p. 139; M. Ia. Sonin, Vosproizvodstvo, p. 207. A. V. Smirnov, "Rabochie kadry tiazhelogo mashinostroeniia SSSR v 1946–1958 gg.," Istoricheskie zapiski 71 (1962): 3, table 1, documents the decline of organized recruitment of rural laborers for work in heavy machine construction enterprises.

by which rural males were transferred to the industrial sector. Rural youths constituted two-thirds of the students at labor reserve schools between 1946 and 1958.[43]

Although organized recruitment and labor reserve schools declined in importance through the postwar years, rural migration continued. Many rural residents independently migrated to join the industrial labor force, and it is reasonable to assume that many of them were young people.[44] Poor working conditions and low pay, which even in 1950 did not reach 1940 levels, contributed to voluntary out-migration.[45] The kolkhoz population had declined by "almost 500,000 in 1948, 1.6 million in 1949, and 1.5 million in 1950," according to an archival source. As a result of the war and migration, "at the end of the Fourth Five-Year Plan, five years after the end of the war, kolkhozy had 26.7 percent fewer [males capable of work] than in 1940."[46] In the early 1950s, according to Sheila Fitzpatrick, "migration from the countryside to town became a flood. In the period 1950–54, 9 million persons are said to have migrated permanently to the towns out of a total rural–urban migration of 24.6 million over the twenty-year period 1939–1959; and the rural share of total population dropped from 61% to 56%"[47] Although direct data documenting the transfer of rural residents to urban industrial jobs is unavailable, postwar labor policies clearly expedited rural migration. Thus labor-intensive agricultural production suffered from labor shortages produced by both wartime losses and the state's efforts to transfer workers from the countryside to the cities. As the rural labor force declined in size, it declined in quality as well.

Soviet postwar labor policies clearly favored the industrial sector, despite the industrial work force's more rapid recovery from the direct effects of the war (see table 2.4). Although the number of workers and white- collar employees had declined by 59 percent

Such workers accounted for 5.6% of those hired in 1949, 1.4% in 1951, and only 0.08% in 1954.

43. Smirnov, "Rabochie kadry," p. 6.

44. See S. L. Seniavskii, "Rabochii klass SSSR," Voprosy istorii, no. 2 (1969), p. 11; M. I. Khlusov, Razvitie sovetskoi industrii, 1946–1958 (Moscow: Nauka, 1977), pp. 94–95.

45. Volkov, Trudovoi podvig, p. 257; Fitzpatrick, "Return to Normalcy"; Verbitskaia, "Izmeneniia," p. 128.

46. Volkov, "Kolkhoznoe krest'ianstvo," pp. 6, 7.

47. Fitzpatrick, "Return to Normalcy," p. 149. Fitzpatrick cites Sonin, Vosproizvodstvo, pp. 144, 148.

TABLE 2.4
Percentage change in number of workers employed in industry and in
agricultural sectors, 1940–45 and 1945–50

	1940–45	1945–50
Industrial workers	− 9.1	+ 50.1
Kolkhozniki	− 19.0	+ 17.5
Sovkhozniki	+ 22.0	+ 18.2

Sources: Calculated from *Sel'skoe khoziaistvo SSSR St. sb.* (Moscow: Statistika, 1972), p. 13; M. Ia. Sonin, *Vosproizvodstvo rabochei sily v SSSR i balans truda* (Moscow: Gosplaniz-dat, 1959), p. 51.

in 1942, their numbers had already begun to increase in 1943. By 1945 the number of workers in both classifications in the economy as a whole (including state-sector agricultural workers) was only 13 percent below their 1940 levels.[48] As a result of state labor policies during the Fourth Five-Year Plan, "the number of workers and white-collar employees grew by almost 12 million and in 1950 had attained 119 percent of the prewar level. The proportion of the rural population declined from 67 percent in 1940 to 60 percent by the beginning of 1951.[49]

World War II intensified the problems that arose from the Stalinist model of economic development and further undermined those factors that were essential to agricultural production. The war resulted in the widespread destruction of kolkhoz and sovkhoz capital goods in the most productive areas of the country. From the time of prewar economic mobilization, capital investment in agriculture dwindled to virtually nothing. But perhaps the most significant direct effect of the war on agricultural production was the drastic human losses it imposed. The war seriously disrupted the demographic structure of the rural labor force. These direct consequences were intensified by the regime's policy preferences during postwar reconstruction. This combination of factors created extreme pressure on those responsible for policy implementation.

Clearly, the urban industrial sector also suffered severe losses during the war. Even before the war ended, however, Soviet decision makers adopted policies that promoted the reconstruction of heavy industry in the European part of the Soviet Union. These

48. Mitrofanova, *Rabochii klass*, p. 436, and *Trud v SSSR*, pp. 22–25, 32.
49. Volkov, *Trudovoi podvig*, pp. 218–19.

preferences find their most vivid expression in the regime's policies in regard to capital investment and labor. The industrial sector benefited from the evacuation of at least part of its productive capacity, and as the occupation of European areas ended, the regime immediately sought to concentrate capital investment in the reconstruction of the economy's base in heavy industry. The loss of urban industrial workers was to be compensated for not only by capital investment but by the transfer of rural workers, as we have seen. These efforts led to the further weakening of the rural labor force. Thus the regime's traditional preference for the industrial sector now required the countryside to support the recovery of urban industry.

As a result of the war and the regime's policy preferences, the factors on which agricultural production depended were weakened. Indeed, an agriculture that was already subject to production problems stemming from central planning was further undermined by the direct and indirect consequences of the war. The environment for agricultural policy implementation placed an extraordinary burden on those responsible for policy results. Although industry was not immune to disruption by the war, the evacuation of industrial capacity and the regime's more supportive policies softened its more extreme consequences. Ultimately, the policy environment was more conducive to continual crisis in agricultural production than in industrial production. If conditions of production were thus likely to foster a greater magnitude and frequency of severe problems in agriculture than in industry, it may then be expected that the patterns of economic policy implementation should differ between the two sectors. The pervasive crisis atmosphere in agriculture called for extraordinary measures. The issue of who was to exercise such power depended to a large extent on the party's relation to the economic sector per se and to the sector's population in particular.

The Party and the Countryside

The party's relationship with the countryside had been contentious since the time of the Revolution. The party and the peasants viewed each other with suspicion and at times open hostility. The party's attitude grew out of Marxism's hostility toward peasants as remnants of a past to be overcome. Stalin's policies took these basic attitudes to an extreme: peasants were now adversaries to be controlled, and if they resisted control, they were to be eliminated. Although after the Stalin Constitution of 1936 peasants were no longer formally categorized as a hostile class, the abuses of collectivization left a heritage of mistrust. The rural sector may be viewed as external to the regime until the war. The state's policies toward the countryside were aimed at maximizing the development of the urban industrial sector, which was viewed as critical to the future of the USSR. Rural residents were expected to contribute to the public good but not necessarily to share public benefits.

Despite what was essentially an adversarial relationship before the war brought an upsurge of patriotism, the party nonetheless sought to establish itself in the countryside. From the standpoint of policy implementation, the extent of the party's organizational presence and the depth of party saturation among rural residents, particularly among agricultural workers, is important. The question of who was to exercise authority within a system of rural crisis management depended in part on the ability of the local party to rely on rural leaders and to supervise agricultural production indirectly through the political penetration of the countryside.[50] From this perspective, the distribution of party representatives and the extent of party membership among rural residents was critical. The greater the party presence and political saturation of the countryside as measured by both the number and size of primary party organizations, the greater the ability of middle- and upper-level party organizations to work through their representatives in the countryside, thereby avoiding direct intervention.

The party's presence in the prewar countryside was weak. Party representatives were usually attached to raion party organizations and machine tractor stations.[51] At the time of the Eighteenth Party

50. The important point is to what extent the rural population represented a danger to the interests of the state and whether the party could trust rural administrators to ensure the state's primary interest, the procurement of agricultural production. The issue of agricultural leaders' political reliability will be dealt with in chap. 4.

51. Robert F. Miller, *100,000 Tractors* (Cambridge: Harvard University Press, 1970), p. 207.

Congress in 1939, A. A. Andreev noted that "only 5 percent of kolkhozy (12,000 out of 243,000) had party organizations, and the total membership among kolkhozniki was only 153,000."[52] The majority of rural communists were located in raion party organizations, at sovkhozy, and at machine tractor stations, although the majority of agricultural workers were at kolkhozy.[53] Most rural Communists belonged to territorial party organizations, since there were too few Communists at kolkhozy to form primary party organizations. The few kolkhoz primary party organizations that existed were very small, consisting on the average of from three to five people.[54] After 1939 a major effort was made to increase party membership in the countryside. Though only 12.5 percent of all kolkhozy had primary party organizations on the eve of the war,[55] party membership was substantial in 1940, and it increased dramatically during and immediately after the war, as tables 2.5 and 2.6 indicate.

The effect of the war on party membership and the the party's organizational presence in the countryside warrants attention. During the war the party recruited new members on a massive scale. Membership requirements were temporarily lowered so that large numbers of army recruits, many from the countryside, could join. From 1941 to 1945 the party recruited 8.4 million members and candidates, of whom 6.4 million, or 76.2 percent, were in the armed forces.[56] Although more workers and peasants were recruited during the war than during the 1939–41 period (when they represented 20 and 10 percent, respectively), the trend was toward an increasingly white-collar party membership. Of the civilians and members of the armed forces enrolled during the war, 32.1 percent had working-class backgrounds, 25.3 percent were peas-

52. "Rech' t. Andreeva," *XVIII s"ezd VKP(b) Stenograficheskii otchet 10–12 marta 1939 g.* (Moscow: Politicheskoi Literatury, 1939), p. 109, cited in I. E. Zelenin, *Obshchestvenno-politicheskaia zhizn' sovetskoi derevni, 1946–1958 gg.* (Moscow: Nauka, 1978), p. 11. See also Arutiunian, *Sovetskoe krest'ianstvo*, pp. 60–62.

53. Arutiunian, *Sovetskoe krest'ianstvo*, p. 60.

54. Ibid., p. 61. See also M. A. Vyltsan, *Sovetskaia derevnia nakanune Velikoi Otechestvennoi voiny* (Moscow: Politizdat, 1970), pp. 186–88.

55. Zelenin, *Obshchestvenno-politicheskaia zhizn'*, p. 36.

56. "KPSS v tsifrakh," *Kommunist*, no. 15 (October 1967), p. 93; Iu. P. Petrov, *Partiinoe stroitel'stvo v sovetskoi armii i flote (1918–1961 gg.)* (Moscow: Ministerstva Oborony SSSR, 1964), p. 397.

TABLE 2.5
Number and percentage of rural population in Communist Party organizations, 1940–1950 (in thousands)

	1940		1945		1946		1947		1949		1950	
	No.	%	No.	%	No.	%	No.	%	No.	%	No.	%
Kolkhoz party organizations	350.0	56.0%	n.a.	n.a.	761.2	73.0%	916.7	75.0%	797.9	71.0%	879.2	73.3%
Territorial party organizations	260.0	41.7	n.a.	n.a.	91.1	8.7	n.a.	n.a.	n.a.	n.a.	279.2	23.3
Other	13.4	2.3	n.a.	n.a.	190.1	18.3	n.a.	n.a.	n.a.	n.a.	41.6	3.4
All party organizations	623.4	100.0%	726.7	100%	1,042.4	100.0%	1,208.7	100.0%	1,123.7	100.0%	1,200.0	100.0%

n.a. = not available.
Source: I. E. Zelenin, Obshchestvenno-politicheskaia zhizn' sovetskoi derevni, 1946–1958 gg. (Moscow: Nauka, 1978), p. 35.

TABLE 2.6
Percentage change in number of Communists in agricultural and kolkhoz
populations, 1940–1950

Population	1940–46	1946–47	1947–49	1949–50
Agricultural	+67.2%	+16.0%	−7.0%	+6.8%
Kolkhoz	+117.4	+20.4	−13.0	+10.7

Source: Calculated from I. E. Zelenin, *Obshchestvenno-politicheskaia zhizn' sovetskoi derevni, 1946–1958 gg.* (Moscow: Nauka, 1978), p. 35.

ants, and 42.6 percent were white-collar employees. White-collar
representation is even greater when members are classified by
occupation rather than by social origin.[57] Wartime recruitment and
losses did change the social composition of the party. National
data on party membership show an increase in members with a
white-collar background from 34.1 percent in 1941 to 48.3 percent
in 1947. The proportion of workers dropped from 43.7 percent in
1941 to 33.7 percent in 1947, and that of peasants declined from
22.2 percent to 18.0 percent.[58] So despite the increase in absolute
numbers of rural party members during the war years, peasants'
representation in the party was reduced.

In the initial months of the war, the number of rural Communists
declined as party members were drafted into the armed forces and
Soviet territories came under German occupation. In January 1941,
party members and candidate members numbered 623,400; by
January 1942 they numbered only 294,000; and by January 1943,
277,700.[59] "The number of Communists working in the agricultural sector fell 56 percent during the first one and a half years of
the war," according to a party journal. "As a result of this decline,
many kolkhoz PPOs [primary party organizations] had only three
to five Communists during the war."[60] In the following years, party
ranks in the countryside grew. At the beginning of 1945, according

57. T. H. Rigby, *Communist Party Membership in the U.S.S.R., 1917–1967*
(Princeton: Princeton University Press, 1968), pp. 224–25, 239, 268.
58. V. Beliakov and N. Zolotarev, *Partiia ukrepliaet svoi riady* (Moscow: Politicheskoi Literatury, 1970), p. 143; "KPSS v tsifrakh," *Partiinaia zhizn'*, no. 21
(November 1977), p. 28.
59. Zelenin, *Obshchestvenno-politicheskaia zhizn'*, pp. 10–11.
60. "O partiinykh organizatsiiakh v derevne," *Partiinoe stroitel'stvo*, no. 12 (June
1942), p. 45.

TABLE 2.7
Number of Communist Party members in the countryside ("na sele"), January 1, 1941–January 1, 1948 (in thousands), and as percentage of 1941 membership

Year	Number of members	Percentage of 1941 membership
1941	623.4	100.0%
1945	421.1	67.5
1946	726.7	111.6
1947	1,042.4	165.6
1948	1,192.4	191.3

Sources: "Istoriia KPSS," t. 5, kn. 1, pp. 375, 377; "KPSS v tsifrakh," *Kommunist*, no. 5 (1967), p. 100; *Partiinaia zhizn'*, no. 4 (1946), pp. 1–2; *Pravda*, March 13, 1947; and *Partiinaia zhizn'*, no. 5 (1948), p. 21, cited in V. N. Donchenko, "Perestroika riadov VKP(b) v period perekhoda SSSR ot voiny k miru (1945–1948 gody)," candidate dissertation, Moscow State University, 1972, p. 170, table 19.

to one set of figures, the total number of rural party members and candidate members stood at 421,100, only 67.5 percent of their numbers in January 1941; by the end of 1945, however, the number of Communists in agriculture exceeded the prewar contingent by 16 percent.[61] In 1946, with postwar demobilization, rural Communists surpassed their prewar numbers by 11.6 percent in the countryside (*na sele*) and by 22.8 percent in their primary party organizations.[62]

The increase in rural Communists produced by demobilization was reversed after 1947 (see table 2.5). It should also be noted that only slightly over 1 percent of the total kolkhoz population belonged to the Communist Party.[63] To assess the real impact of the increasing number of rural Communists, we must distinguish between the total number in the countryside and those who actually worked in agriculture (see table 2.7). "For the period 1948–1949," writes I. E. Zelenin, "the total number of Communists in agriculture declined by 85,000 persons (from 1,208,700 to 1,123,700, or approximately 8 percent). In 1950, in connection with a growth in recruitment and the sending of Communists to rural raions, a

61. Zelenin, *Obshchestvenno-politicheskaia zhizn'*, p. 11.
62. V. N. Donchenko, "Perestroika riadov VKP (b) v period perekhoda SSSR ot voiny k miru (1945–1948 gody)," candidate dissertation, Moscow State University, 1972, p. 170. These figures differ from those in tables 2.5 and 2.6.
63. The kolkhoz population was 66.6 million in 1947 and the number of Communists at kolkhozy in that year is variously given as 761,194 (Verbitskaia, "Izmeneniia," p. 126; "KPSS v tsifrakh," *Partiinaia zhizn'*, no. 21 [November 1977], p. 34) and 916,700 (see table 2.5).

general increase in the ranks of rural Communists took place."[64] This growth in absolute numbers, however, does not account for the magnitude of the increase in the number of kolkhoz PPOs. This increase resulted from the transfer of territorial party members to PPOs.

The party's organizational presence was critical to its ability to exercise indirect supervision over agricultural activities. Among the war's most immediate consequences was a dramatic decline in the number of primary party organizations. During the first six months of the war, PPOs declined by 987,000 organizations (or more than 50 percent). Economic PPOs declined from 98,000 to 63,000.[65] Although the dissolution of PPOs in occupied areas accounts for most of this decline, the number of kolkhoz PPOs fell in areas behind the lines also. As the level of party membership in rural areas was low to begin with, some PPOs collapsed when its members were drafted; others were transformed into candidate-komsomol groups.[66] In 1940, 12.6 percent of kolkhozy had PPOs; in 1945, 15.5 percent.[67] These figures, however, are somewhat misleading. From the beginning of the war until 1943 the number of kolkhoz primary party organizations declined, with the exception of those in western Siberia and Central Asia.[68] The disproportionately high percentage of kolkhozy with PPOs in Central Asia stems from the larger size of kolkhozy there. The expansion of the party network in Siberia reflects the influx of evacuees and urban cadres. The region's importance increased when the Nazis occupied the country's most fertile areas, and the party's attention to Siberia's agriculture and society increased accordingly. Al-

---

64. Zelenin, Obshchestvenno-politicheskaia zhizn', p. 27.

65. L. N. Ul'ianov, Trudovoi podvig rabochego klassa i krest'ianstvo Sibiri, 1945–1953 gg. (Tomsk: Izdatel'stvo Tomskogo Universiteta, 1979), p. 28.

66. Zelenin, Obshchestvenno-politicheskaia zhizn', p. 12; Arutiunian, Sovetskoe krest'ianstvo, pp. 67–68. Although the Eighteenth Party Congress had encouraged the establishment of kolkhoz PPOs, most rural Communists remained in territorial party organizations. In 1939 only 4.9 percent of all kolkhozy had PPOs (N. N. Shushkin, Vo imia pobedy [Petrozavodsk: Kareliia, 1970], p. 87).

67. Zelenin, Obshchestvenno-politicheskaia zhizn', p. 36.

68. "O partiinykh organizatsiiakh v derevne," Partiinoe stroitel'stvo, no. 12 (June 1942), pp. 44–45; Beliakov and Zolotarev, Partiia ukrepliaet, p. 155; N. Ia. Grishchin et al., Obshchestvenno-politicheskaia zhizn' sovetskoi sibirskoi derevni (Novosibirsk: Nauka, 1974), p. 110. The complete data necessary to document the exact nature of the decline in kolkhoz PPOs are unavailable.

though the number of kolkhoz PPOs grew during the postwar period, as table 2.8 indicates, much of their growth represents the redistribution of rural Communists and the influx of urban ones. In 1947, although the rural population represented over 60 percent of the total Soviet population, only 23.4 percent of Communist Party members worked in the countryside.[69] In fact, many of those classified as rural Communists worked in state, economic, and party administrative posts or were members of the rural intelligentsia; only 17.4 percent of party members were actually involved in agriculture.[70] Party members numbered 740 per 10,000 population in urban areas and 155 per 10,000 in rural areas.[71] Out of a total Communist Party membership of 7 million in 1953, 3 million worked in the countryside, but only approximately 1 million were actually at kolkhozy, machine tractor stations, and sovkhozy.[72] And most of those who worked in agricultural enterprises held administrative positions.

From 1946 until the amalgamation of kolkhozy in 1950, personnel policies transferred Communists from territorial party organizations to kolkhoz PPOs. The amalgamation increased the proportion of kolkhozy with PPOs to nearly 70 percent in 1950 and to 80 percent by 1953 (see table 2.8). As personnel policies concentrated on recruiting the rural intelligentsia, the increased number of kolkhoz PPOs resulted from the redistribution of Communists in the rural sector rather than a substantial growth in the absolute numbers of party members.[73] Thus, although the war served to increase the number of rural Communists and the percentage of kolkhozy with primary party organizations and to de-

---

69. "KPSS v tsifrakh," *Partiinaia zhizn'*, no. 21 (November 1977), p. 34; *Strana sovetov za 50 let: Sbornik statisticheskikh materialov* (Moscow: Statistika, 1967), p. 15.

70. Donchenko, "Perestroika riadov," p. 131. The distribution of Communists in the economy changed after 1941. The proportion of total party members in the armed forces was 14.4% in 1941, 23.0% in 1947; in industry, 23.3% in 1941, 19.7% in 1947; in transport, 7.5% in 1941, 6.0% in 1947; in agriculture, 16.1% in 1941, 17.4% in 1947; and other, 38.7% in 1941, 33.9% in 1947 (ibid., p. 131, table 10).

71. Rigby, *Communist Party*, p. 491.

72. V. M. Rezvanov, ed., *Organizatorskaia i politicheskaia rabota partii na sele: Mezhdu XIX i XXI s"ezdami KPSS* (Rostov-on-Don: Izdatel'stvo Rostovskogo Universiteta, 1966), pp. 168–69.

73. Rigby, *Communist Party*, pp. 292–93.

TABLE 2.8
Number of kolkhoz primary party organizations (PPOs) and percentage of kolkhozy with PPOs, 1940–1953

	1940	1945	1946	1947	1949	1950	1953
Kolkhoz PPOs	29,700	35,200	61,200	86,800	93,900	84,400	73,000
Kolkhozy with PPOs	12.6%	15.5%	27.0%	38.4%	37.2%	69.5%	80.0%

Sources: I. E. Zelenin, *Obshchestvenno-politicheskaia zhizn' sovetskoi derevni, 1946–1958 gg.* (Moscow: Nauka, 1978), pp. 35, 60; *Sel'skoe khoziaistvo SSSR statisticheskii sbornik* (Moscow: Gosstatizdat, 1960), p. 41; calculations for 1953 by the author.

crease the scope of territorial party organizations, the party's penetration and saturation of the countryside remained limited.

The Party Organizations of Leningrad
and Rostov

Given the particular importance of party penetration and saturation of the rural population for policy implementation, a somewhat closer examination of the Leningrad and Rostov provincial party organizations (whose behavior will be analyzed in chapter 6) is warranted. Clearly, the Leningrad party organization was preoccupied with industrial production in the city of Leningrad and in other cities in the oblast. Rostov represented a major area of agricultural production, and it also produced substantial amounts of industrial products for agriculture. As the two areas were dominated by different economic concerns, the characteristics of the party organizations should be expected to differ. Such differences should contribute to distinctive political contexts shaping the policy environment. Of particular interest is whether differences in policy focus and natural conditions produced distinctive party behavior in the implementation of agricultural policy.

Although party representation in the countryside was more extensive in Rostov Oblast than in Leningrad Oblast, it was surprisingly weak in both regions. One measure of party penetration is the social composition of party membership (see table 2.9). Workers were represented better and peasants less well in the Leningrad party than in the party as a whole. The social composition of the Rostov party more closely mirrored national party averages.[74] Data on the social composition of oblast party organizations show a clear tendency for the major economic preoccupation of a region to be reflected in the balance between workers and peasants. Representation of party members claiming white-collar origins remained relatively stable.[75]

Perhaps an even more important indicator of rural political pen-

74. National data show that in 1947 33.7% of the party was composed of workers and 18% of peasants (Beliakov and Zolotarev, *Partiia ukrepliaet*, p. 143; "KPSS v tsifrakh," *Partiinaia zhizn'*, no. 21 [November 1977], p. 28).

75. This assessment is based on data from numerous statistical handbooks on local party organizations.

TABLE 2.9

Percentage of workers and peasants in party organizations of Leningrad and Rostov oblasts, 1946–1953

Oblast	1946	1950	1952	1953
Leningrad				
Workers	49.2%	46.0%	n.a.	45.9%
Peasants	4.1	5.2	n.a.	5.7
Rostov				
Workers	35.8	36.5	35.6%	n.a.
Peasants	18.0	16.6	16.2	n.a.

n.a. = not available

Sources: S. S. Dmitiev et al., eds., *Leningradskaia organizatsiia KPSS v tsifrakh, 1917–1973* (Leningrad: Lenizdat, 1974), p. 74; A. M. Stepanov, "Partino-organizatsionnaia rabota kommunisticheskoi partii v gody chetvertoi piatiletki," candidate dissertation, Rostov State University, 1971, pp. 212–213; I. M. Kriulenko et al., eds., *Rostovskaia oblastnaia organizatsiia KPSS v tsifrakh, 1917–1975* (Rostov-on-the-Don; Rostovskoe knizhnoe izdatel'stvo, 1976), pp. 88, 109.

etration than party members' social origins is their location and involvement in the economy. Between 1946 and 1949 only 3.4 to 4.8 percent of the total membership of the Leningrad party lived in the countryside. The actual percentage of those members involved in agriculture during this period reached a high of only 1.7 percent.[76] Of course, the preponderance of Leningrad Oblast's population was urban. Indeed, rural party saturation in Leningrad Oblast appears to be roughly the same as the national average, 159 party members per 10,000.[77]

Although party representation in the Rostov countryside should be expected to vary significantly from that found in Leningrad because of the oblast's preoccupation with agricultural production, the percentage of Rostov party members actually involved in agriculture remained small. In 1947, 46.5 percent of the Rostov

76. L. V. Kruglova, "Deiatel'nost' leningradskoi partiinoi organizatsii po ukrepleniiu raidov partii i marksistko-leninskomu prosveshcheniiu kommunistov v pervoi poslevoennyi piatiletke (1946–1950 gg.)," candidate dissertation, Leningrad State University, 1971, p. 46; S. S. Dmitriev et al., eds., *Leningradskaia organizatsiia KPSS v tsifrakh, 1917–1973* (Leningrad: Lenizdat, 1974), p. 74.

77. Because of the lack of data, my calculations are only suggestive. If party and population data available for 1956 are used and the proportion of the party involved in the countryside is assumed to be 2.02%, as Kruglova suggests, then the Leningrad party's rural saturation rate would be 159 members per 10,000. See Dmitriev, *Leningradskaia organizatsiia*, p. 71, and *Leningrad entsiklopedicheskii sprovochnik* (Moscow and Leningrad: Bol'shaia Sovetskaia Entsiklopediia, 1957), p. 44.

party organization was located in the countryside.[78] By 1953 this figure had declined slightly, to 43.5 percent. Closer examination reveals, however, that 30 percent of those rural party members were located at raion institutions, 20 percent at industrial enterprises, 31 percent at kolkhozy, 8 percent at machine tractor stations (MTS's), and 4.3 percent at sovkhozy.[79] In fact, only approximately 13 percent of the total party organization was involved with the work of kolkhozy. (It should be remembered that agricultural production was dominated by kolkhozy and that MTS's represent more of an administrative presence.) Indeed, one Soviet scholar noted that in one raion, "of 1,109 members and candidates, only 142 people worked at kolkhozy" in 1953.[80] Thus, even in Rostov Oblast, the party's presence at the dominant institution of agricultural production remained relatively limited.

The number and location of primary party organizations provide another indication of rural party penetration. Once again party data suggest a greater and more rapid postwar penetration of the countryside in Rostov than in Leningrad (see table 2.10). Rostov's membership figures are unavailable, but we know that the PPOs in Leningrad Oblast (excluding the city of Leningrad) had small memberships.[81]

The available evidence indicates, then, that the Rostov party organization had a greater presence in the countryside than the Leningrad party organization. Nonetheless, party saturation rates for Leningrad did conform to the national average. These data, however, include people who were not directly involved in agriculture. As in Rostov Oblast in 1953, few party members were actually located at kolkhozy. Although the Rostov party organization maintained a greater presence in the countryside than did the Leningrad party organization, in neither case was party penetration of the productive environment particularly extensive.

78. D. I. Dubonosov, "Deiatel'nost' kommunisticheskoi partii po vosstanovleniiu i razvitiiu sel'skogo khoziaistva (1945–1950 gg.)," doctoral dissertation, Rostov State Pedagogical Institute, 1970, p. 57; I. M. Kriulenko et al., eds., *Rostovskaia oblastnaia organizatsiia KPSS v tsifrakh, 1917–1975* (Rostov-on-Don: Rostovskoe Knizhnoe Izdatel'stvo, 1976), p. 79.

79. Rezvanov, *Organizatorskaia i politicheskaia rabota*, p. 169. Rezvanov fails to locate the remaining 6.7%.

80. Ibid.

81. Dmitriev, *Leningradskaia organizatsiia*, pp. 134–35.

TABLE 2.10

Percentage of kolkhozy with PPOs in Leningrad and Rostov oblasts and in all USSR, 1940–1953

	1940	1945	1946	1950	1953
Leningrad	1.9%	2.3%	10.8%[a]	77.0%	79.4%
Rostov	46.0[b]	10.0	60.0	100.0	100.0[c]
USSR	12.6	15.5	27.0	69.5	80.0

[a]Data are for 1947.

[b]Data are for 1941. If alternate data for the number of kolkhoz PPOs in Rostov are used (945 as opposed to 852), then 51.4% of Rostov's kolkhozy had PPOs.

[c]Data are for 1952.

Sources: Narodnoe khoziaistvo leningradskoi oblasti (Moscow: Gosudarstvennoe Statisti-cheskoi Izdatel'stvo, 1957), pp. 69, 83; S. S. Dmitriev et al., eds., Leningradskaia organizatsiia KPSS v tsifrakh (Leningrad: Lenizdat, 1974), pp. 130–31, 171; Iu. V. Arutiunian, Sovetskoe krest'ianstvo v gody Velikoi Otechestvennoi voiny (Moscow: Nauka, 1970), p. 390; Propaganda i agitatsiia, no. 6 (1947), p. 3; I. M. Kriulenko et al., eds., Rostovskaia oblastnaia organizatsiia KPSS v tsifrakh, 1917–1975 (Rostov-on-Don: Rostovskoe Knizhnoe Izdatel'stvo, 1976), pp. 126–27; Narodnoe khoziaistvo Rostovskoi oblasti St. sb. (Rostov-on-Don: Statisticheskoe Upravlenie Rostovskoi Oblasti, 1961), p. 120; Rostovskaia oblast' za 50 let: Stat. sb. (Rostov-on-Don: Statistika, 1967), p. 54; D. I. Dubonosov, "Deiatel'nost' kommuniticheskoi partii po vosstanovleniiu i razvitiiu sel'skogo khoziaistva (1945–1950 gg.)," doctoral dissertation, State Pedagogical Institute, Rostov-on-Don, 1970, p. 57; S. G. Mogilevskii, "Partiino-organizatsion-naia rabota na sele v gody chetvertoi piatiletki (1946–1950 gg.)," candidate dissertation, Rostov State University, 1972, p. 90.; I. E. Zelenin, Obshchestvenno-politicheskaia zhizn' sovetskoi derevni, 1946–1958 gg. (Moscow: Nauka, 1978), p. 35; Sel'skoe khoziaistvo SSSR St. sb. (Moscow: Gosstatizdat, 1960), p. 41.

The factors that shaped the agricultural policy environment—the nature of the Soviet economy, the impact of World War II on the economy and its consequence for the rural sector, and the party's penetration of the countryside—formed the basis for the ongoing crisis of agricultural production during the postwar years. To understand how a system of crisis management actually arose, however, we must analyze the tasks that confronted the men and women responsible for policy implementation. The interaction of the policy environment with the tasks that confronted local leaders sets the stage on which local agricultural and party leaders act. The system of agricultural production required extraordinary measures. The characteristics of agricultural and party leaders helped to determine the nature of their informal authority rela-tionship. Before we examine these candidates for the role of ag-ricultural crisis manager, however, we must assess the demands that arose from agricultural policy itself. The demands of the ag-ricultural plan confronted local leaders with a series of problems. The difficulties they encountered in their efforts to fulfill the plan shaped the characteristics associated with the role of agricultural crisis manager.

CHAPTER 3

Postwar Agricultural Policies

Postwar agricultural policies evolved as the Soviet Union embarked upon peacetime reconstruction and development. The turbulence of industrialization, collectivization, and political terror gave way to rising Soviet patriotism and the party's increased legitimacy during the war. A return to the prewar Stalinist system under the new generation of state and party leaders seemed unlikely in the immediate postwar atmosphere, which was marked by pride in the victorious war effort and optimism about the future. At least for a brief time at the end of the war, economic and political liberalization seemed to be realistic possibilities. These expectations were soon dashed as the Soviet Union assumed a new conservative form. The postwar priorities cast an ominous shadow over the future of agriculture.

Soviet agriculture's future depended on the policy choices that would determine the form of collectivized agriculture, the degree of central control in the sector, and the extent of state economic support. Postwar agricultural policies emphasized central control with only limited increases in state investment. These policies sought to complete the structural transformation of agricultural production begun by collectivization and to maintain centrally planned production targets that afforded little local flexibility. Agricultural production was to be raised without a significant increase in material assistance to the kolkhozy, the sector that dominated agriculture. The tremendous pressure exerted by these policies on local agricultural and political leaders contributed directly to a system of crisis management in agriculture.

What features of these policies produced the extraordinary pressure under which local leaders sought to fulfill their plans? A partial answer can be found in the regime's attempt to complete the socialization of agriculture and to maintain a system of command farming. The basic problem that confronted all rural leaders, party and state, continued to be: How can I carry out central policies and successfully meet plan targets?

The Stalinist Agricultural Revolution Continues

In agriculture, unlike industry, Soviet leaders sought not only to reestablish the institutions of the 1930s while adjusting the roles of state and party cadres but to socialize agricultural production further. After reconfirming their permanent commitment to collectivized agriculture, they sought to complete the transformation of agricultural production and to strengthen the state's and party's control over the sector. Neither the rural population nor agricultural leaders were particularly receptive to these policies. The politically sensitive tasks they required called for the close supervision and active involvement of the party.

Moscow's attitude toward agriculture was evident in the 1946 resolution "On Measures for the Liquidation of Violations of the Charter of Agricultural Artels of Kolkhozy," which sought to strengthen kolkhozy politically and economically.[1] By calling for the observance of kolkhoz democracy, the regime notified the rural population that their participation and support of Soviet institutions were expected. The warning also reminded kolkhoz leaders that they did not have the right to control agriculture personally. Kolkhoz democracy served as a form of social control. The state sought to strengthen kolkhozy economically by excluding state and party employees who had illegally received salaries and land from kolkhozy and by returning land given to industrial

1. *Resheniia partii i pravitel'stva po khoziaistvennym voprosam (1917–1967 gg.)*, vol. 3, *1941–1952 gody* (Moscow: Politicheskoi Literatury, 1968), pp. 336–41.

enterprises and kolkhozniki during the war.[2] These measures gave notice that private profit at the expense of public interest would not be tolerated. The importance attached to the reimposition of central control over agriculture was reflected in the founding of a special committee to supervise the sector, the Council on Kolkhoz Affairs.[3]

Once the kolkhoz system was reestablished, agricultural policies focused on socializing production. These policies closely resemble those announced (though not implemented) from 1939 to 1941.[4] Indeed, it might be argued that if the purges and the war had not intervened after collectivization was completed in 1937, these policies would have formed part of a continuous process restructuring agriculture.[5] The most important of these policies, the May 1950 resolution "On the Strengthening of Weak Kolkhozy and the Tasks of Party Organizations in This Matter," signaled the return to policies aimed at structural transformation.[6]

The campaign to amalgamate kolkhozy initiated by the May 1950 resolution had both economic and political motivations. In 1949 only 37.2 percent of kolkhozy in the USSR had primary party organizations.[7] Indeed, only 40 percent of all kolkhoz chairmen were party members in 1948.[8] After the amalgamation, 69.5 per-

2. Ibid.

3. "O Sovete po delam kolkhozov," in ibid., pp. 349–50.

4. During 1937 to 1940, for example, the kolkhoz amalgamation policy was adopted, but only 3 percent of kolkhozy were actually amalgamated (V. G. Venzher, *Ispol'zovanie zakona stoimosti v kolkhoznom proizvodstve* [Moscow, 1965], p. 108, cited in I. M. Volkov, *Trudovoi podvig sovetskogo krest'ianstva v poslevoennye gody* [Moscow: Mysl', 1972], p. 200). In 1939 a resolution called for the elimination of private plots (M. A. Vyltsan, *Sovetskaia derevnia nakanune Velikoi Otechestvennoi voiny* [Moscow: Politizdat, 1970], pp. 40–41; "O merakh okhrany obshchestvennykh zemel' kolkhozov ot razbazarivaniia" [May 27, 1939], in *Resheniia*, vol. 2, *1929–1940 gody* [1967], pp. 707–13).

5. In 1937, 93 percent of all peasant households were collectivized (Vyltsan, *Sovetskaia derevnia nakanune*, p. 24).

6. "Ob ukrupnenii melkikh kolkhozov i zadachakh partiinykh organizatsii v etom dele," in *Resheniia*, 3:614–16.

7. I. E. Zelenin, *Obshchestvenno-politicheskaia zhizn' sovetskoi derevni, 1946–1958 gg.* (Moscow: Nauka, 1978), p. 35.

8. T. H. Rigby, *Communist Party Membership in the U.S.S.R., 1917–1967* (Princeton: Princeton University Press, 1968), p. 434; Jerry F. Hough, "The Changing Nature of the Kolkhoz Chairman," in *The Soviet Rural Community*, ed. James R. Millar (Urbana: University of Illinois Press, 1971), pp. 107–8.

cent of all kolkhozy had PPOs, and by 1953, 79.6 percent of all
kolkhoz chairmen were party members.[9]

Amalgamation also promoted economic objectives. The small
size of postwar kolkhozy made mechanization inefficient. Wartime population losses intensified the regime's commitment to
mechanization. The policy of kolkhoz amalgamation received the
support of Stalin, who, like other Soviet leaders, associated economies of scale with increased efficiency and productivity. Beyond
ideological preferences, a reduction in the number of kolkhozy
did indeed permit a more rational distribution of agricultural experts. A greater reliance on agricultural experts, especially on
those who served as kolkhoz chairmen, it was argued, could improve agricultural performance.[10] Thus the regime's policies suggest that the Stalinist revolution in the countryside continued
during the postwar reconstruction period. Such policies required
the active involvement of local party organizations if they were
to achieve their objectives.

While kolkhoz amalgamation may have seemed both politically
and economically desirable to Soviet leaders in Moscow, what
was its actual effect at the local level? How were such policies
implemented? Did they exert additional pressure on agricultural
administrators?

Like collectivization, amalgamation went forward rapidly—so
rapidly that it produced substantial chaos in the countryside.[11]
By October 1950, five months after the policy was announced,
44.7 percent of all kolkhozy were amalgamated. The weak kolkhozy of the central, north, and western regions were united particularly rapidly (see table 3.1). By the end of the year, the number
of kolkhozy had declined by 47 percent. Although some amalgamations were reversed in a step similar to Stalin's "dizzy from
success" tactic, this was only a temporary measure. At the beginning of 1951, 79.3 percent of all Soviet kolkhozy were amalga-

9. Zelenin, *Obshchestvenno-politicheskaia zhizn'*, p. 35; Roy D. Laird,
"Khrushchev's Administrative Reforms in Agriculture: An Appraisal," in *Soviet
and East European Agriculture*, ed. Jerzy F. Karcz (Berkeley: University of California Press, 1967), p. 34.

10. Volkov, *Trudovoi podvig*, p. 230.

11. Zelenin, *Obshchestvenno-politicheskaia zhizn'*, p. 311. Soviet sources note
the similarity of the party's mobilizational and organizational roles in collectivization and the amalgamation campaign.

TABLE 3.1
Percentage decline in the number of kolkhozy, January–November 1950, by region

Region	Percent decline
South	40.5%
Southeast	35.0
Kazakhstan and Urals	47.6
Central and northwest	58.7
Northern Caucasus	30.4
Caucasus	34.0
Siberia and East	35.0
Central Asia	46.2
USSR	47.0

Source: Calculated from M. A. Vyltsan, *Vosstanovlenie i razvitie material'no-tekhnicheskoi bazy kolkhoznogo stroia (1945–1958)* (Moscow: Mysl', 1976), p. 102, table 24.

mated.[12] The rapid amalgamation of kolkhozy adversely affected agricultural production.

Originally the amalgamation campaign may have been intended to produce a greater structural transformation in the rural sector than actually took place. The campaign was accompanied by a resolution reducing the size of kolkhozniki's private plots.[13] This policy undoubtedly contributed to disaffection among peasants: as kolkhoz work paid poorly, most kolkhozniki survived by raising food on their private plots and selling the excess.[14] The same resolution called for the creation of *agrogorody* (agricultural cities) to replace traditional villages. This policy, closely associated with Nikita Khrushchev, came under attack in the spring of 1951.[15] Indeed, the struggle between Khrushchev and Georgi Malenkov contributed to the chaos of agricultural production. Stalin's last contribution to theory, *Economic Problems of Socialism in the USSR*, published in 1952, also touched on agricultural policy. His

12. Volkov, *Trudovoi podvig*, pp. 206–7.
13. "O meropriiatiiakh v sviazi s ukrupneniiem melkikh kolkhozov" (July 17, 1950), in *Direktivy KPSS i Sovetskogo pravitel'stva po khoziaistvennym voprosam*, vol. 3, *1946–1952 gody* (Moscow: Politicheskoi Literatury, 1958), pp. 534–36.
14. I. M. Volkov et al., eds., *Sovetskaia derevnia v pervye poslevoennye gody, 1946–1950* (Moscow: Nauka, 1978), pp. 461–63.
15. *Pravda*, April 25, 1950, cited in Werner C. Hahn, *Postwar Soviet Politics* (Ithaca: Cornell University Press, 1982), p. 137.

arguments suggested the further transformation of kolkhozy into sovkhozy, a more advanced form of socialist production.[16]

Thus, unlike industry, agriculture continued to undergo a structural revolution during the immediate postwar period. Agricultural policies emphasized central control, thereby further limiting the autonomy of local agricultural leaders. At the same time, these policies required local party organizations to mobilize the rural work force and to carry out structural changes. Thus the political nature of agricultural policy reinforced the party's active involvement in the rural sector.

The Economics of Agricultural Policy

Agricultural recovery confronted Soviet leaders and the nation with a monumental task. Unlike the industrial sector, in which machinery evacuated to the East provided at least a partial basis for expanded production, agriculture had been virtually destroyed in nearly half of the country's productive regions: 47 percent of sown acreage and 45 percent of livestock were affected by the Nazi occupation.[17] Unoccupied areas also suffered during the war, as investment, manpower, and industrial production were focused exclusively on military objectives. These regions tended to be less productive than those occupied, with the possible exception of areas in which commercial crops were cultivated.[18] Thus the question is not so much whether agricultural policies set difficult production goals as whether such goals were attainable at all. Were agricultural goals realistic from an economic perspective? How much pressure did they place on those responsible for plan fulfillment? Did they permit measures that could promote efficient production, or did they hinder them? The key question is whether agricultural policies provided the necessary material support to pursue economic goals. Answers to these questions pro-

16. I. V. Stalin, "Ekonomicheskie problemy sotsializma v SSSR," in *Works of Joseph Stalin*, vol. 3, *1946–1953*, ed. Robert H. McNeal (Stanford: Hoover Institution on War, Revolution, and Peace, 1967), pp. 188–245.

17. N. A. Voznesenskii, *The Economy of the USSR during World War II* (Washington, D.C.: Public Affairs Press, 1948), p. 94. Gross agricultural production declined 60 percent as a result of the war (A. V. Krasnov et al., eds., *Bor'ba partii i rabochego klassa za vosstanovlenie i razvitie narodnogo khoziaistva SSSR [1943–1950 gg.]* [Moscow: Mysl', 1978], pp. 220–21).

18. M. A. Vylstan, *Vosstanovlenie i razvitie material'no-tekhnicheskoi baza kolkhoznogo stroia (1945–1958)* (Moscow: Mysl', 1976), p. 15.

vide an important glimpse into the factors that shaped the crisis of agricultural production..

The characteristics of the postwar economic plans clearly contributed to the crisis of agricultural production. Constant revisions of plan targets provided an unstable basis for agricultural production. Postwar agricultural policies can perhaps be most accurately depicted as a constant flow of demands emanating from Moscow. The Fourth Five-Year Plan was supplanted by the resolution of the February 1947 Plenum of the Central Committee and the 1949 three-year program to increase livestock. At the same time, local leaders were directed to implement the specific policies espoused by T. D. Lysenko and V. R. Vil'iams, although these policies were of questionable scientific value.[19] If a deluge of demands from Moscow confused local leaders during the initial recovery period, the subsequent period, 1951–55, was marked by adhocism. Indeed, the Fifth Five-Year Plan was not even presented until the 19th Party Congress, in 1952. Rather than lowering overambitious targets when performance faltered, as it did in industry, Moscow raised agricultural targets higher still. The combination of central policy making and the frequent revision of plan targets prevented local leaders from adjusting plans to prevailing conditions and from establishing the long-term expectations necessary for efficient performance. As a result of these practices, local policy implementation became a process of crisis management.

While the style of central planning disrupted efficient agricultural policy implementation, the goals created a crisis of production. The Fourth Five-Year Plan set the official targets and priorities for postwar economic recovery. Although the plan recognized the importance of agricultural production, the recovery of heavy industry remained the basis for future economic development. This emphasis limited the state's support for agriculture but did not result in the adoption of lower production goals. Though the targets for particular crops and livestock varied significantly, agricultural production as a whole was expected to rise 27 percent above its prewar level by 1950 and to exceed its 1945 level (measured in 1926–27 prices) by 211.4 percent.[20] This was

19. See Zhores Medvedev, *The Rise and Fall of T. D. Lysenko*, trans. I. Michael Lerner (New York: Columbia University Press, 1969); David Joravsky, *The Lysenko Affair* (Cambridge: Harvard University Press, 1970).

20. "Zakon o piatiletnem plan vosstanovleniia i razvitiia narodnogo khoziaistva SSSR na 1946–1950 gg.," *Resheniia*, 3:272–79; Eugene Zaleski, *Stalinist Planning*

an extraordinary goal. Even in the more favored sovkhoz sector, plan targets were extremely demanding. Not even these targets were always supported by the plan itself. According to general plan objectives, sovkhoz production was to surpass its prewar level, but actual plan targets did not sustain the necessary growth rate for such an achievement.[21]

The goals of the Fourth Five-Year Plan were replaced in February 1947 by the Central Committee's resolution "On Measures for Improving Agriculture in the Postwar Period."[22] Although the 1946 drought had devastated agricultural production, plan targets were actually increased. To the extent that any plan governed agricultural production, these goals remained in force until the Fifth Five-Year Plan (1951–55).

Between the February Plenum in 1947 and the 19th Party Congress, at which the Fifth Five-Year Plan was announced, agricultural policy was strongly influenced by Lysenko and Vil'iams. Policies aimed at changing soil structure and the climate through irrigation and afforestation promised benefits far in the future at best. Lysenko, at the height of his power in 1948, contributed to the dire straits in which agriculture, and especially livestock raising, found itself through the destruction of genetics.[23] In 1949 a new "Three-Year Plan for the Development of Kolkhoz and Sovkhoz Production of Livestock" raised the original targets posted by the Fourth Five-Year Plan.[24] The ideas of Lysenko and Vil'iams met resistance from agricultural leaders at the local level because they contradicted firsthand experience. Vil'iams' crop-rotation scheme led to a decline in grain cultivation and was finally condemned in 1950.[25]

for Economic Growth, 1933–1952, trans. and ed. Marie-Christine MacAndrews and John H. Moore (Chapel Hill: University of North Carolina Press, 1980), p. 349.

21. I. E. Zelenin, Sovkhozy SSSR, 1941–1950 (Moscow: Nauka, 1969), p. 140.

22. "O merakh pod'ema sel'skogo khoziaistva v poslevoennyi period," in KPSS v rezoliutsiiakh i resheniiakh s"ezdov, konferentsii i plenumov TsK, chast' 3, 1930–1954, 7th ed. (Moscow: Politicheskoi Literatury, 1954), pp. 502–52; Pravda, May 13 and June 4 and 18, 1949, cited in Sovetskaia derevnia, ed. Volkov et al., p. 249.

23. Medvedev, Lysenko, pp. 103–39; Joravsky, Lysenko Affair, pp. 130–57.

24. "Trekhletnii plan razvitiia obshchestvennogo kolkhoznogo i sovkhoznogo produktivnogo zhivotnovodstva (1949–1951 gg.)" (April 18, 1949), in Direktivy, 3:341–68. Also see Volkov, Trudovoi podvig, p. 157.

25. Volkov et al., eds., Sovetskaia derevnia, p. 229.

If the numerous policies of the 1946–50 period caused confusion, the long delay of the Fifth Five-Year Plan compounded the problems. Although the plan itself was never published, M. Z. Saburov, the chairman of Gosplan, presented directives allegedly based on it at the 19th Party Congress in 1952. As might be expected, production targets again rose. The gross harvest of grain was to increase by 40 to 50 percent: wheat by 55 to 65 percent, raw cotton by 55 to 65 percent, flax fiber by 40 to 50 percent, sugar beets by 65 to 70 percent, and potatoes by 40 to 45 percent. The critical lack of fodder for livestock was to be eased by increases of 80 to 90 percent in hay production, 300 to 400 percent in tubers and roots, and 200 percent in silage. The importance of agricultural zones surrounding cities was again stressed. Livestock quotas were targeted for substantial increases. These ambitious goals depended on increases in the capabilities of machine tractor stations. The number of tractors and their productivity were to rise by 50 percent.[26]

Although the postwar goals were extremely demanding, they were not altogether out of touch with reality. In comparison with those of the prewar period, postwar production targets appear almost reasonable.[27] It can be argued that the low level of absolute production made the high percentage increases less harsh. Nonetheless, the comparison of prewar and postwar production goals does not adequately reflect the difficulties they posed for local leaders. The agricultural policies of the 1930s, after all, called for mass mobilization and virtual expropriation. The postwar regime's attempts to create a stable, conservative administrative system formally disowned such methods.

The logic of Soviet agricultural policy was derived from the Stalinist model of unequal development. Such logic tended to equate economic rationality with state procurements rather than with the absolute growth or economic welfare of agricultural production. As the terms of trade during postwar recovery strongly

26. M. Z. Saburov, "Directives of the 19th Party Congress for the Fifth Five-Year Plan of Development in the USSR, 1951–1955," *Pravda*, October 12, 1952, trans. in *Current Soviet Policies*, vol. 1, ed. Leo Gruliow (New York: Praeger, 1953), pp. 23–24. The number of tractors at sovkhozy was to increase by 21.7% between 1950 and 1953 (M. L. Bogdenko, *Sovkhozy SSSR, 1951–1958* [Moscow: Nauka, 1972], p. 48).

27. Zaleski, *Socialist Planning*, p. 348.

favored the industrial/urban sector at the expense of the agrarian/
rural sector, procurement prices remained low, often failing to
cover the cost of kolkhoz production.[28] Although kolkhoz income
from the state increased during the late 1940s as some procurement prices rose, the state's contribution to kolkhoz total income
remained strikingly low. In 1947 state payments accounted for
only 30 percent of total kolkhoz income. This figure grew to 40
percent in 1948, to 51.6 percent in 1949, and to 59.6 percent in
1950.[29]

Other kolkhoz economic activities had to subsidize state procurements. The state, however, sought to profit from these activities, too. The sale of kolkhoz produce at peasant markets and
consumption within the kolkhoz were discouraged through rural
taxation.[30] After 1947, central procurements were adjusted according to agricultural performance.[31] More successful regions had
their quotas increased, while poorer areas maintained lower quotas. After state procurements and the payment of MTS personnel,
however, the poorer areas frequently had little to sell or con-
sume.[32] Thus the logic of the Stalinist economic model was ir-
rational from the perspective of agriculture's own welfare. Subject
to programs based on this implicit logic, agriculture struggled to
avoid further impoverishment.

Given the extraordinarily difficult production targets, how well
were local leaders able to implement agricultural policy? A partial
answer is provided by data on plan fulfillment and agricultural
production. Data published during the late Stalin period are frequently erroneous, often exaggerating actual production. The most
egregious cases of data manipulation, such as the use of biological
yields data, however, were corrected during the Khrushchev era.

Data on plan fulfillment and agricultural performance show
mixed results. Agricultural production rose during the postwar
period, a real achievement given the dire conditions affecting pro-

28. A. N. Malafeev, *Istoriia tsennobrazovaniia v SSSR (1917–1963 gg.)* (Moscow, 1964), p. 266, cited in I. M. Volkov, "Kolkhozy SSSR v gody chetvertoi
piatiletki (1946–1950 gg.)," in *Razvitie sel'skogo khoziaistva SSSR v poslevoennye
gody (1946–1970 gg.)*, ed. I. M. Volkov et al. (Moscow: Nauka, 1972), p. 68.

29. Volkov, *Trudovoi podvig*, p. 184.

30. Alec Nove, *Economic Rationality and Soviet Politics, or Was Stalin Really
Necessary?* (New York: Praeger, 1964), p. 175.

31. Abram Bergson, *The Economics of Soviet Planning* (New Haven: Yale University Press, 1964), pp. 192–93.

32. Volkov, *Trudovoi podvig*, pp. 192, 194.

TABLE 3.2

Percentage of Fourth Five-Year Plan targets fulfilled by production of selected agricultural products, 1950

Product	Plan fulfillment
Raw cotton[a]	141.7%
Grain[b]	121.0
Sugar beets[a]	93.4
Grain[a]	79.5
Sunflowers[a]	62.2
Milk	78.5
Meat and fat[c]	76.0
Flax fiber[a]	51.6

[a]Barn yield.
[b]Biological yield.
[c]Includes rabbits and poultry.
Source: Adapted from Eugene Zaleski, *Stalinist Planning for Economic Growth, 1933–1952*, trans. and ed. Marie-Christine MacAndrews and John H. Moore (Chapel Hill: University of North Carolina Press, 1980), p. 397, table 93.

duction. Nonetheless, upon more careful examination, the data yield a picture of growth rates with significant fluctuation, especially by crop and type of livestock.[33] Production of many crops during the Fourth Five-Year Plan neither met plan targets nor surpassed 1940 production levels (see table 3.2).[34] Official Soviet data show gross production at 99 percent of the 1940 level at the end of the plan period, somewhat higher than estimates by Western experts.[35] The Fifth Five-Year Plan (1951–55) produced even more disappointing results: gross production declined in 1951 and remained stagnant at approximately 1950 levels during 1952 and 1953 (see table 3.3).[36] Livestock producers also failed to reach the

33. Zaleski, *Stalinist Planning*, p. 368. Official Soviet estimates indicated annual growth rates in gross agricultural production of 10.5% in 1946, 28.4% in 1947, 11.5% in 1948; animal products were expected to increase 20.8, 2.3, and 7.9% in the three years, and grain (barn yield) 16.3, 66.4, and 2.0%.

34. It should be noted that poor climatic conditions in 1940 led to a harvest in that year below those of 1936, 1937 (a record harvest), and 1938 (an average harvest) (G. A. Chigrinov, "Meropriiatiia partii po razvitiiu sel'skokhoziaistvennogo proiz-vodstva v predvoennye gody," *Voprosy istorii KPSS*, no. 1 [1962], pp. 139–40).

35. *Strana sovetov za 50 let* (Moscow: Statistika, 1967), p. 30. See Zaleski, *Stalinist Planning*, pp. 400–401, for Western and Soviet plan fulfillment data based on the value of agricultural production. Differences averaged approximately 10%. Soviet figures (based on 1926–27 prices) estimated plan fulfillment of 89.9%, Western figures 79.4%.

36. *Istoriia sotsialisticheskoi ekonomiki SSSR*, 7 vols. (Moscow: Nauka, 1980), vol. 6, *Vosstanovlenie narodnogo khoziaistva SSSR: Sozdanie ekonomiki razvi-*

TABLE 3.3

Gross production of selected agricultural products, 1940–1953 (in thousands of head, thousands of tons)

	Cattle	Grains	Beets	Potatoes	Vegetables
1940	—	95,600	18.0	76,100	13,700
1941	57.0	—	—	—	—
1945	—	47,300	5.5	58,300	10,300
1946	46.3	—	—	—	—
1950	58.9	81,200	20.8	88,600	9,300
1953[a]	60.3	82,500	23.2	72,600	11,400

[a]The number of cows and horses in 1953 did not reach 1941 levels. Only swine, sheep, and goats attained their 1916 levels.

Sources: Narodnoe khoziaistvo SSSR v 1958 (Moscow: Gosstatizdat, 1959), pp. 419, 421, 427, 431; Sel'skoe khoziaistvo SSSR (Moscow: Statistika, 1971), pp. 148, 245.

targets set by their special three-year program (1949–51).[37] Total agricultural production during 1946–49 grew 47.4 percent, while during 1950–53 it grew only 4.3 percent.[38] The uncertainty associated with volatile growth rates and the inability to attain plan targets contributed to agriculture's crisis atmosphere. The pressure produced by agricultural plan targets on local leaders was probably even greater than these data suggest.

Gross agricultural performance still depended on the noncollectivized sector. In 1950 the state purchased only 69 percent of all poultry and livestock, 57 percent of milk, 39 percent of eggs, and 85 percent of wool from kolkhozy and sovkhozy.[39] The remainder was purchased from private plots. Livestock data mask the complexities of this sector's performance. From 1946 through 1948, for example, kolkhozy purchased 9.7 million head of cattle but increased their holdings by only 5 million head.[40] Insufficient shelter and fodder led to heavy losses. Overall, national economic data on agricultural production provide an overly optimistic assessment of the collectivized sector's performance.

The difficulty of fulfilling plan targets was also an artifact of the low level of material support received by agriculture during the

---

togo sotsializma 1946-nachalo 1960-kh godov, p. 420; Razvitie sotsialisticheskoi ekonomiki SSSR v poslevoennyi period (Moscow: Nauka, 1965), p. 259.

37. Volkov, Trudovoi podvig, pp. 165–66.

38. Razvitie sotsialisticheskoi ekonomiki, p. 259.

39. Sel'skoe khoziaistvo, SSSR: St. sb. (Moscow: Statistika, 1971), p. 29; Volkov et al., eds., Sovetskaia derevnia, p. 280.

40. Volkov, Trudovoi podvig, p. 160.

Fourth and Fifth five-year plans. As local leaders were unable to adjust production goals, capital and labor inputs strongly influenced the potential success of policy implementation. Capital and labor were inextricably linked by the Stalinist model of development. Long-term undercapitalization had forced Soviet agriculture to rely heavily on labor and extensive cultivation. The substitution of labor for capital was upset by the huge loss of life during the war.

The Soviet rural population fell from 67 percent of the country's total population in 1940 to 60 percent in 1951. The decline in rural population, especially as a result of World War II, was felt by kolkhozy throughout the country.[41] Kolkhozniki capable of work declined by a third; the number of male workers declined 65 percent.[42] The kolkhoz population was dominated by women, the young, and the retired—the least productive elements of the labor force. This demographic structure was virtually the same at all kolkhozy, whether the region had been occupied or was behind the lines during the war.[43] Thus agriculture throughout the USSR was particularly sensitive to the state's capital and labor policies.

During the war, agriculture received negligible amounts of capital investment from the state. The Fourth Five-Year Plan increased agricultural investment, but the level and source of this investment intensified the crisis (see table 3.4). Only 7.6 percent of total state capital investment during 1946–50 was devoted to agriculture.[44]

When capital investment from kolkhozy is added to state investment, total capital investment in the agrarian sector reaches

41. Ibid., p. 219; *Trud v SSSR: St. sb.* (Moscow, 1968), pp. 19–20, brought to my attention by Volkov et al., *Sovetskaia derevnia*, p. 106. The kolkhoz population was 18% below its 1940 level in 1944, 15% below in 1945, and 16% below in 1946 (Iu. V. Arutiunian, *Sovetskoe krest'ianstvo v gody velikoi otechestvennoi voiny*, 2d ed. [Moscow: Nauka, 1970], p. 323).

42. Volkov et al., eds., *Sovetskaia derevnia*, p. 42; I. M. Volkov, "Ukreplenie material'no-tekhnicheskoi bazy sel'sko-khoziaistva v pervye poslevoennye gody (1946–1950)," *Vestnik Moskovskogo Universiteta*, no. 6 (1968), p. 3.

43. The population capable of work was 36% of total kolkhoz population in areas of the RSFSR that had been behind the lines during the war, 35% in formerly occupied territories. Men capable of work represented 7% and 6% of total populations in occupied and unoccupied areas, respectively; women capable of work, 29% and 29%; youths capable of work, 10% and 11%; and adults and youths incapable of work, 54% and 54% (Arutiunian, *Sovetskoe krest'ianstvo*, p. 327).

44. Volkov, *Trudovoi podvig*, p. 283.

TABLE 3.4

Capital investment in agriculture, 1941–1955 (in billions of constant rubles)

Period	State capital investment	Capital investment by kolkhozy	All capital investment in agriculture	Percent of capital investment in economy
1941–46	R3.0	R14.8	R17.8	11%
Fourth FYP[a]				15
1946–50	25.1	31.2	56.3	
Fifth FYP[a]				
1951	10.2	9.1	19.3	16
1952	9.7	10.6	20.3	15
1953	8.8	11.7	20.5	15
1954	15.4	14.3	29.7	18
1955	19.9	21.0	40.9	22
1951–55	R64.0	R66.7	R130.7	18

[a]Five-Year Plan.

Source: Sel'skoe khoziaistvo SSSR. Stat. sb. (Moscow: Gosstatizdat, 1960), p. 387. See also Eugene Zaleski, Stalinist Planning for Economic Growth, 1933–1952, trans. and ed. Marie-Christine MacAndrews and John H. Moore (Chapel Hill: University of North Carolina Press, 1980), pp. 404–5, 424–27.

15 percent. The original Fourth Five-Year Plan called for capital investment funds of 19.9 billion rubles, including 8.8 billion for the recovery and development of MTS's, 2 billion for irrigation and drainage projects, and 2 billion for the purchase of livestock by sovkhozy. Thus little state capital investment was to be directed to the kolkhoz sector. An additional 38 billion rubles were to be contributed by kolkhozy themselves.[45] Given the poor financial situation of many kolkhozy, such a contribution made their financial plight desperate.

The capital provided by the Fourth Five-Year Plan was insufficient to offset the long-term undercapitalization of agriculture and the effects of the war. The Fifth Five-Year Plan more than doubled capital investment.[46] This statement is misleading, however. Capital investment in agriculture from 1951 through 1953 actually fell. Only after the Korean War did capital investment in agriculture increase substantially, as table 3.4 indicates.

The sector's need for large-scale capital infusions was particularly urgent in such vital areas as agricultural machinery, the

45. Resheniia, 3:274. Plan figures differ from those published in Soviet statistical handbooks.

46. Bogdenko, Sovkhozy, p. 47.

TABLE 3.5
Percentage of kolkhozy, sovkhozy, and machine tractor stations (MTS's) equipped to use electricity, 1946–1953

Year	Kolkhozy	Sovkhozy	MTS's
1946	7%	25%	60%
1950	15	76	80
1953	22	88	96

Sources: I. M. Nekrasova, "Razvitie elektrifikatsii sel'skogo khoziaistva v 1945–1965 gg.," in *Razvitie sel'skogo khoziaistva SSSR v poslevoennye gody (1946–1970 gg.)*, ed. I. M. Volkov et al. (Moscow: Nauka, 1972), pp. 105, 107; *Narodnoe khoziaistvo SSSR v 1958 godu* (Moscow: Gosudarstvennoe Statisticheskoe Izdatel'stvo, 1959), pp. 507, 508, 523.

development of seed varieties, cattle, transportation, housing, and electricity. In some of these areas, such as cattle and seed stocks, Lysenkoism prevented any real progress. Housing construction and transportation had to wait another decade to receive attention. Agricultural machinery and electrification, however, were singled out for immediate action.

Rural electrification was pursued from the very beginning of recovery in the hope of increasing productivity.[47] While this policy expanded rural electrification (see table 3.5), it did little to increase production. The kolkhoz system, which dominated agricultural production, derived little benefit from the expansion of rural electrification. Only 9 percent of kolkhozy used electricity in production, in part because they were forced to establish their own power stations, which often produced too little power to run machinery. Overall, agriculture consumed only 2 percent of the nation's electrical output in 1950.[48] Agricultural mechanization did not employ electricity on a large scale until after Stalin's death.

The mechanization of Soviet agriculture remained a major postwar objective of agricultural policy. Capital investment in the MTS system rose from 767.7 million rubles in 1946 to 6.135 million rubles in 1950, or 28.7 percent of total state investment in agriculture. Mechanization proceeded, but not without difficulties. Although the number of MTS's increased, the number of tractors had still not achieved prewar levels by 1950 (see table 3.6). The production of agricultural machinery did increase during the im-

47. "O razvitii sel'skoi elektrifikatsii" (February 8, 1945) and "O plane razvitiia sel'skoi elektrifikatsii na 1948–1950 gg." (May 29, 1948), in *Resheniia*, 3:224–29, 490–502. See also I. M. Nekrasova, "Razvitie elektrifikatsii sel'skogo khoziaistva v 1945–1965 gg.," in *Razvitie sel'skogo khoziaistva*, ed. I. M. Volkov et al. (Moscow: Nauka, 1972), pp. 105–7.
48. Nekrasova, "Razvitie elektrifikatsii," p. 108.

TABLE 3.6
Numbers of machine tractor stations (MTS's) and tractors and percentage of
kolkhozy serviced, 1940–1950

	MTS's	Tractors[a]	Percent of Kolkhozy serviced
1940	7,069	410,937	83.9%
1945	7,465	291,162	76.7
1950	8,414	406,459	80.5[b]

[a]In working condition.
[b]Reflects the amalgamation of kolkhozy.
Source: Adapted from M. A. Vyltsan, Vosstanovlenie i razvitie material'no-tekhnicheskoi bazy kolkhoznogo stroia (1945–1958) (Moscow: Mysl', 1976), p. 36, table 6.

mediate postwar years, but with renewed military production for the Korean War it declined from 1951 to 1953.[49]

Despite the limited success achieved in increasing the availability of agricultural machinery, did mechanization nonetheless serve to intensify agricultural production? In general, this question must be answered in the negative. Although mechanization undoubtedly aided agricultural performance, its role remained limited. Livestock and such crops as potatoes and vegetables benefited relatively little from mechanization.[50] The poor quality of MTS work also limited its impact on production. A number of palliative measures, such as the strengthening of kolkhoz–MTS agreements, increasing the responsibility of MTS personnel for the quality of their work, and the basing of MTS salaries on merit, sought to remedy these problems.[51] Poor repair facilities and the lack of qualified, experienced cadres also hindered mechanization. Thus, despite the increased number of tractors, combines, and MTS's, mechanization could not effectively substitute for the loss of rural labor.

The Politics of Labor Policies

As we saw in chapter 2, postwar Soviet labor policies favored the industrial sector in spite of rural labor shortages. Such policies

49. M. A. Vyltsan, "Vosstanovlenie i razvitie material'no-tekhnicheskoi bazy sel'skogo khoziaistva v 1946–1958 gg.," in Razvitie sel'skogo khoziaistva, ed. Volkov et al., pp. 81, 86.
50. Ibid., p. 84.
51. Vylstan, Vosstanovlenie, pp. 75, 76.

as the organized recruitment of rural labor for industrial production drew off both demobilized soldiers and youths from the countryside. In the course of five years (1943–48), more than 2.75
million rural residents were trained for industrial jobs. Even after
organized industrial recruitment declined in the late 1940s, rural
youths continued voluntarily to enter industrial training schools.[52]
Of the students accepted at schools within the state labor reserve
system, rural youths represented 77 percent during 1946–50 and
66 percent during 1951–55, after the system had declined in
importance.[53]

The overall effect of labor policy contributed to a 5.7 percent
decline in rural population from 1946 through 1950. The central
RSFSR, in particular, witnessed a steep decline in kolkhoz population.[54] On January 1, 1951, the kolkhoz population fell to 82.2
percent of its 1941 complement and 96.6 percent of the 1945
level.[55] Rural out-migration, encouraged by Soviet authorities in
most areas, made labor-intensive policies increasingly difficult to
pursue.

While official Soviet policy promoted out-migration, it also
sought to mitigate the problems created by labor shortages and
the lack of agricultural experts. Soviet policies sought to improve
rural labor productivity through increased education, the use of
material incentives, and administrative reorganization. New agricultural schools were established (see table 3.7). In order to train
agricultural workers and leaders rapidly, the government established six-month leadership courses, three-year agricultural pro-

---

52. M. I. Khlusov, *Razvitie sovetskoi industrii, 1946–1958* (Moscow: Nauka,
1977), p. 95. In 1948, 80% of those accepted entered voluntarily. In 1949, this
figure reached 94%.

53. *Narodnoe khoziaistvo SSSR v 1959 gody* (Moscow: Gosudarstvennoe Statisticheskoe Izdatel'stvo, 1960), p. 623, brought to my attention by S. L. Seniavskii
and M. I. Khlusov, "Industrial'nye kadry SSSR v 1946–1955 godakh," *Voprosy
istorii*, no. 10 (1965), p. 31.

54. O. M. Verbitskaia, "Izmenenie chislennost' kolkhoznogo krest'ianstva
RSFSR v gody chetvertoi piatiletki," in *Problemy istorii sovetskogo krest'ianstva:
Sb. st.*, ed. M. P. Kim (Moscow: Nauka, 1981), pp. 201–2. Tambov Oblast lost 19.1%
in 1945, Velikolusk Oblast 17.5%, the non-black-earth and northern oblasts 10–
15%, Povol'zhe and the Urals 4–6%. Exceptions to this trend—areas in which the
kolkhoz population increased—included Dagestan, 1%; Chuvash, 3.4%; Altai,
4.3%; Astrakhan, 4.5%; Kemerov Oblast, 6.3%; Molotov Oblast (Saratov), 2%;
Tomsk Oblast, 5.4%; and Iaroslavl', 6.7%.

55. Volkov, *Trudovoi podvig*, p. 221. The exceptions to this trend were Central
Asia, the Transcaucasian republics, and Krasnodar (ibid., p. 220).

TABLE 3.7
Number of agricultural educational institutions, entering students, and graduates, 1940/41–1954, by type of institution

	1940/41	1945/46	1950/51	1954
Agricultural educational institutions				
Specialized secondary schools	751	539	619	753[a]
Institutions of higher education (VUZY)	91	92	94	99[b]
Entering students				
Specialized secondary schools	48,078	48,983	59,295	97,687
Institutions of higher education	11,938	17,858	28,473	47,541
Graduates				
Specialized secondary schools	21,505	19,825	48,654	55,204
Institutions of higher education	10,344	32,882	12,705	20,148

[a]Data for 1952/1953: 760 in 1955/56.
[b]Data for 1955/56.

Sources: Narodnoe obrazovanie, nauka i kul'tura v SSSR St. sb. (Moscow: Statistiki, 1971), pp. 168, 177, 188, 192; Kul'turnoe stroitel'stvo SSSR St. sb. (Moscow: Gosstatizdat, 1956), pp. 213–15, 236–39; Vysshee obrazovanie v SSSR St. sb. (Moscow: Gosstatizdat, 1961), pp. 81, 91, 95, 238, 244–45; Sel'skoe khoziaistvo SSSR St. sb. (Moscow: Gosstatizdat, 1960). p. 476; A. P. Tiurina, Formirovanie kadrov spetsialistov i organizatorov kolkhoznogo proizvodstva, 1946–1958 gg. (Moscow: Nauka, 1973), pp. 56, 64. 65.

grams at technical institutes (normally four years), and one- and two-year special agricultural schools, in addition to the traditional, specialized secondary technical institutes and institutions of higher education. Overall, the regime's postwar efforts concentrated on short courses and specialized secondary education as a means to train rural workers quickly and inexpensively.[56]

The number of agricultural specialists with secondary qualifications doubled from 1946 to 1952, but the abbreviated educational programs that they completed provided little technical expertise. The poor educational backgrounds of many entering students, the short periods of instruction, and the lack of equipment necessary for practical experience undermined the program's effectiveness. By the early 1950s, many of the special agricultural schools were converted into technical institutes or were abandoned. Nonetheless, by 1953 Soviet educational programs had more than tripled the number of students at agricultural institutions of higher education and doubled the numbers at agricultural technical institutes over the 1940 levels.[57] Nonetheless, agriculture still suffered from a scarcity of agricultural experts.

The continued deficit of agricultural experts was due in part to the fact that many of the new graduates chose not to enter agricultural production work. Only 13.4 percent of graduates of both higher and technical agricultural institutions assumed jobs at MTS's and kolkhozy in 1950. Although this problem received special attention after the amalgamation of kolkhozy, the majority of newly trained agricultural specialists still did not enter kolkhoz and MTS work, preferring administrative work in the urban sector.[58]

With capital and labor lacking, Soviet agricultural policy pursued the logical option—increased labor productivity. In addition to socialist competition, more innovative strategies were intro-

---

56. A. P. Tiurina, *Formirovanie kadrov spetsialistov i organizatorov kolkhoznogo proizvodstva, 1946–1958 gg.* (Moscow: Nauka, 1973), pp. 63–64.

57. Ibid., pp. 72–73, 75, 79.

58. Ibid., pp. 82, 84–85, 93. See the resolution by the Central Committee and the Council of Ministers "O zadachakh partiiny i sovetskikh organizatsii podal'neishemu ukrespleniiu sostova predsedatelei i drugikh rukovodiashchikh rabotnikov kolkhozov," in *KPSS v rezoliutsiiakh i resheniiakh s"ezdov, konferentsii i plenumov TsK*, vol. 6, *1941–1954*, 8th ed. (Moscow: Politicheskoi Literatury, 1971), pp. 323–31.

duced during the postwar period: material incentives and the reorganization of the rural work force. The Fourth Five-Year Plan sought to expand the role of the workday in the distribution of salaries and to increase supplementary pay for kolkhozniki.[59] This policy was revised in 1948 to base supplementary pay on the work of the link (team) within a work brigade rather than on the entire kolkhoz's performance.[60] This measure sought to establish a closer connection between the individual's work and financial reward. Incentives were also created for administrative and MTS personnel, but of a negative kind. Agricultural experts were to lose 25 percent of their salary if they remained in administration. The object, of course, was to induce them to take jobs in production at sovkhozy, kolkhozy, and MTS's. The salaries of MTS personnel, although guaranteed by kolkhozy, were to be adjusted on the basis of independent monitoring of their work.[61]

Programs for the provision of material incentives were in principle logical, but they suffered from a fatal flaw: the absence of monetary income and excess produce at kolkhozy. Monetary pay received by kolkhozniki illustrates this problem. Over 50 percent of all kolkhozy paid 40 or fewer kopeks per workday.[62] In 1950, 77.3 percent of all kolkhozy paid the smallest permissible amount of grain (1.5 kilograms) per workday compared with 90.4 percent in 1945 and 70.5 percent in 1940.[63]

Kolkhoz pay per workday varied significantly by area. The average payments in the central non-black-earth zone, the central black-earth zone, and Povol'zhe fell below those for the USSR in 1950, while those in Central Asia, Kazakhstan, and the Transcaucasian republics exceeded them. Northern Caucasia remained borderline. Payment in kind also varied widely, but differences in crops cultivated make comparisons difficult. The poor material

59. Supplementary pay was derived from income received from production in excess of the plan target. Workdays were used as the basis of distribution.

60. "O merakh po uluchsheniiu organizatsii povysheniia proizvoditel'nosti i uporiadocheniiu oplaty truda v kolkhozakh" (April 19, 1948), in *Resheniia*, 3:469–88.

61. "O merakh pod'ema sel'skogo khoziaistva v poslevoennyi period" (Central Committee Plenum, February 21–26, 1947), in *KPSS v rezoliutsiiakh*, 6:255, 242.

62. Volkov et al., eds., *Sovetskaia derevnia*, p. 456.

63. V. B. Ostrovskii, *Kolkhoznoe krest'ianstvo SSSR* (Saratov, 1967), p. 59, cited by ibid., p. 456.

conditions of production along with major droughts during the recovery period (1946, 1948, and 1951) made private plots continue to be a major source of food and monetary income for kolkhozniki during the postwar period.[64]

The role of labor organization in agricultural production, frequently viewed as a means to greater efficiency, was more overtly political than economic. The "link" within brigades, at first promoted as a unit of cost accounting, later was attacked for impeding mechanization. These organizational units had short lives during the early postwar period, and the real controversy over these policies was rooted in high politics. The faction that supported a more pragmatic approach to agriculture was weakened by the purge of Nikolai Voznesenski and the death of Andrei Zhdanov. The debate over agriculture grew more intense as Georgi Malenkov and Nikita Khrushchev vied over who would control agricultural policy in the waning Stalin era. The politicization of agricultural policies and the influence of Lysenko made the exploration of alternative modes of organization, incentives, and scientific agronomy virtually impossible.[65] The nature of national political life inhibited efforts that might have attenuated the objective difficulties of postwar agricultural production.

Postwar agricultural policies produced a tension-ladden, crisis-prone system of agricultural production. The structural transformation of agriculture and the economic goals of agrarian policy placed particular pressure on local cadres responsible for policy results. The chaos and dislocation produced by the amalgamation campaign and the frequent revision of policy strengthened the authority of the party as the center's most trusted rural representative while undermining local agricultural leaders. Both structural and economic aspects of agricultural policy encouraged extraordinary methods. The party apparatus was the most likely agent to assume responsibility for policies promoting social and structural economic change. Even purely economic aspects of agricultural policy, such as meeting agricultural production targets,

64. Volkov et al., eds., *Sovetskaia derevnia*, pp. 456, 459, 461–63.

65. See Hahn, *Postwar Soviet Politics*; Medvedev, *Lysenko*; Joravsky, *Lysenko Affair*.

fostered party intervention when goals appeared to be threatened, as they frequently did. The plan's agricultural targets simply could not be met, given agriculture's low level of capital investment and inadequate labor force. Even such measures as mechanization, rural electrification, material incentives for labor, and labor reorganization stood little chance of rescuing the sector. Perhaps postwar conditions made successful agricultural production impossible. Nonetheless, the logic of the Stalinist model of economic development prevented the major policy shifts necessary if agriculture was to recover and grow in an orderly manner. Thus, unable or unwilling to devote substantial economic resources to kolkhozy or to apply scientific measures, the regime left agricultural production to its own devices.

Given the poor conditions of agricultural production caused by its long-term undercapitalization, the effects of the severe droughts of the postwar period, and a shortage of productive labor, it is not surprising that agricultural leaders found life a constant struggle to meet the plan. The people responsible for plan fulfillment at the district or kolkhoz level had to resort to extraordinary measures to survive professionally. Thus the demands and the style of agricultural policy set the parameters of the agricultural crisis. To understand the response to this crisis, we must investigate the people responsible for policy implementation at the local level.

CHAPTER 4

Agricultural Leaders

Postwar agricultural leaders played a crucial role in the evolution of policy implementation in the countryside. Their low
level of scientific expertise and questionable political reliability
strongly influenced their relations with local party officials. Given
agricultural and local party leaders' shared responsibility for agricultural production, a potentially interdependent relationship
based on mutual needs and respective strengths might have developed. It did not. Unlike the industrial sector, in which expertise
increasingly served as a basis of authority, encouraging a new
postwar relationship between secretaries of oblast party committees (obkoms) and factory directors, agriculture continued to be
dominated by political authority.

The nature of Soviet agricultural leadership and ultimately its
effectiveness were shaped by the consequences of World War II
and the Soviet regime's own policy preferences. The wartime mobilization of local agricultural leaders forced often inexperienced
kolkhozniki to assume positions of authority. These leaders and
those who were to replace them during the postwar years confronted virtually insoluble problems of agricultural production.
Soviet policy made little allowance for the deficiencies of agricultural leaders' backgrounds and the adverse conditions of production. As I have argued, the Soviet regime's strong economic

and political preference for industry served once again during the postwar period to relegate the rural sector to a secondary position in the recovery process—secondary not in terms of demands for results but as measured by capital investment and expertise. Central policy, while espousing agricultural mechanization and increased reliance on qualified rural leaders, did not in fact allocate the resources necessary to attain these goals. Conditions of postwar scarcity contributed to this situation. Although Soviet personnel policy sought to improve the training and increase the number of agricultural leaders, political considerations and basic administrative skills played a greater role in their selection than any technical knowledge of agriculture they may have acquired. Agricultural leadership was to remain rooted in the exercise of political power rather than in economic expertise or traditional authority. The centrality of high politics in agriculture is not confined to the Kremlin's elite politics; it permeates behavior at the local level.

The qualifications of local agricultural leaders during the early postwar years reflected the party's desire for control over agriculture—a policy that stressed organizational ability over expertise. This was a relatively low-cost policy. Efforts to improve the education of agricultural leaders foundered in the face of inadequate resources. Environmental factors that made professional success difficult at best and life in the countryside unappealing encouraged better-educated cadres and those with scarce skills to seek urban employment. If these observations are valid, agricultural leaders' level of expertise, job tenure, geographical origins, and political qualifications should support them. In turn, local agricultural leaders' background characteristics serve as tangible measures of their ability to carry out policy. Agricultural leaders' ability to attain policy goals shaped their relations with local party leaders.

Defining the Soviet Agricultural Elite

Which agricultural positions gained their holders membership in the rural agricultural elite? The most important positions at the production level were those of kolkhoz chairman, sovkhoz director, and machine tractor station director. Although the personnel

of raion (district) agricultural departments might warrant inclu-
sion, these cadres often attempted to avoid direct involvement in
policy implementation.

MTS directors' positions clearly differed from those of kolkhoz
chairmen and sovkhoz directors. In charge of mechanized services
crucial to agricultural production, MTS directors were responsible
to raion party officials. They supervised the mechanized work
carried out at kolkhozy by their skilled and semiskilled staffs. The
success of their work and their pay for at least part of the period
under consideration depended on services rendered, not agricultural results. Given their critical role in agricultural production
and their familiarity with relatively large territorial units, they
were often called upon by the party to assume administrative and
supervisory functions not officially part of their duties. Indeed,
MTS directors, along with MTS assistant directors for political
affairs, played an instrumental role in agriculture.[1] The narrow
and specialized nature of the services they performed, the wide
scope of the territory they served, the nature of their remuneration,
and the standards by which their performance was judged all
distinguish the MTS director's role from that of other agricultural
leaders. Theirs was a specialized role that, while integral to agricultural production, was not itself a primary factor in agricultural
policy implementation. Indeed, it might be argued that MTS directors and certainly their assistants for political affairs often
served as instruments of local party organizations. In this role,
they frequently acted as special representatives of raion party committees.[2] From a purely quantitative perspective, however, the
relatively small number of MTS's[3] limited their leaders' influence
on the evolving role of the party in agriculture.

The central figures in agricultural production were the kolkhoz
chairmen and sovkhoz directors. Although from a political per-

1. Robert F. Miller, *100,000 Tractors* (Cambridge: Harvard University Press,
1970), pp. 220–89; "O merakh pod'ema sel'skogo khoziaistva v poslevoennyi period" (Plenum TsK VKP[b], February 21–26, 1947), in *KPSS v rezoliutsiia i resheniiakh s"ezdov, konferentsii i plenumov TsK*, vol. 6, *1941–1954*, 8th ed.
(Moscow: Politicheskoi Literatury, 1971), pp. 210–60.

2. Machine tractor stations had a separate administrative hierarchy to which
names of candidates for appointment had to be submitted; MTS officials do not
appear to have competed for authority with raion-level party officials. See "O
merakh pod'ema."

3. See table 3.6.

spective the kolkhoz was seen as less progressive than the sovkhoz, it nonetheless remained the dominant type of production
unit measured by absolute numbers, acreage cultivated, and size
of work force.[4] Owing both to the regime's political preference for
the sovkhoz as a form of production and the often commercial
nature of its crops, this sector received substantially more investment than its kolkhoz counterpart.[5] The privileges enjoyed by
sovkhozy as state enterprises (as opposed to collectives) helped
the sovkhoz director to fulfill the plan. Although sovkhoz directors
were officially appointed by the Ministry of Sovkhozy USSR, in
fact these appointments often amounted to confirmation of decisions already taken by local party organs. The formal functions of
the Ministry of Sovkhozy at least theoretically allowed sovkhoz
directors a separate line of authority in the event of conflicts at
the local level, though they were unlikely to resort to it, given the
ministry's low status. Kolkhoz chairmen, as heads of democratic
collectives, were elected by the farm's members, the election results being subject to confirmation by the obkom. In reality, raikom
secretaries often selected kolkhoz chairmen, who were confirmed
by the obkom and even by the kolkhoz itself after the fact.[6] The
privileged position of sovkhoz directors suggests a more selective
personnel policy in regard to them than in regard to kolkhoz chair-

4. Data from *Sel'skoe khoziaistvo SSSR St. sb.* (Moscow: Gosstatizdat, 1960),
pp 47, 56, 57, 450, show the dominance of the kolkhoz sector (figures are in
thousands):

	Kolkhozy			Sovkhozy		
	1940	1950	1953	1940	1950	1953
Number	236.9	123.7	93.3	4.2	5.0	4.9
Work force	29,000.0	27,600.0	25,600.0	1,373.0	1,665.0	1,844.0
Hectares cultivated	117,700.0	121,000.0	132,000.0	11,559.0	12,894.0	15,155.0

5. Much of the investment in the kolkhoz sector was to come from the kolkhozy
themselves rather than from the state budget. See Eugene Zaleski, *Stalinist Planning for Economic Growth, 1933–1952*, trans. and ed. Marie-Christine MacAndrews
and John H. Moore (Chapel Hill: University of North Carolina Press, 1980), p. 424,
table 104; V. S. Dolgov, "Razukrupnenie kolkhozov v pervye poslevoennye gody
(1945–1950 gg.)," in *Problemy otechestvennoi istorii*, chast' 2, ed. A. M. Anfinmov
(Moscow: Institut Istorii SSSR, 1973), p. 82.

6. A. P. Tiurina, *Formirovanie kadrov spetsialistov i organizatorov kolkhoznogo proizvodstva, 1946–1958 gg.* (Moscow: Nauka, 1973), p. 95.

men, a factor that might have contributed to the superior qualifications of sovkhoz directors. Surprisingly, however, their actual
qualifications remained strikingly low during the immediate postwar years.

The position of kolkhoz chairmen changed somewhat during
the postwar period as a consequence of kolkhoz amalgamations
during the early 1950s. Kolkhozy that had coincided with a single
village before the amalgamation campaign now encompassed
three to five villages.[7] Thus the responsibility of kolkhoz chairmen
increased. At the same time, the decline in the number of positions
available after amalgamation permitted greater selectivity in the
appointment of kolkhoz chairmen. Whether the regime's conscious efforts to improve their qualifications was realized is a
matter to be examined.[8] The qualifications of kolkhoz chairmen,
like those of sovkhoz and MTS directors, reveal the regime's inability to carry out its stated cadre policy or possibly its unwill-
ingness to devote the resources necessary for success.

Kolkhoz chairmen's qualifications helped define their roles in
two respects. First, the better qualified the agricultural leader, the
more competent he or she should be, and the greater the likelihood
of successful implementation of policy. Second, to the extent that
greater selectivity resulted in greater numbers of party members
among kolkhoz chairmen, the party should have been willing to
grant them greater autonomy. Improvement in job performance as
a result of enhanced expertise and political reliability should have
made them more likely candidates for partnership with local political leaders. The direct effect of improved qualifications on kolkhoz chairmen's informal relations with party leaders also
depended on the latter's qualifications. The interaction of the two
roles and of the people who held them determined informal authority relations in the countryside.

7. The amalgamated kolkhozy were formed by combining three to five of the
former kolkhozy (I. M. Volkov et al., eds., Sovetskaia derevnia v pervye poslevoennye gody, 1946–1950 [Moscow: Nauka, 1978], p. 303; Dolgov, "Razukrupnenie," p. 84).
8. "O zadachakh partiinykh i sovetskikh organizatsii po dal'naishemu ukrepleniiu sostava predsedateli i drugikh rukovodiashchikh rabotnikov kolkhozov"
(Postanovlenie Soveta Ministrov SSSR i TsK VKP[b], July 9, 1950), in KPSS v
rezoliutsiiakh, 6: 323–31.

The Background Characteristics of Agricultural Leaders

The evolution of postwar party and state roles reflected the ambiguity of their formal functions, the influence of exogenous factors that shaped the policy environment, and the effect of agricultural leaders' background characteristics on their ability to perform satisfactorily. To the extent that expertise was officially stressed, better education and professional training might have contributed to a greater reliance on local agricultural officials in policy implementation. A knowledge of local conditions and the presence of local ties might also enhance local agricultural leaders' status and contribute to their ability to implement policy successfully. Knowledge of local conditions may be measured by cadres' geographic origin and length of job tenure. Finally, the issue of political reliability also affected the party's willingness to delegate authority to these leaders. The need to ensure political reliability led to the appointment of urban party members to rural jobs. Taken together, education, job tenure, and party membership reveal a great deal about the sources of local agricultural leaders' authority and their potential relations with local party representatives.

Expertise in Agriculture

Soviet agriculture has long suffered from a lack of trained personnel. The low qualifications of leading Soviet agricultural personnel limited their ability to surmount the uncertainties of agricultural production. This lack of expertise, along with the formal definition of their positions, helped shape their role in policy implementation.

In 1941 only 134,000 agricultural specialists were working under the auspices of the Ministry of Agricultural USSR. Among those specialists, only 54 had higher education and 80 had specialized secondary education. Just as striking was the distribution of these agricultural specialists. Forty-seven percent were located in administrative organs not directly involved in agricultural production. Only 22 percent occupied positions at machine tractor stations and kolkhozy. After the war, the number of specialists dropped to 104,600—78 percent of their 1940 level. This decline was particularly acute at raion agricultural departments and

MTS's, where the number of agronomists shrank by 20 and 41.5 percent, respectively.[9] In 1946, according to I. M. Volkov, "only 7 percent of all kolkhozy had agronomists, 3.6 percent had zoological technicians, and 17 percent had veterinarians and veterinary assistants."[10]

Soviet postwar policies sought to increase the number of agronomists working directly in agricultural production.[11] The results, however, were disappointing. Even after 1947, the majority of rural oblasts had 20 to 40 percent fewer specialists than they needed.[12] In 1948 only 3.7 percent of the agronomists within the Ministry of Agriculture system worked at kolkhozy. By 1951 this figure had risen only to 5.3 percent, despite salary incentives offered to encourage the transfer of specialists from administrative positions and to improve their retention at the production level.[13]

Efforts to increase the number of agronomists with higher and secondary education at kolkhozy during the Fourth Five-Year Plan met with little success. In 1946, 8,506 agronomists with higher and secondary education served at kolkhozy; in 1950 their numbers had grown to only 8,765.[14] Agricultural production benefited relatively little from the rise in agricultural graduates during the postwar years. With agricultural experts in short supply, the leading agricultural cadres, especially kolkhoz chairmen, had little opportunity to seek advice on problems of production. In light of this situation, the attempts by central authorities to raise the qualifications of agriculture's leading cadres take on even greater importance.

Postwar personnel policies had initially to confront the widespread decline in agricultural leaders' qualifications produced by wartime mobilization. The 60 to 70 percent of kolkhoz chairmen who were mobilized during the war were most frequently replaced by inexperienced and poorly educated women and elderly men from the countryside.[15] In 1945, before the great influx of demo-

9. Tiurina, *Formirovanie kadrov spetsialistov*, pp. 41–43.

10. I. M. Volkov, *Trudovoi podvig sovetskogo krest'ianstva v poslevoennye gody* (Moscow: Mysl', 1972), p. 230.

11. "O merakh pod'ma sel'skogo khoziaistva," p. 214.

12. Tiurina, *Formirovanie kadrov spetsialistov*, p. 230.

13. Volkov, *Trudovoi podvig*, p. 230.

14. Ibid.

15. Volkov et al., eds., *Sovetskaia derevnia*, pp. 44–45.

bilized soldiers, 90.7 percent of all kolkhoz chairmen had only primary education and 5.5 percent were semiliterate. Only 0.3 percent had higher and 3.5 percent secondary education.[16]

The lack of formal education among wartime agricultural leaders was not offset by the experience they gained: at the end of the war they were replaced by demobilized soldiers.[17] In 1945, 41.3 percent of all kolkhoz chairmen had less than one year's tenure. According to the archives of the Ministry of Agriculture, in 1946 two-fifths of all kolkhozy changed their chairman every year.[18] Consequently, in many areas demobilized soldiers comprised a high proportion of the total number of kolkhoz chairmen: 45.6 percent in Chkalovsk Oblast, for example, and 93.0 percent in Kaluga Oblast.[19] In the sovkhoz system, more than half of those appointed to positions of responsibility from July 1, 1945, to November 1, 1947, were demobilized soldiers.[20] Leadership ability demonstrated during the war appears to have been the major criterion for selection of agricultural leaders, as opposed to job experience or expertise. At the 1947 February Plenum of the Central Committee, after the initial influx of demobilized soldiers, the party adopted policies aimed at improving the qualifications of agricultural leaders. Although formal attention focused on establishing programs and institutions for agricultural education, in fact many urban cadres were simply transferred to the countryside.[21] Relatively few highly qualified agricultural specialists were appointed as kolkhoz chairmen.[22]

After the kolkhoz amalgamation campaign in 1950, which should have facilitated a more selective personnel policy, 87.6 percent of all kolkhoz chairmen still had only primary education.[23]

16. I. M. Volkov, "Kolkhoznaia derevnia v pervyi poslevoennyi god," *Voprosy istorii* 1 (1966): 19.

17. V. N. Donchenko, "Demobilizatsiia sovetskoi armii i reshenie problemy kadrov v pervye poslevoennye gody," *Istoriia SSSR*, no. 3 (May/June 1970), p. 102.

18. Volkov, "Kolkhoznaia derevnia," pp. 19, 29.

19. Donchenko, "Demobilizatsiia," p. 102.

20. M. L. Bogdenko and I. E. Zelenin, *Sovkhozy SSSR* (Moscow: Politicheskoi Literatury, 1976), p. 136.

21. Volkov, "Kolkhoznaia derevnia," p. 29; Jerry F. Hough, "The Changing Nature of the Kolkhoz Chairman," in *The Soviet Rural Community*, ed. James R. Millar (Urbana: University of Illinois Press, 1971), pp. 106–8.

22. Tiurina, *Formirovanie kadrov spetsialistov*, pp. 89–90.

23. Volkov, *Trudovoi podvig*, p. 241.

By 1953 the proportion of kolkhoz chairmen with higher and secondary education had increased to only 18 percent.[24] Clearly, in spite of financial incentives and political pressure, recent graduates of institutions of higher education and technical institutes did not seek positions directly involved in agricultural production, particularly that of kolkhoz chairman.[25] Although 133,700 newly trained agricultural experts (including 81.5 percent with specialized secondary education and 18.5 percent with higher education) were sent to work in agriculture, only 5.2 percent of all local agricultural specialists worked at kolkhozy in 1951 and only slightly more than half of them were agronomists.[26] Thus, despite the regime's attempts to increase the pool of agricultural experts, expertise at the local level remained relatively rare. Of course, the quality of agricultural education during this time was also questionable.[27]

The qualifications of sovkhoz and MTS directors and specialized agricultural personnel clearly surpassed those of their kolkhoz counterparts. Of the directors of sovkhozy under the all-union system, 16.3 percent had specialized agricultural educations in 1947 and 13.8 percent in 1948. By 1950 the proportion of sovkhoz directors with higher or secondary education had risen to 70 percent from 39 percent in 1947.[28] This improvement was achieved by the expedient of sending young specialists to work in rural areas. This strategy also encountered obstacles, however. From 1947 through 1950, 11,840 graduates of institutions of high education were sent to the countryside, but only 6,388 actually arrived. Nonetheless, 24.7 percent of all sovkhoz directors had specialized higher education by 1950 and 31.9 percent by 1953. Renewed criticism of sovkhoz directors' qualifications led to in-

24. *Narodnoe khoziaistvo SSSR v 1960 godu st. ezhegodnik* (Moscow: Gosstatizdat, 1961), p. 526.

25. "O zadachakh partiinykh i sovetskikh organizatsii po dal'neishemu ukrepleniiu sostava predsedatelei i drugikh rukovodiashchikh rabotnikov kolkhozov" (Postanovlenie Soveta Ministrov SSSR i TsK VKP[b], July 9, 1950), in *Direktivy KPSS i Sovetskogo pravitel'stva po khoziaistvennym voprosam*, vol. 3, *1946–1952 gody* (Moscow: Politicheskoi Literatury, 1958), pp. 521–28.

26. Tiurina, *Formirovanie kadrov spetsialistov*, pp. 48, 52.

27. See ibid., pp. 59–85, for a detailed description of the achievements and weaknesses of Soviet agricultural education.

28. I. E. Zelenin, *Sovkhozy SSSR, 1941–1950* (Moscow: Nauka, 1969), pp. 188, 186; see also Volkov et al., eds., *Sovetskaia derevnia*, p. 132.

creased attention to their qualifications during the early 1950s.[29] Although many of the more highly qualified cadres left agriculture after a short time, the favored position of sovkhozy, the centralized personnel system, and the smaller number of positions to be filled led to greater success in the attempt to raise sovkhoz leaders' qualifications than comparable efforts focused on kolkhoz chairmen had managed to achieve.

The qualifications of MTS personnel also rose during the postwar years. By January 1950, 40.6 percent of all (7,891) MTS directors had higher and secondary education, while 17.2 percent had incomplete secondary and 42.2 percent primary education.[30] Those with at least secondary education increased to 45.1 percent by 1951.[31] In 1952, 23.5 percent of all MTS directors had higher education.[32] This level of education was roughly the same as that found among sovkhoz directors and substantially higher than that of kolkhoz chairmen.

Given regional variations within the USSR, differences among the local agricultural elites are also germane, particularly in regard to the dominant agricultural leaders, the kolkhoz chairmen, whose appointment was not centrally controlled. The widespread desire among agricultural specialists to avoid positions directly responsible for implementation of agricultural policy affected kolkhoz chairmanships, and better-educated kolkhoz chairmen clearly preferred positions close to cities or in more productive areas of the country.[33] These two trends were not unrelated. The availability

29. M. L. Bogdenko, Sovkhozy SSSR (1951–1958) (Moscow: Nauka, 1972), pp. 40, 64, 54–58.

30. A. P. Tiurina, "Ukreplenie kolkhozov i MTS kadrami rukovoditelei i spetsialistov (1946–1958 gg.)," in Razvitie sel'skogo khoziaistva SSSR v poslevoennye gody (1946–1970 gg.), ed. I. M. Volkov (Moscow: Nauka, 1972), p. 236.

31. Volkov et al., eds., Sovetskaia derevnia, p. 143.

32. V. M. Rezvanov, ed., Organizatorskaia i politicheskaia rabota partii na sele (Rostov-on-Don: Izdatel'stvo Rostovskogo Universiteta, 1966), p. 22.

33. In 1950, for example, 73.2% of kolkhoz chairmen in fertile Georgia were agricultural specialists; in Armenia, 71.8%; in Krasnodar, 54.4%; and in Astrakhan, 47.8%. Specialists comprised only 13.9% in Orlov, 9.9% in Chkalovsk, 8.5% in Kalinin, 8.8% in Tul', and 3.8% in Tomsk (Tiurina, "Ukreplenie kolkhozov i MTS kadrami," pp. 237–38.) See the data for Leningrad Oblast below. In Moscow Oblast 30.1% of kolkhoz chairmen had higher and specialized secondary education (N. S. Ivanov, "Chislennost' i sostav krest'ianstva tsentral'nykh oblastei nechernozemnoi zony RSFSR [1951–1958 gg.]," in Problemy istorii sovetskogo krest'ianstva, ed. M. P. Kim [Moscow: Nauka, 1981], p. 212). See also Iu. P. Denisov, "Kadry predsedatelei kolkhozov v 1950–1968 gg.," Istorii SSSR 15 (1971): 40.

of transportation was crucial if the kolkhoz was to sell produce at the peasant market—a factor critical to its financial well-being.

The qualifications of kolkhoz chairmen were correlated with a region's agricultural potential. "In the Caucasian republics," Volkov relates, "55.9 percent of kolkhoz chairmen at the end of the Five-Year Plan (1950) had secondary and higher education; in Krasnodar Krai, 38 percent; and in the Ukraine, 15 percent. But in Pskov Oblast, kolkhoz chairmen with such preparation number only 2 percent, in Velikoluksk Oblast 5 percent."[34] The low educational levels found among kolkhoz chairmen in non-black-earth regions and Siberia remained a problem throughout the recovery period. In Siberia, 86 percent of all kolkhoz chairmen did not even have secondary education by 1953.[35]

The trend in poorer agricultural areas was sometimes moderated by the presence of industry. Despite unfavorable natural conditions, if an area had a large urban center generally associated with industry, agricultural leaders tended to have superior levels of education. This was certainly the case in Leningrad Oblast. Nonetheless, after the February Plenum of the Central Committee in 1947, P. S. Popkov, the first secretary of the Leningrad obkom, noted that "1,790 (97.8 percent) of all kolkhoz chairmen [in Leningrad Oblast] have only primary education, only 20 incomplete secondary education, and 20 completed secondary education." This situation dramatically improved during the recovery period.[36] By 1952, 30 percent of all kolkhoz chairmen were classified as agricultural specialists.[37] Here as elsewhere, the increase in kolkhoz chairmen's qualifications was achieved by the strategy of sending urban cadres formerly employed in industry and recent graduates of agricultural schools to rural areas.[38]

---

34. Volkov, Trudovoi podvig, p. 238. In Belorussia in 1953 only 1.4% of kolkhoz chairmen had higher education, 20.2% secondary, and 50% primary (V. K. Shatik, "Deiatel'nost' KPB po ukrepleniiu sostava predsedatelei kolkhozov respubliki v piatoi piatiletke [1950–1955 gg.]," in Deiatel'nost' kompartii Belorusii v period sotsialisticheskogoi kommunisticheskogo stroitel'stva, ed. V. M. Sikorskii [Minsk: BGU, 1969], p. 113).

35. L. N. Ul'ianov, Trudovoi rabochego klassa i krest'ianstva Sibiri 1945–1953 gg. (Tomsk: Izdatel'stvo Tomskogo Universiteta, 1979), p. 89.

36. Leningradskaia Pravda, March 20, 1947.

37. Ibid., April 1, 1952.

38. Tiurina, Formirovanie kadrov spetsialistov, p. 82.

In Rostov Oblast in 1946, 92.5 percent of all kolkhoz chairmen had only primary education. By 1950, 89.1 percent of kolkhoz chairmen remained in this category; only 4.9 percent had completed secondary and higher education. Those classified as agricultural specialists constituted slightly less than 7 percent of all kolkhoz chairmen.[39] From 1949 to 1951, 900 kolkhoz chairmen in Rostov Oblast were replaced by individuals with agricultural educations.[40] By September 1953, of a total of 867 kolkhoz chairmen, those with higher and secondary education (171) slightly surpassed the national average at 19.7 percent.[41]

Data for Rostov Oblast permit a detailed analysis of the process by which the educational qualifications of kolkhoz chairmen improved. A significant increase among those with secondary education occurred in 1948, the final year of demobilization. The departure of recently demobilized soldiers who had been appointed as kolkhoz chairmen for industrial jobs resulted in a slight decline in kolkhoz chairmen's qualifications. The next significant increase occurred with the 1950 kolkhoz amalgamation campaign. Although the number of kolkhoz chairmen with higher education was fairly stable by 1951, those with secondary education increased by 44.4 percent, or from 13.3 to 27.2 percent of all kolkhoz chairmen in Rostov Oblast. Rostov's kolkhoz chairmen were still far from constituting a highly qualified agricultural elite, but the increase among those with secondary education was real, not due to the decline in the number of kolkhozy. Yet the magnitude of these increases in the qualifications of kolkhoz chairmen failed to create a new Soviet technical agricultural elite analogous to that found in industry.

39. S. G. Mogilevskii, "Partiino-organizatsionnaia rabota na sele gody chetvertoi piatiletki (1946–1950 gg.) (Na materialakh partiinykh organizatsii Rostovskoi oblasti, Krasnodarskogo i Stavropol'skogo kraev)," candidate dissertation, Rostov State University, 1972, pp. 193–94, 196; P. V. Barchugov, ed., Ocheri istorii partiinykh organizatsii Dona, 1921–1971, chast' 2 (Rostov-on-Don: Rostovskoe Knizhnoe Izdatel'stvo, 1973), p. 477. The sources provide no information about the 6% of kolkhoz chairmen who had neither primary nor secondary education; presumably they had no formal schooling at all.

40. Mogilevskii, "Partiino-organizatsionnaia rabota," p. 197.

41. Barchugov, Ocheri istorii, p. 516. Leaders' qualifications tended to be better than average in areas where grain was cultivated.

Job Tenure

Despite the limited expertise of kolkhoz chairmen, they might have claimed expanded authority on the basis of their knowledge of local conditions or extensive agricultural experience. Such expertise was often attributed to them by Soviet writers of the early postwar period. Upon examination, however, these alternative sources of authority disappear. Knowledge of agriculture in general and of local conditions in particular may be indirectly measured by length of service at the kolkhoz and the geographic origins of cadres.

Cadre stability was a conscious objective of Soviet policy. Nonetheless, this goal was inconsistent, at least in the short run, with policies aimed at improving cadres' qualifications. Some agricultural leaders were removed because their education was inadequate; others left voluntarily in order to retrain. The option of retraining while on the job, popular during the early postwar years, was ultimately unsatisfactory. Efforts to increase education had two unanticipated consequences. First, they contributed to the relatively high turnover rates found among kolkhoz chairmen, already substantial as a result of policy failures. Second, better educational qualifications facilitated the transfer of young, recently trained agricultural leaders to the urban sector and administrative jobs.

During the initial postwar period, the influx of demobilized soldiers to replace ill-prepared, makeshift administrative teams contributed to substantial turnover rates. From 1947 to 1949, one-third to half of all kolkhoz chairmen were changed each year.[42] The source of cadre instability changed after the demobilization concluded. Beginning in 1948, new graduates arrived to replace agricultural cadres. Though turnover rates declined, they remained significant. The amalgamation of kolkhozy maintained an average national turnover rate of slightly under 25 percent among kolkhoz chairmen during the early 1950s. By 1953, a majority of kolkhoz chairmen still had held their positions for less than three years, as table 4.1 indicates.

Although national data on turnover rates among kolkhoz chairmen remain incomplete, a complete set of data is available for

42. Volkov et al., eds., *Sovetskaia derevnia*, p. 414.

TABLE 4.1
Tenure of kolkhoz chairmen, USSR, 1946–1953 (percent)

Tenure	1946	1947	1948	1952	1953
Less than 1 year	41.3%	38.0%	27.0%	23.5%	23.8%
1–3 years	30.0	34.0	39.7	36.1	35.6
3 years +	28.7	28.0	33.3	40.4	40.6

Sources: I. M. Volkov, Trudovoi podvig sovetskogo krest'ianstva v poslevoennye gody (Moscow: Mysl', 1972), p. 223; speech by A. A. Andreev, published in Molot, March 8, 1947; Narodnoe khoziaistvo SSSR v 1960 gody St. ezhegodnik (Moscow: Gosstatizdat, 1961), p. 526.

Rostov Oblast. The data show a trend toward increasing stability among kolkhoz chairmen until the beginning of the amalgamation campaign in 1950 (see table 4.2).

As might be expected, turnover rates among kolkhoz leaders vary by region. Once again, those areas with the greatest potential for agricultural success tended to retain cadres, while poorer areas suffered from greater instability. From 40 to 60 percent of chairmen in the Caucasian republics and Central Asia at the end of 1950 had held their posts more than three years, but only 30 to 35 percent had done so in Pskov, Briansk, Smolensk, and other oblasts.[43] A contributing factor in this regional variation was the regime's policy of sending party cadres and recent agricultural graduates to the poorest agricultural areas and to those newly

TABLE 4.2
Tenure of kolkhoz chairmen, Rostov Oblast, 1945–1951 (percent)

Year	Number of kolkhoz chairmen	Less than 1 year	1–3 years	3 years +
1945	1,854	44.5	29.8	25.7
1946	1,866	41.9	30.2	27.9
1947	1,872	31.2	39.7	29.1
1948	1,876	23.8	36.1	40.1
1949	1,872	26.5	26.7	46.8
1950	1,276	34.9	22.4	42.7
1951	896	30.6	30.2	39.2

Source: N. V. Grebeniuk, "Partiinoe rukovodstvo osushchestvleniem demokraticheskie printsipov upravleniia v kolkhozakh (1946–1950 gg.)," candidate dissertation, Rostov State University, 1974, p. 201, table 8.

43. Volkov, Trudovoi podvig, p. 238.

incorporated into the USSR.[44] This policy resulted not only in the initial removal of cadres but in continued personnel instability, as many experts left their posts as soon as they could. In 1950, 403 specialists arrived in Azerbaidzhan, but in the same year 291 left; in the Ukraine the corresponding figures were 3,437 and 2,326; in Belorussia, 363 and 233; in Georgia, 744 and 381; and in Kazakhstan, 510 and 211. This trend can also be seen in relatively poor areas, especially those with large industrial cities that attracted rural migrants. In 1950 Moscow Oblast welcomed 582 agricultural specialists, but in the same year 524 (90 percent) left. Leningrad fared only slightly better: in the same year the oblast gained 327 specialists and lost 233 (over 71 percent).[45] Although these figures are not a direct indication of turnover rates among kolkhoz chairmen, they do indirectly illustrate an important factor in cadre instability.

The short tenures of kolkhoz chairmen prevented them from acquiring comprehensive knowledge of local conditions, and they did not have time to develop personal relationships with the local population which might have helped them in their efforts to implement policy. These problems were exacerbated by the fact that many of the new kolkhoz chairmen came from urban areas.[46]

As these observations suggest, the high turnover rates among kolkhoz chairmen were partially produced by the regime's own changing personnel criteria. During the immediate postwar years, leadership and general administrative ability were emphasized; later specialized education came to dominate the selection process.[47] One additional qualification was to become increasingly important for kolkhoz chairmen at the beginning of the 1950s: party membership.

Party membership was particularly important during the postwar years because of peasants' distress at the recollectivization of agriculture and the superficial political penetration of the countryside.[48] Inhabitants of areas that had been occupied by the Ger-

44. Tiurina, *Formirovanie kadrov spetsialistov*, p. 82.

45. Volkov et al., eds., *Sovetskaia derevnia*, p. 140.

46. Tiurina, *Formirovanie kadrov spetsialistov*, pp. 46–47.

47. Volkov, "Kolkhoznaia derevnia," p. 29; Hough, "Changing Nature of the Kolkhoz Chairman," pp. 106–7.

48. Volkov et al., eds., *Sovetskaia derevnia*, p. 416; I. E. Zelenin, *Obshchestvenno-politicheskaia zhizn' sovetskoi derevni, 1946–1958 gg.* (Moscow: Nauka,

mans during the war were often suspect, particularly because the Nazis had co-opted large numbers of them as slave labor. The isolation of kolkhozy on their all but impassable roads intensified official suspicion.

Soviet policy sought to increase party membership among members of the rural intelligentsia and to further the political penetration of kolkhoz agriculture. T. H. Rigby has estimated that in 1948 only 40 percent of all kolkhoz chairmen were party members.[49] The amalgamation campaign dramatically improved this situation. By 1953, 79.6 percent of the nation's kolkhoz chairmen were either party members of candidates for membership.[50]

Party membership had long been an important factor in the selection of MTS and sovkhoz personnel. Special political officials were put in charge during collectivization and during the war, and these positions were reintroduced in 1947. Such representatives frequently were drawn from among full-time party workers.[51] Although it is probably safe to assume that party membership was substantially higher among MTS and sovkhoz directors than among kolkhoz chairmen, few Soviet data exist to document such a conclusion.[52] It is known that 96 percent of MTS directors in the RSFSR in 1946–47 and 98.9 percent of all MTS directors in the USSR in 1952 were party members.[53] In the spring of 1947, a quarter of all MTS assistant directors for political affairs (zampolity) had been party members for more than seventeen years and 55 percent for not less than seven years. By the end of the year, only 3.4 percent of all MTS's did not have special political

---

1978), pp. 35 (table 3), 38; M. L. Gutin, "Vosstanovlenie partiinykh organizatsii na osvobozhdennoi territorii v gody Velikoi Otechestvennoi voiny," Voprosy istorii KPSS, no. 7 (1974), p. 84. See chap. 2.

49. T. H. Rigby, Communist Party Membership in the U.S.S.R., 1917–1967 (Princeton: Princeton University Press, 1968), p. 474.

50. Sel'skoe khoziaistvo SSSR (1960), p. 474.

51. Miller, 100,000 Tractors, p. 280.

52. In 1953 all 107 sovkhoz directors in Leningrad Oblast were party members (S. V. Stepanov, Za krutoi pod'em sel'skogo khoziaistva: Iz opyta raboty partiinykh organizatsii Leningradskoi oblasti [1953–1960 gg.] [Leningrad: Lenizdat, 1961], p. 34).

53. Tiurina, Formirovanie kadrov spetsialistov, p. 113; V. B. Chistiakov, "Deiatel'nost' partii po podgotovke spetsialistov sel'skogo khoziaistva i rukovodiashchikh kadrov kolkhozov RSFSR v pervy poslevoennye gody (1946–1950 gg.)," abstract, candidate dissertation, Moscow Institute of Economics im. G. V. Plekhanov, 1976, p. 23.

departments.[54] Thus it is reasonable to assume that the leaders of all MTS's and sovkhozy were probably party members. Even if they themselves were not members, their special assistants for political affairs certainly were.

Four major factors critical to the behavior of agricultural leaders emerge from this analysis: their low levels of formal and specialized education, their high turnover rates, their urban origins, and initially their low levels of party membership. These characteristics apply most clearly to kolkhoz chairmen, who dominated Soviet agricultural leadership positions; they are seen to a lesser degree in sovkhoz and MTS directors. It can be argued that because of their informal subordination to raion party committees and the nature of their functions, MTS directors should not be viewed as functional equivalents of kolkhoz chairmen and sovkhoz directors. While sovkhoz directors were beneficiaries of the Soviet regime's political preference for the state sector, they nonetheless exhibit many of the characteristics associated with their kolkhoz counterparts. The most notable exception was their high rate of party membership. Although formally subordinated to the Ministry of Sovkhozy, sovkhoz directors were subject to many of the same pressures as kolkhoz chairmen. The factors that distinguished sovkhoz directors from their more numerous kolkhoz counterparts, however, were not so extensive as to cause the party's role in the implementation of agricultural policy to vary substantially in the two types of enterprise.

The characteristics of local agricultural leaders clearly distinguish them from their industrial counterparts and make them unlikely candidates for the role of either crisis manager or equal partner with local party leaders. Plant directors during the recovery period fall into two categories, the postpurge generation and the group that Jerry Hough has called "post-revolutionary professionals."[55] The former group enjoyed a greater degree of technical

54. Zelenin, Obshchestvenno-politicheskaia zhizn', p. 42; "Pis'ma zamestitelei direktorov MTS po politchasti," Partiinaia zhizn', no. 13 (1947), p. 37.

55. Jerry F. Hough, The Soviet Prefects (Cambridge: Harvard University Press, 1969), pp. 42–43, 49. The typical person who because a plant director after the Great Purges was a graduate of a provincial engineering institute who had spent a brief period at technical or political work before completing his education. Careers were marked by rapid advancement. The directors who assumed their positions in the late 1940s and early 1950s were younger than their predecessors.

expertise than the latter, who nonetheless had some formal education and long years of professional experience. Factory directors did not necessarily, however, remain at the same posts throughout the postwar period. A Leningrad sample shows some evidence of lateral transfers, and of course many careers were interrupted by wartime service.[56] Some members of the sample eventually entered ministerial work or became involved in the work of soviets. As a group, industrial managers were considered politically reliable. Thus the background characteristics of factory directors suggest a group of increasingly expert, experienced, and politically reliable managers. These beneficiaries of the Stalinist industrialization drive and the Great Purges were to form the new social elite of the mature Stalinist system. Their independent base of authority, derived from their expertise, and the regime's own preferences helped form a system of industrial management in which the party increasingly assumed a coordinating staff role.[57]

The background characteristics that enabled industrial managers to expand their authority and eventually to enter into a partnership with provincial party leaders were missing among postwar agricultural leaders. Lacking expertise and local experience, agricultural leaders enjoyed neither a formal basis of independent authority promoted by the regime nor an informal basis of authority derived from their own ability to fulfill the plan. Policy failures, of course, cannot be laid solely at their door; they were victims of the desperate state of the policy environment and unremitting pressure to meet impossible plan targets. Although the regime encouraged agricultural education and training, it could not neutralize the lure of the cities: people with higher or specialized education were needed there, too, and they went. The

---

They joined the party in their early thirties and had little work experience before enrolling in rigorous institute programs. Their career mobility was moderate.

56. The Leningrad sample included twenty factory directors and two chief engineers. Data used to assemble their biographies were drawn from *Leningradskaia Pravda*, 1946–53; *Deputaty Verkhovnogo Soveta SSSR* (Moscow: Izdatel'stvo Izvestiia, 1959, 1962, 1966); *Directory of Soviet Officials* (Washington, D.C.: U.S. Government Printing Office, 1955); *Leningradtsy—geroi sotsialisticheskogo truda* (Leningrad: Lenizdat, 1967); M. S. Kurtynin, *Pokoleniia udarnikov* (Leningrad: Leninzdat, 1963); V. A. Kutuzov and E. G. Levina, eds., *Vozrozhdenie: Vospominaniia, ocherki, i dokumenty o vosstanovlenii Leningrada* (Leningrad: Lenizdat, 1977).

57. See Hough, *Soviet Prefects.*

quick fix of importing urban industrial cadres for positions of rural leadership only temporarily improved incumbents' qualifications. The transfer of cadres helped to eliminate illiteracy and to increase party membership among agricultural leaders, but economic success continued to elude them. A large proportion of these urban migrants fled the countryside within a short time.

The regime's postwar personnel policies did achieve some positive results. After 1950, party membership among kolkhoz chairmen grew substantially. The regime achieved this gain by appointing party members, not by increasing political saturation among agricultural professionals. Increases in party membership surpassed gains in cadres' education. Although fewer agricultural leaders had only primary education now, relatively little progress was made in creating a specialized, technical elite. Ultimately, the attributes of local agricultural leaders during the postwar recovery period contributed little to their capacity to achieve economic goals. Nor did these attributes serve to increase local agricultural leaders' status vis-à-vis local party leaders, whose own background characteristics still were superior. Unlike industrial managers after the war, agricultural leaders had little opportunity to develop an interdependent, cooperative relationship with local party leaders. Political authority remained central to the evolving postwar pattern of agricultural policy implementation.

CHAPTER 5

The Party and Rural Party Leaders

Postwar local party leaders represented a new political generation, receptive to the influence of policy tasks, the policy environment, and the regime's efforts to define a new role for the party.
Their sensitivity to these factors was heightened by the absence
of long-established patterns of party organizational behavior after
the disruptions of the purges and the war. Indeed, the purges and
the war had severed the human link necessary for the replication
of learned behavior. The ambiguity implicit in the regime's attempts to construct new political and economic functions for the
party enhanced local leaders' ability to shape their emergent roles.
Accordingly, the party sought to increase these new leaders' political and educational qualifications, which varied widely.

The nature of economic policies, the structure of the workplace,
the formal structure of administration, and the economic and political environments in which policy was implemented all helped
to determine the extent to which local party leaders' qualifications
affected party behavior. Thus the characteristics of these leaders
are important from the organizational perspective, even though
they probably did not determine particular types of behavior. Indeed, the chaos resulting from the transformation of the Soviet
political system at the end of the Stalinist revolution, the war, and

86

the absence of older leaders accustomed to established patterns of behavior served to enhance the influence of leaders' background characteristics on the evolution of informal behavior.[1]

As we saw in chapter 4, local party leaders shared their responsibility for policy results with their economic counterparts. The party's official economic role was to become increasingly indirect, however, as economic leaders enjoyed the right of one-man management. As party leaders were urged to focus on the supervision and verification of policy implementation, their relations with economic leaders were supposed to become increasingly interdependent. This tendency was fostered by the parallel structure of party and state economic lines of authority. The evolution of roles and patterns of behavior as party leaders worked to implement policy contributed to expectations later associated with party functions and to what Robert K. Merton has termed "patterned behavior and relationships" that came to characterize the structure of policy implementation.[2]

The postwar model of indirect party leadership implicitly required economic leaders whose expertise could be relied on to ensure plan fulfillment and primary party organizations that could monitor workplace activities and carry out propaganda and agitation. These prerequisites, as we shall see, were more fully met in industry than in agriculture. Given postwar conditions, economic policies, historical and political preferences, and the nature of industrial and agricultural production, the industrial sector was able to maximize the effect of expertise, while agriculture continued to rely heavily on political authority. Thus both consciously pursued central policies and the unintended consequences of postwar conditions caused local political and agricultural leaders to develop a working relationship quite different from that found in the industrial sector. These factors, in conjunction with the background characteristics of local party leaders, led them to create the role of agricultural crisis manager.

1. See Seweryn Bialer, *Stalin's Successors* (New York: Cambridge University Press, 1980), p. 101; Arthur L. Stinchcombe, *Constructing Social Theories* (New York: Harcourt, Brace & World, 1968), pp. 105, 107–17.

2. Robert K. Merton, *Social Theory and Social Structure*, enl. ed. (New York: Free Press, 1968), pp. 422–23.

Local Party Leaders

A focus on the actual pattern of behavior exhibited by party apparatchiki in rural areas inevitably raises the issue of whether the loci of informal authority in the process of policy implementation differed in urban and rural areas. After the war, the first secretary of the obkom (of the city committee, or gorkom, after the division of the positions in provinces with major cities, such as Leningrad and Moscow) had general responsibility for the oblast and particular responsibility for industrial production, especially all-union industry.[3] The first obkom secretary enjoyed the authority to modify local policy in order to ensure successful policy implementation. In agricultural areas, the first obkom secretary also retained overall authority and responsibility for plan fulfillment, but the dispersion of agricultural work over a large area and the inability to standardize the production process caused the real work of implementing agricultural policy to fall to the rural raion party organization. Indeed, the Soviet party theoretician Lazar Slepov stated that in the area of "agriculture, the obkom influences the work of kolkhozy, MTS's, and sovkhozy above all through party raikoms, increasing their responsibility for the state of affairs."[4] On the most vital issues of economic performance, such as planting decisions, procurement quotas, and on-site verification of activities, it was thus the rural raikom apparatus that exercised authority. The background characteristics of these leaders are most crucial to an understanding of local party leaders' relations with agricultural leaders. What were the background characteristics of these rural party apparatchiki? How did rural party leaders differ from their urban counterparts? The answers to these questions provide a measure of rural/urban party differentiation that contributed to distinctive patterns of party behavior.

Despite a centralized cadre policy that sought to create generalists with extensive experience in both industry and agriculture, an urban/rural cleavage based on qualifications existed at the ob-

3. Lazar Slepov, *Mestnye partiinye organy* (Moscow: Vysshei Partiinoi Shkole pri TsK KPSS, 1954), pp. 25–26.
4. Ibid., p. 27.

last party level.[5] Obkom secretaries as a group survived the purges. Those in agricultural oblasts in 1941 tended to be somewhat older and more poorly educated than those in industrial oblasts. After the war, these immediate beneficiaries of the purges, particularly those in industrial areas, began to give way to a slightly younger and better-educated cohort who had joined the party during industrialization and collectivization. The political tenure of obkom first secretaries in 1955 reflected these postwar changes. Only about a fifth of the obkom first secretaries in industrial and RSFSR oblasts had held their posts before 1950.[6] As a group, the secretaries of obkoms, kraikoms (territory party committees), and republican party committees were now better educated than their predecessors. Those with at least some higher education increased from 50.2 percent in 1946 to 77.8 percent in 1952; those with no more than secondary education declined from 27.9 percent to 17.8 percent.[7]

Most leaders had received a political education, though industrial specializations also showed an increase. A relatively small percentage of first obkom secretaries had pursued agricultural specialties before 1953.[8] General education levels as well as the extent and type of specialized training suggest Moscow's increased attentiveness to expertise among obkom secretaries in industrialized areas. This emphasis is consistent with the dominance of engineers in the higher echelons of the party.

Obkom first secretaries are the most carefully selected members of the apparatus beneath the Politburo; they are really an elite at the top of the local apparatus. While the party's organizational

5. Brezhnev was a prime example of this pattern. See Bialer, *Stalin's Successors*, pp. 114–15.

6. Jerry F. Hough, *The Soviet Prefects* (Cambridge: Harvard University Press, 1969), pp. 50, 52, 65, 71. In 1941 the average birth date of RSFSR obkom secretaries in agriculture was 1900, and average age at party entry was 22. One of eight secretaries was an engineer. The average obkom secretary in industry was born in 1904 and joined the party at age 21; nearly half were engineers (ibid., p. 39).

7. Data for 1946 are from V. N. Donchenko, "Perestroika riadov VKP(b) v period SSSR ot voiny k miru (1945–1948 gody)" candidate dissertation, Moscow State University, 1972, p. 213. Data for 1952 are from "KPSS v tsifrakh," *Partiinaia zhizn'*, no. 14 (July 1973), p. 25.

8. Robert E. Blackwell, Jr., "Elite Recruitment and Functional Change: An Analysis of the Soviet Obkom Elite, 1950–1968," *Journal of Politics* 34 (1972): 136.

behavior was influenced by these leaders, however, it was more forcefully shaped by the local parties more broadly defined. The differences in characteristics between first secretaries in agricultural and industrial obkoms were even more pronounced at the level of raion and primary party organizations.

Like the obkom secretaries, many apparatchiki at the city and district levels assumed their positions immediately after the purges.[9] Unlike most obkom first secretaries, however, this group was subject to large-scale mobilization during the war.[10] Many of those who served in the armed forces or joined partisan movements did not survive.[11] As a whole, these leaders lacked prewar professional party experience.

In all parts of the country the party apparatchiki who replaced them also tended to be politically inexperienced; this was the first professional party position that most of them had held. In Rostov Oblast, for example, only 17 of 155 oblast party workers had prewar experience, just under 11 percent.[12] During the war years, 78.0 percent of the Rostov Obkom party apparatus was replaced, 86.4 percent of raion committee members, and 98.7 percent of

9. V. K. Beliakov and N. A. Zolotarev, *Organizatsiia uesiateriaet sily* (Moscow: Politicheskoi Literatury, 1975), p. 85.

10. Within the first two years of the war Leningrad sent 1,786 of its leading party members; Belorussia sent 19 of its 69 obkom secretaries and 285 of its 600 gorkom and raikom secretaries; Ivanovo sent 600 responsible workers and 2,400 PPO secretaries; Volgograd sent 519 of the 1,509 members of its obkom nomenklatura; Uzbekistan sent 25% of obkom, gorkom, and raikom secretaries; Kirgizia sent 1,300 of its central committee nomenklatura, and Tadzhikistan 1,079; Kirov sent 32.5% of the heads of raikom departments in the first two and a half months (N. A. Krasnov, *Partiinye mobilizatsii na front v gody Velikoi Otechestvennoi voinu* [Moscow: Izdatel'stvo Moskovskogo Universiteta, 1978], pp. 17–25). In Kazakhstan by the end of 1942, 15.7% of gorkom and raikom secretaries, 65.4% of department heads, and 42.2% of PPO secretaries had left for the front (S. B. Beisembaev and P. M. Pakmurnyi, *Kommunisticheskaia partiia Kazakhstana v dokumentakh i tsifrakh* [Alma Ata: Kazakhskoe Gosudarstvennoe Izdatel'stvo, 1960], p. 256). In Siberia, 71.7% of the Irkutsk party secretaries were mobilized (Iu. A. Vasil'ev, *Sibirskii arsenal, 1941–1945* [Sverdlovsk: Sredne-Ural'skoe Knizhnoe Izdatel'stvo, 1965], p. 233).

11. T. H. Rigby, *Communist Party Membership in the U.S.S.R., 1917–1967* (Princeton: Princeton University Press, 1978), p. 272.

12. P. I. Dubonosov, "Organizatorskaia i politicheskaia rabota kommunisticheskoi partii po vosstanovlenniiu i razvitiiu narodnogo khoziaistva v poslevoennyi period (1946–1950 gg.)," doctoral dissertation, Rostov State Pedagogical Institute, 1972, p. 133.

primary party secretaries.[13] In Leningrad, 82.6 percent of the party apparatus was new by the end of the war.[14] In Belorussia, 28 percent of the raikom and gorkom secretaries were elected for the first time in 1946; so were 45 percent of the raikom and gorkom bureau members and 64 percent of the total raikom and gorkom membership.[15] In Smolensk, another area devastated by the war, of 1,037 prewar raikom and gorkom members, only 178 (17.2 percent) remained at its conclusion.[16] Party organizations located away from front-line areas were also affected. Saratov's gorkom and raikom membership sharply declined during the war.[17] Even Siberia's gorkom and raikom secretaries underwent a substantial renewal.[18]

Data from Kalinin Oblast provide a somewhat more detailed picture of cadre changes caused by the war. According to the first secretary of the Kalinin obkom, I. Boitsov, Kalinin's experience was fairly typical. Of the total number of raikom and gorkom members on January 1, 1945, 28.9 percent had less than one year of job tenure, 57.6 percent had one to three years, and only 13.5 percent had more than three years. Among the 396 members of the Kalinin party apparatus, 319 had embarked upon party work during the war. Though more raikom first secretaries retained their posts than other members of the apparatus, according to Boitsov,

13. S. G. Mogilevskii, "Partiino-organizatsionnaia rabota na sele v gody chetvertoi piatiletki (1946–1950 gg.) (Na materialakh partiinykh organizatsii Rostovskoi oblasti, Krasnodarskogo i Stavropol'skogo kraev)," abstract, candidate dissertation, Rostov State University, 1972, p. 16.

14. P. P. Danilov, "Bor'ba kommunisticheskoi partii sovetskogo soiuza za vypolnenie chetvertogo piatiletnego plana v oblasti promyshlennosti," candidate dissertation, Leningrad State University, 1972, p. 16.

15. T. I. Baradulina, "Povyshenie ideino teoreticheskogo urovnia kommunistov v raionakh o svobozhdennykh ot fashistskoi okkupatsii," in *Deiatel'nost' KPSS v pervye gody posle Velikoi Otechestvennoi voiny*, ed. L. V. Shivikov (Moscow: Akademiia Obshchestvennykh Nauk pri TsK KPSS, 1978), p. 2.

16. P. I. Kurbatova, *Smolenskaia partiinaia organizatsiia v gody Velikoi Otechestvennoi voiny* (Smolensk: Smolenskoe Knizhnoe Izdatel'stvo, 1958), p. 113.

17. D. F. Frolov, *Edinstvo tyla i fronta* (Saratov: Saratovskoe Knizhnoe Izdatel'stvo, 1961), p. 114.

18. Vasil'ev, *Sibirskii arsenal*, pp. 75, 233, 234. For example, 48% of the raikom and aikom secretaries in the Buriat party organization were new during the war, as were 80% of department heads.

most cadres were still young and had no leadership experience beyond what they had picked up during the war.[19]

The Kalinin findings are supported by data from other party organizations. Few middle-level apparatchiki enjoyed prewar professional party experience. Their lack of experience was attributable not only to the war but also to the large turnover among members of the local apparatus immediately after it. Moscow's urban raikoms and gorkoms, for example, had a turnover rate of 32.5 percent in 1943. From 1944 through the beginning of 1945, half of the urban raikom and gorkom members were replaced, as were 68 percent of those in the rural oblast.[20] In Kuibyshev during 1945–46, more than 75 percent of gorkom and raikom secretaries were replaced.[21] One-fourth to one-third of all party secretaries in western Siberia were newly elected to their positions after the war.[22] In Belorussia 494 raikom secretaries were removed in 1945–46; in Kaluga 36.2 percent of party workers, including 23 raikom secretaries, were replaced in 1946; in Vologda 41 percent of raikom secretaries were replaced in 1946, in Kirov 46 percent in 1947, and in Vladimir 60 percent in the same year.[23] Thus, by the conclusion of the first party electoral meetings after the war, local party apparatuses had undergone substantial renewal throughout the country. Among raikom secretaries 39.9 percent were newly elected, 27.5 percent of them for the first time. Similarly, 52.2 percent of raion bureau members were newly elected, 35.3 percent for the first time.[24]

As a result of cadre changes during and immediately after the war, party leaders were increasingly drawn from the 1931–40 political generation as table 5.1 shows. Turnover among party cadre did not lead to a change in political generation, although some

19. I. Boitsov, "Vydvizhenie i rost kadrov v gody voiny," Partiinoe stroitel'stvo, no. 11 (June 1945), p. 36.

20. Ocherki istorii Moskovskoi organizatsii KPSS (1883–65 gg.) (Moscow: Moskovskii Rabochii, 1966), pp. 601, 603.

21. Ocherki istorii Kuibyshevskoi organizatsii KPSS (Kuibyshev: Kuibyshevskoe Knizhnoe Izdatel'stvo, 1967), p. 492.

22. L. N. Ul'ianov, Trudovoi podvig rabochego klassa i krest'ianstva Sibiri, 1945–1953 gg. (Tomsk: Izdatel'stvo Tomskogo Universiteta, 1979), p. 28.

23. Donchenko, "Perestroika riadov," pp. 214–15.

24. "Povyshat' rol' raikomov kak organov politicheskogo rukovodstva (S raionnykh partiinykh konferentsii)," Partiinaia zhizn', no. 5 (March 1948), p. 27.

TABLE 5.1

Period in which postwar raion party secretaries, bureau members, and committee members joined the Communist Party (percent)

Period	Secretaries	Bureau members	Committee members
1930 or earlier	31.0%	28.3%	20.2%
1931–1940	54.0	49.4	39.2
1941 or later	15.0	22.3	40.6
All periods	100.0%	100.0%	100.0%

Source: "Povyshat' rol' raikomov kak organov politicheskogo rukovodstva," *Partiinaia zhizn'*, no. 5 (March 1948), p. 27.

apparatchiki at the lowest level (PPOs) were drawn from among wartime recruits. Given the suspension of recruitment during the purges, many of the 1931–40 group probably entered the party during prewar mobilization. Thus they had little, if any, professional party experience before the abnormal conditions of wartime.

Many of these new party leaders, a generation that was to dominate the postwar party, had white-collar social origins or occupied white-collar positions.[25] This recruitment pattern, which began at the end of the 1930s, survived the war. In 1946 a Central Committee directive reinforced a restrictive recruitment policy by further focusing on people with white-collar backgrounds.[26] Party members who had white-collar social backgrounds rose from 34.1 percent of the entire party membership in 1941 to 48.3 percent in 1947.[27] This trend can be seen throughout the Soviet Union.[28]

There was some broadening of the party's social base (generally associated with Khrushchev) after Zhdanov's death in 1948, but the more restrictive approach was reinstated at the 19th Party

25. Rigby, *Communist Party Membership*, pp. 224–25, 268; see also chap. 2.

26. *Pravda*, August 8, 1946, brought to my attention by ibid., pp. 278–79.

27. V. Beliakov and N. Zolotarev, *Partiia ukrepliaet svoi riady* (Moscow: Politicheskoi Literatury, 1970), p. 143; "KPSS v tsifrakh," *Partiinaia zhizn'*, no. 21 (November 1977), p. 28.

28. Data from Leningrad, Kuibyshev, Saratov, Kalinin, Cheliabinsk, Perm, Altai, Kazakhstan, and Uzbekistan may be found in Cynthia S. Kaplan, "The Impact of World War II on the Party," in *The Impact of World War II on the Soviet Union*, ed. Susan Linz (Totowa, N.J.: Rowman & Allanheld, 1985), table 3.

Congress in 1952.[29] Over the entire postwar period, according to an official source, "some 55 to 60 percent of new candidate members were in white-collar positions at the time of their admission while some 25 percent were workers and some 15 percent to 20 percent were collective farmers."[30] The need for stricter admission standards at the local level was duly noted. P. S. Popkov, for example, observed at the joint plenum of the Leningrad obkom and gorkom in August 1946 that future recruitment was to increase the party's presence in the "decisive branches of the economy" and among the rural intelligentsia.[31]

The party's social recruitment policy, aimed more at increasing the level of expertise within the party than at showing preference toward a social stratum, promoted a new soviet elite to positions of authority. Clearly we cannot infer the social origins of local party leaders from their political generation, but we can explore the related issue of whether the party's recruitment policy translated social preference into expertise as measured by the educational attainment of local party leaders and its consequences for agriculture.

Party Cadre Policy: The Importance of Education

Immediately after the war the party confronted two major cadre problems that would directly affect its role in the economy. The first was the need to socialize and train a new generation of local party leaders. The second was to increase the level of expertise within the party—a necessity if party members were to supervise effectively an increasingly complex economy run by experts and a highly desirable means of increasing the party's saturation rate among leading economic personnel. These goals were reflected in

29. Rigby, *Communist Party Membership*, p. 285.
30. N. A. Petrovichev, ed., *Partiinoe stroitel'stvo*, 3d ed. (Moscow: Politizdat, 1973), p. 18, cited in Jerry F. Hough and Merle Fainsod, *How the Soviet Union Is Governed*, rev. and enl. ed. (Cambridge: Harvard University Press, 1979), p. 334.
31. *Leningradskaia pravda*, September 6, 1946; V. A. Kutuzov, "Nekotorye voprosy partiinogo stroitel'stva v leningradskoi organizatsii v pervye poslevoennye gody (1946–1948 gg.)," *Uchenie zapiski* 1 (Institut Istorii Partii Leningradskogo Obkoma KPSS) (1970): 224.

the party's general recruitment policy and more specifically through its cadre policies.

The cadre policy carried out during the postwar period actually began at the end of the Stalinist revolution. As early as the Feb-ruary–March plenum of the Central Committee in 1937, Stalin stated that a renewed emphasis on political qualifications should not be understood to signify a disregard for economic qualifica-tions.[32] Stalin's admonition that economic and political issues cannot be separated was repeated at the 18th Party Congress and later in numerous articles in the party press.[33] Thus we may at-tribute the large-scale influx of new party members to central cadre policy without necessarily attributing it directly to conflict among the elite.[34] Whatever may have motivated party cadre policy, its components—the removal of party cadres, high levels of party recruitment, and a desire to change the character of the party and its role in society—were not necessarily contradictory.[35] Indeed, they may be viewed as a coherent attempt to transform the party and its role in the Soviet system.

Wartime recruitment served to raise the level of educational attainment within the party as a whole. Education levels of local apparatchiki were quite low immediately after the war, but they rose as the years passed. Data from the oblasts of Iaroslavl', Che-liabinsk, Kalinin, Kostromsk, Krasnodar, Leningrad, Moscow, and Rostov show a trend toward rising education levels among local

32. "O nedostatkakh partiinoi raboty i merakh likvidatsii trotskistskikh i inykh dvurushnikov: Doklad T. Stalina na Plenume TsK VKP(b) 3 marta 1937," *Za in-dustrializatsiiu*, March 29, 1937.

33. *XVIII s"ezd vsesoiuznyi kommunisticheskoi partii (b) 10–12 marta 1939 g. Stenograficheskii otchet* (Moscow: Politicheskoi Literatury, 1939), p. 107; Lazar Slepov, "Stalinskaia programma pod'ema partiino-politicheskoi raboty (K piat-nadtsatiletiiu doklada I. V. Stalina na febral'sko-martovskom Plenume TsK VKP[b] v 1937 godu)," *Bolshevik*, no. 3 (1952), pp. 21–34; "Nedstano vopityvat' kadry na ideiakh leninizma," *Partiinaia zhizn'*, no. 1 (January 1947), pp. 1–6.

34. During the year and one month between the 18th Party Congress and the 18th Party Conference, party membership increased by 1,399,219 (D. Bakhshiev, *Partiinoe stroitel'stvo v usloviiakh pobedy sotsializma v SSSR [1934–1941 gody]* [Moscow: Politicheskoi Literatury, 1954], p. 85).

35. The scope of postpurge party renewal is suggested by changes in the ap-paratus. Among those elected for the first time during 1937–38 were 35% of the members of party committees and secretaries of PPO bureaus, 41% of raikom members, 46% of gorkom members, and 60% of obkom, kraikom, and central committee members (Bakhshiev, *Partiinoe stroitel'stvo*, pp. 116–17).

TABLE 5.2

Educational attainment of okruzhkom,* gorkom, and raikom secretaries, 1946 and 1952 (percent)

Year	Higher and incomplete higher education	Secondary education	Incomplete secondary education	Primary education
1946	18.7%	32.0%	23.9%	25.4%
1952	62.3	25.5	9.2	3.0

*Party committee of an okrug, an administrative district based on nationality.
Sources: For 1946: V. N. Donchenko, "Perestroika riadov VKP(b) v period perekhoda SSSR ot voiny k miru (1945–48 gody)," candidate dissertation, Moscow State University, 1972, p. 213; for 1952: "KPSS v tsifrakh," Partiinaia zhizn', July 14, 1973, p. 25.

party secretaries (see table 5.2).[36] Local apparatchiki's improved educational level during the immediate postwar years can be attributed largely to the party's intense program of political education. In a resolution of July 26, 1946, the Central Committee cited the need for political education among recent party recruits

36. Information on the educational backgrounds of gorkom and raikom secretaries for the late 1940s and early 1950s is selective. In Iaroslavl' Oblast, 34.5% of gorkom and raikom secretaries had at least some higher or secondary education in 1947, 67% in 1949. In Cheliabinsk Oblast, 32.8% had some higher education in 1946, 53.8% in 1949. In Kalinin Oblast, 13.5% had some higher education in 1945, 50.3% secondary, and 36.2% primary; in 1950 the respective figures were 42.6%, 50.6%, and 6.8%. In Kostromsk Oblast, 51% of gorkom and raikom first secretaries and 86% of second secretaries did not have complete secondary education. In Krasnodar Krai, 21% had some higher education in 1948, 54% in 1950 (Ocherki istorii Iaroslavskoi organizatsii KPSS [Iaroslavl': Verkhne-Volzhskoe Knizhnoe Izdatel'stvo, 1967], p. 442; E. M. Tiazhel'nikov, ed., Ocherki istorii Cheliabinskoi oblastnoi partiinoi organizatsii [Cheliabinsk: Iuzhno-Ural'skoe Knizhnoe Izdatel'stvo, 1967], p. 369; A. V. Egrova, ed., Kalininskaia oblastnaia organizatsiia KPSS v tsifrakh 1917–1977 gg. [Moscow: Moskovskii Rabochii, 1979], p. 112; M. L. Siniazhnikov, ed., Ocherki istorii Kostromskoi organizatsii KPSS [Iaroslavl': Vernkhna-Volzhskoe Knizhnoe Izdatel'stvo, 1967], p. 305; Ocherki istorii Krasnodarskoi organizatsii KPSS, 2d enl. ed. [Krasnodar: Krasnodarskoe Knizhnoe Izdatel'stvo, 1976], p. 407). Data for Rostov, Leningrad, and Moscow appear below. See Leningradskaia pravda, December 23, 1948; Kutuzov, "Nekotorye voprosy," p. 231; A. M. Stepanov, "Partiino-organizatsionnaia rabota kommunisticheskoi partii v gody chetvertoi piatiletki," candidate dissertation, Rostov State University, 1971, p. 106; I. A. Zelenkov, "Deiatel'nost' Moskovskoi partiinoi organizatsii po vosstanovlenniiu i razvitiiu sotsialisticheskogo narodnogo khoziaistva (1945–1952 gg.)," candidate dissertation, Akademiia Obshchestvennykh Nauk pri TsK KPSS, 1965, p. 205.

and men demobilized from the Soviet Army. The scarcity of adequately prepared cadres to carry out propaganda and agitation in rural areas was especially decried.[37]

A second major resolution on cadre policy, on August 2, 1946, announced plans to establish an elaborate system of political schools throughout the USSR. At the apex of this system was the Higher Party School in Moscow and the Academy of Social Sciences, under the auspices of the Central Committee. Applicants to these schools were required to have completed at least secondary school. The first class was to include 300 three-year students and 600 nine-month students from party committees of oblasts, krais (territories), republics, okrugs (administrative districts based on nationality), and major cities. Two-year party schools at the republican, krai, and oblast levels were to train leading party and soviet workers at the district level, especially in rural areas. These schools were to accept 8,000 students in their two-year programs and 5,000 in a six-month retraining course.[38]

These schools did in fact provide a major source of cadres during the late 1940s. By 1947, 192 former party secretaries, 273 leaders of departments of provincial and republican organizations, 113 former editors of local party newspapers, and 130 chairmen of oblast and krai executive committees of soviets of workers' deputies and their assistants were attending the Higher Party School. In 1948, 270,000 party members took political correspondence courses at institutions of higher education.[39] Of course, attendance at such schools reveals more about the desirability of the qualifications they offered and pressure to pursue such programs than the quality of the education itself.

The large number of political school graduates contributed to the influx of new cadres into the apparatus and the transfer of retrained cadres. The first students graduated in 1948. Approxi-

37. "O roste partii i o merakh po usileniiu partiino-organizatsionnoi i partiino-politicheskoi raboty s vnov' vstupivshimi v VKP(b)," in *KPSS v rezoliutsiia i resheniiakh s"ezdov, konferentsii i plenumov TsK*, vol. 6, *1941–1954*, 8th ed. (Moscow: Politicheskoi Literatury, 1971), pp. 154–61.

38. "O podgotvke i perepodgotovke rukovodiashchikh partiinykh i sovetskikh rabotnikov," in *KPSS v rezoliutsiia*, 6: 162–72.

39. *Kultura i zhizn'*, September 19, 1947; *Partiinaia zhizn'*, no. 1 (1947), p. 4; *Pravda*, December 20, 1948; all cited in E. F. Agafonenkov, "Podgotovka i perepodgotovka partiinykh i sovetskikh kadrov (1946–1950 gg.)," *Voprosy istorii KPSS* 11 (1970): 104.

mately 10,000 leading party and soviet workers from party schools were directed to work in oblasts, krais, and republics. Among more than 800 graduates of the Higher Party School, 355 were sent to Moscow, 627 to the Ukraine, 363 to Belorussia, and 222 to Uzbekistan. From 1946 to 1950, 25,000 people completed the full programs of the Central Committee's Academy of Social Sciences and Higher Party School and the somewhat shorter programs of republic, krai, and oblast schools, and 26,000 more completed one-year and nine-month courses at these institutions.[40] Even if not all of the 51,000 graduates embarked upon full-time party work, they nonetheless represent a major influx of new leading cadres and were largely responsible for the high turnover rates among holders of leading party and state positions. Rural cadres usually were drawn from local and regional schools. As early as 1947, approximately 30,000 students were enrolled in 177 two-year schools and six-month courses.[41]

Data from Rostov and Leningrad oblasts provide a more detailed picture of the impact of these attempts to improve cadres' qualifications. Rostov Oblast sent 55 people to the Higher Party School in Moscow, while 3,424 Communists and 935 nonparty students attended 196 local two-year schools, 6 evening universities of Marxism-Leninism, 199 political schools, more than 600 study groups, and 131 seminars.[42] These schools and groups were functioning by 1946. Two-year schools graduated 419 students in 1947 and 817 in 1948. The oblast party school's ten-month course enrolled 148 students, most of them raikom and gorkom secretaries, heads of departments, obkom instructors, and chairmen and department heads of city and district soviet executive committees. In 1948, 78 received diplomas. Among the 554 graduates of the six-month course at the Rostov Oblast Party School were 168 gorkom and raikom secretaries, 60 chairmen of raisoviet (district

40. Bol'shevik, nos. 14 (1948), p. 3, and 17 (1950), p. 20; Stalinets, July 22, 1948; Pravda, July 31, 1948; Pravda ukrainy, July 29, 1948; Sovetskaia Belorussiia, July 31, 1948; Pravda vostoka, July 31, 1951; all cited in ibid., p. 107.

41. Pravda, December 9, 1947, cited in V. A. Abramov, "Organizatsionno-partiinaia rabota KPSS v gody chetvertoi piatiletki," Voprosy istorii KPSS, no. 3 (1973), p. 59.

42. P. V. Barchugov, ed., Ocherki istorii partiinykh organizatsii Dona, vol. 2, 1921–1971 (Rostov-on-Don: Rostovskoe Knizhnoe Izdatel'stvo, 1973), p. 437.

council) executive committees, and 62 heads of departments.[43] Evening universities of Marxism-Leninism enrolled 4,500 leading workers and raion party evening schools approximately 7,000.[44]

The postwar history of political education in Leningrad Oblast closely resembled that of Rostov. Among the 1948 graduates of the Higher Party School were 50 Leningraders, and 320 additional Leningraders were correspondence students. From 1945 through 1948 a total of 5,427 Communist Party members graduated from party schools. The number of party schools in Leningrad Oblast rose from 177 in 1946, with 4,500 party members attending, to 1,158, with more than 15,000 students. Eighty percent of these students had joined the party during or shortly after the war.[45]

Party policy clearly promoted continuing political education for local party cadres. To what extent, however, was this emphasis on political education and improved education in general translated into rising levels of expertise among local party cadres? Was a preference shown for industrial fields at the implicit expense of agricultural instruction? Although data on the party elite are unavailable, information on the fields of specialized education entered by party personnel as a whole provides a sense of the general distribution of expertise.

In 1947, 9.8 percent of party members had at least some higher education and 47.1 percent had at least some secondary education. Of those with higher education, 40.1 percent were in the field of engineering and 6.3 percent in agronomy, veterinary science, and other agricultural specialties. The strong preference for fields related to industry was also found among party members with secondary education: 25.8 percent had technical training, while only 5.1 percent had training in agronomy, veterinary science, and other agricultural fields.[46] The disparity in educational levels and fields of specialization suggests a more technically competent leadership in urban party organizations, particularly at the district level, than in rural areas.

Although these data do not permit a direct assessment of the educational qualifications of rural party leaders, they do suggest

43. *Molot*, February 9, 1948, and October 8, 1950.
44. Barchugov, *Ocherki istorii*, p. 439.
45. Kutuzov, *Nekotorye voprosy*, pp. 231, 234.
46. "KPSS v tsifrakh," pp. 29–30.

that relatively few members of the pool from which they were drawn had agricultural training. Most of the improvement in educational levels found among rural party leaders can be attributed to cadres' newly acquired political education. The emphasis on political education rather than economic expertise not only suggests the status of the professions involved but, given the centralized nature of Soviet policy, also indirectly indicates the basis of party leaders' authority. Once again, the industrial arena required specialized knowledge for the exercise of authority, while authority in agricultural affairs depended primarily on political training.

A closer look at Rostov Oblast reveals the impact of rising levels of education among local party cadres. By 1950 the proportion of secretaries and heads of raikom departments with at least some higher education was 57 percent; while those with primary and incomplete secondary education declined from 11 percent in 1949 to 6 percent. At the end of 1950, more than 70 percent of the obkom nomenklatura had higher, incomplete higher, or secondary education.[47] By 1953, 74 percent of raikom and gorkom secretaries had higher education.[48] The turnover rate among the obkom nomenklatura was 16.3 percent in 1948 and 16.4 percent from January 1949 to October 1950. Among those who left their jobs, 17.0 and 24.5 percent, respectively, were appointed to higher positions. The number of leading workers at rural party raikoms removed for unsatisfactory performance declined. One-third of those removed were sent to study.[49]

Data from the national and oblast levels conceal important educational disparities both among and within party organizations which correspond to urban/rural differences. In some oblasts the proportion of leading party workers with only primary education was much higher than the national average, especially among secretaries of rural raikoms: 27.5 percent of raikom secretaries in the Gor'kii Oblast party organization had only primary education, 38 percent in Nizhnii Povolzh'e, 40 percent in Kurgansk, 43.2 percent in Kaluga, and 61 percent in Stalingrad.[50] In Leningrad,

47. Mogilevskii, "Partiino-organizatsionnaia rabota," p. 144.
48. Barchugov, Ocherki istorii, p. 429.
49. Mogilevskii, "Partiino-organizatsionnaia rabota," p. 147.
50. Donchenko, "Perestroika riadov," p. 214.

58 percent of city raikom secretaries had higher education in 1946, while only 8.5 percent of the raikom and gorkom secretaries in the oblast organization had attained a comparable level.[51] By 1948, a year after the party began its concerted effort to increase educational levels within the apparatus, 77.4 percent of Leningrad's urban raikom secretaries had some higher education, while only 34 percent of rural raikom and gorkom secretaries had attained this level.[52] Among raikom secretaries in Moscow, 70 percent had at least some higher education, while only 45 percent in the oblast had attained comparable levels.[53] Thus, despite the improvement in educational level among raikom secretaries during the postwar period, the education gap between urban and rural party secretaries was not closed.

At the lowest level of the professional party apparatus is the secretary of the primary party organization. In theory, the PPO secretary was to play an important role in the implementation of economic policy through the verification of economic activities, propaganda, and agitation. During the immediate postwar period, however, relatively few kolkhozy had primary party organizations, even though the creation of kolkhoz PPOs was stressed during the late 1940s. Only after the 1950 kolkhoz amalgamation campaign did the proportion of kolkhozy with PPOs increase significantly. Despite the relatively small number of positions to be filled, the party was hard put to find qualified PPO secretaries for agricultural organizations. Most PPO secretaries either were new party members or had recently transferred from urban areas. The former often had little understanding of the nature of party work and the latter frequently knew little about agriculture.

The lack of experience of rural PPO secretaries was perpetuated by high turnover rates. The scenario of cadre instability was associated with youth, recent party entry, lack of higher education, and political inexperience. Almost two-thirds of all PPO secretaries joined the party during or shortly after World War II.[54] In

---

51. *Leningradskaia pravda*, December 23, 1948.

52. Kutuzov, "Nekotorye voprosy," p. 231.

53. A. Ia. Utenkov, *Bor'ba KPSS za vosstanovlenie narodnogo khoziaistva i dal'neishee razvitie sotsialisticheskogo obshchestva, 1946–1955 gg.* (Moscow: Vysshaia Shkola, 1974), p. 58.

54. A. V. Krasnov, ed., *Bor'ba partii i rabochego klass za vosstanovlenie i razvitie narodnogo khoziaistva SSSR (1943–1950 gg.)* (Moscow: Mysl', 1978), p. 64.

the eyes of higher party officials, such leaders' political reliability was open to question.

The weakness of PPO secretaries' political qualifications was not mitigated by expertise. Among all PPO secretaries in 1946, only 9.6 percent had some higher education, 32.4 percent secondary, and 58.0 percent primary.[55] The party did attempt to raise the leaders' educational levels during the postwar years. In Leningrad Oblast, for example, only 27.7 percent of PPO secretaries had higher and secondary education before the war; this figure rose to 31.3 percent by January 1947 and to 34.9 percent in 1948.[56] In 1952, the educational level of PPO secretaries throughout the Leningrad party rose to 32.5 percent with at least incomplete higher education and 30.9 percent with secondary, although approximately 40 percent still lacked a complete secondary education.[57]

The qualifications of rural party apparatchiki were poorer than those of primary party secretaries as a whole. In 1951 kolkhoz party organization secretaries were singled out as having insufficient prior experience in political work.[58] As late as 1952, after the kolkhoz amalgamation campaign, an editorial in *Leningradskaia pravda* admonished, "Never forget that party groups at kolkhozy are something new; their leaders for the most part are people who are unfamiliar with party work."[59]

The findings from Leningrad Oblast, primarily an industrial province, are confirmed by those from Rostov Oblast, a province with a mixed economy that includes an important agricultural component. PPO secretaries in Rostov, like those in Leningrad, were drawn from among the young and inexperienced. Indeed, 56.5 percent were young party members in 1947 and 84.4 percent had less than three years' experience in party work.[60] Their educational attainment was low and turnover rates were predictably high (see tables 5.3 and 5.4). After the immediate changes pro-

55. Donchenko, "Perestroika riadov," p. 213.

56. Kutuzov, "Nekotorye voprosy," p. 222.

57. *Leningradskaia pravda*, September 23, 1953.

58. Ibid., April 31, 1951.

59. Ibid., January 12, 1952.

60. A. A. Zobov, "KPSS v bor'ba za vosstanovlenie i dal'neishii pod'em promyshlennosti v chetvertoi piatiletke (1946–1950 gg.)," abstract, candidate dissertation, Rostov State University, 1960, p. 8.

TABLE 5.3
Educational attainment of PPO secretaries, Rostov Oblast, 1945–1951 (percent)

Year	Higher education	Secondary education	Incomplete secondary and primary education
1945	8.0%	29.0%	63.0%
1946	7.0	25.0	68.0
1947	8.7	18.3	73.0
1948	8.5	21.7	69.8
1949	8.4	23.1	68.5
1950	8.4	25.1	66.5
1951	9.3	27.2	63.5

Source: Calculated from A. M. Stepanov, "Partino-organizatsionnaia rabota kommunisti-cheskoi partii v gody chetvertoi piatiletkii," candidate dissertation, Rostov State University, 1971, p. 124.

duced by the end of the war and a period of PPO expansion (1946–47) during which many party secretaries were transferred, the turnover rate rose again at the end of the 1940s and the beginning of the 1950s. Ostensibly these changes stemmed not from poor performance but from a desire to improve the qualifications of party personnel. Nonetheless, these replacements did not appreciably raise educational levels within the local party apparatus, as table 5.3 indicates. The causes of this professional and geographical mobility are not apparent, but the available Rostov data clearly indicate a high degree of instability among PPO secretaries throughout the reconstruction period. As this instability limited the party's ability to rely on PPO representatives, it promoted increased dependence on district and oblast representatives.

Thus, beyond the initial issue of party saturation of the rural population and the replacement of rural territorial party organizations by PPOs, the instability and inexperience of PPO secretaries in the postwar years enhanced the importance of rural raikom apparatchiki. In fact, not only did they share with economic leaders the responsibility for plan fulfillment, but circumstances encouraged their active role in the implementation of agricultural policy. The new indirect party role, with its reliance on PPOs, never developed in the countryside. As rural party lead-

TABLE 5.4
Turnover rate and prior experience of PPO secretaries, Rostov Oblast, 1945–1951 (percent)

	1945	1946	1947	1948	1949	1950	1951
Total number	2,165	2,893	4,623	5,489	5,788	6,013	5,666
Turnover rate	42.0%	14.0%	16.0%	41.0%	44.5%	24.6%	35.0%
Elected PPO secretary for first time	37.2	13.2	6.6	30.0	29.4	14.9	19.3
Less than one year's experience in party work	47.7	45.8	58.8	49.8	41.8	32.6	33.2

Source: A. M. Stepanov, "Partino-organizatsionnaia rabota kommunisticheskoi partii v gody chetvertoi piatiletki," candidate dissertation, Rostov State University, 1971, p. 110, table 2.

ers' low levels of education and expertise make evident, the agricultural arena continued to be dominated by political authority. As we shall see, the rural raion party organization chose to act through its own representatives.

CHAPTER 6

The Local Party and Agricultural Crisis Management

Postwar party behavior evolved in the course of the party's search for a new role within a conservative political system. The discussions found on the pages of the major theoretical journals of the postwar period document Moscow's concern about defining new functions for the party apparatus in this period of relative normality.[1] The initial formal role prescriptions gave way to new realities in light of party praxis. The ultimate criterion applied to party behavior was the success or failure of plan implementation.

During World War II the party had served as a highly centralized administrative organization, often making decisions and implementing them alone. This was a marked departure from the so-called conveyor belts or competing hierarchies of the 1930s. The change reflected both the loss of state cadres and the need for quick, authoritative decisions under emergency conditions. Now that the war was won at last, the time had come to reestablish the state and economic systems and to renounce the extraordinary powers entrusted to the party. The emergent party role was not that of a centralized competing hierarchy but rather that of a com-

---

1. Major discussions of the party's role are to be found in *Bol'shevik*, *Partiinoe stroitel'stvo*, and *Partiinaia zhizn'*.

plex organization. As Lazar Slepov, a leading party theoretician of the period, noted:

> Party committees are organs of political leadership. Their task is the coordination and direction of the activity of all state and public organizations. Party committees bear the responsibility for the economy. The party judges the work of this or that party organization on the basis of the actual results in the various economic and cultural areas and in the standard of living provided for workers. It is possible for party organizations to exert necessary influence over the course of economic construction and the behavior of economic organs, though they do not displace economic administration or take it upon themselves to decide all economic questions directly.[2]

These sentiments, echoed throughout the postwar period, signaled a concerted attempt to transform the party from an instrument for direct implementation of economic policy to a political organ indirectly responsible for policy success.

In agriculture, however, theory yielded to organizational imperatives. The increasingly indirect role of the party in theory was synonymous with the increased authority of state and economic organs. From some perspectives, the obstacles to the party's adoption of this new indirect style should have been relatively easy to surmount in the immediate postwar period. Organizational inertia, for example, was probably a lesser problem than usual because of the large number of new cadres who lacked the imprint of past standardized operating procedures. Yet the questionable expertise of many soviet and economic experts made it seem risky to stake one's career or even survival on their ability to implement the plan successfully. These considerations, along with the very real difficulties encountered during economic reconstruction, militated against the transference of authority from the party to other organs. The sharing of authority cannot have been easy for the many party secretaries who had become accustomed to making decisions alone during the war. The situation gave rise to tension between authorized behavior and central demands for plan fulfillment, with resultant violation of the party's formal role.

2. Lazar Slepov, "Stalinskaia programma pod'ema partiino-politicheskoi raboty," *Bol'shevik*, no. 3 (February 1952), p. 26.

The new official party role required the weighing of economic and political responsibilities and activities. As the party emphasized its political leadership, it came increasingly to focus on so-called principled questions of the economy as a means of encouraging its members to develop a broad, future-oriented perspective. The party was to disengage itself from current substantive issues.

Party literature sketches an ambiguous division of labor between party and state organs. This ambiguity can be traced in part to the party's right and duty of supervision (*kontrol'*) over the activities of economic and state organizations and verification (*proverit'*) of policy implementation. Neither of these functions was possible without an intimate knowledge of the details of economic and state activities. A mastery of such details was an inextricable part of supervision and verification. A clear administrative dilemma arose within the party organization: how was one to discuss only questions of policy "principle" while maintaining mastery over the details of policy implementation? In the agricultural sector this tension led inevitably to behavior that contradicted the role officially stipulated for the avant- garde party of the postwar years.

One way to overcome this apparent dilemma was to increase the responsibility of local party organizations. With increased responsibility came a new type of active engagement. *Partiinaia zhizn'* reported in 1946: "The Central Committee of the Party pointed out that the main direction of our work in the immediate period must be to strengthen our local party organs, to count on our party organs to be capable of exercizing real supervision over the activities of state and economic organs locally, to criticize and to correct mistakes in their work, and to carry out their political and organizational work with the masses."[3]

This attempt to transfer authority to oblast and raion party organizations was consistent with the complexities of policy implementation. A totally centralized system had become an ineffective means of dealing with the problems of economic reconstruction. Thus the natural strains of policy decision making and implementation favored decentralization or at a minimum the deconcentration of authority. All the same, it would be erroneous

3. "Zadachi partiinoi raboty v sovremennykh usloviiakh," *Partiinaia zhizn'*, no. 1 (November 1946), p. 18.

to characterize central party leaders as seeking to promote the decentralization of authority for the purpose of making policy.

Active involvement by local party organizations in the processes of supervision and verification required an extensive knowledge of policy implementation to be used in the ideological mobilization of the work force. Indeed, mass mobilization was a prominent aspect of political organizational work throughout this period. Such an intimate knowledge of other organizations' policy behavior, which clearly affected the apparatchik's own career, exerted strong pressure for direct intervention at the expense of indirect functions whenever policy threatened to go awry.

When local party organizations encountered problems, the correct response was to report them to superior party organizations and to work through lower party organizations, such as PPOs. Local activities were to be supervised through personnel policy rather than through direct party intervention. Thus the party, by suggesting responsible personnel for political, economic, and state positions, was to ensure its indirect control. In fact, policy success was not to be attained so simply. Indeed, the party's manipulation of personnel policy resulted in high turnover rates that ultimately contributed to the unanticipated disruption of the economy. Such problems were more intense in agriculture than in industry because personnel matters were under the authority of central industrial ministries.

Many of the themes found in the party's theoretical literature— mass mobilization, internal party democracy, cadre policy, delegation of authority to the masses and lower party organizations, an enhanced role for economic experts, and the necessity of increased political training—cast the widely held view of the Stalinist postwar system into question. With the advantage of hindsight, the issues and problems encountered by the party seem more reminiscent of the Khrushchev years than of the Stalin regime. Close examination of the party's actual activities during the postwar years, however, suggests a link between the party's role as an instrument of societal revolution during the 1930s and its experiments of the 1950s. Indeed, the postwar years may be seen as the beginning of the party's search for a new role in an increasingly complex society.

The New Party Role and Agriculture

The tensions apparent in the party's official postwar functions created new dilemmas for local party organizations in agriculture. The new party role was designed to accommodate the emergent conservatism of the late Stalin period's approach to running institutions created before the war, yet in agriculture the process of institution building continued. The instrumental role that party cadres played during the creation of state institutions was still required in the countryside, since collective agriculture not only was to be reestablished after the war but was to be further developed through the amalgamation of kolkhozy and perhaps by the conversion of kolkhozy into sovkhozy. In these circumstances it would be difficult for party leaders to withdraw from direct involvement in the economy unless other organizations or methods could substitute for them.

The regime called upon local party leaders to share authority with nonparty organizations and their leaders and to develop a greater reliance on indirect supervision of economic activities through primary party organizations. In agriculture these demands could not be met. Rural economic and state leaders lacked experience, expertise, and political reliability—the preconditions for a cooperative relationship. If the party allowed these leaders to exercise primary authority over economic activities, the outcome could be economic and political disaster. In addition, wartime authority patterns had so subordinated these state and economic organs to local party organizations that change would be extremely difficult. The party's control over personnel appointments (nomenklatura) was an insufficient mechanism by which to ensure plan fulfillment.

Another necessary condition for the party's indirect supervisory role was its ability to rely on primary party organizations. But the rural party lacked sufficient representatives at the farm for economic supervision and political organizational work. Because so few primary party organizations existed and those few had minimal memberships and inexperienced leaders, the party had too few local representatives capable of monitoring state economic leaders and mobilizing the rural labor force.[4] These factors con-

4. Territorial party organizations lacked the right of *kontrol'* enjoyed by workplace primary party organizations.

tributed to rural party leaders' continued direct involvement in the details of policy implementation, even though party theoreticians explicitly condemned such activities. The populist propaganda of the era, typified by the campaign for kolkhoz democracy, further justified the severe criticism of so-called party bureaucratic behavior, that is, the party's direct involvement in policy implementation and displacement of economic leaders. Ultimately, of course, the regime insisted on plan fulfillment and political control, restricting populist sentiments to mobilization campaigns. Thus economic policies, rural conditions, and the characteristics of both leaders and followers shaped local party behavior in agriculture in a way that clearly distinguished it from that found in the urban industrial sector. Rural party leaders developed a distinct pattern of crisis intervention.

We can see the effect of such factors on the behavior of agricultural and party leaders in Soviet rural fiction of the late 1940s and early 1950s. Although such stories clearly do not offer an unbiased view of the countryside or a precise picture of actual conditions, they do mingle their didacticism with the new realism that emerged during the thaw and provide vivid portraits of local party and agricultural leaders. They afford a glimpse of what the Soviet regime considered appropriate and inappropriate roles for local leaders and a strong sense of the rural atmosphere that helped to shape their behavior.[5]

Vera Dunham has brilliantly synthesized this material in her portrayal of the dilemmas that confronted fictional local party leaders and kolkhoz chairmen and the forces that molded them.[6] From her analysis emerge pictures of local party leaders who are adrift. They are no longer praised for being the "boss" of the region and fulfilling plans at all costs. Basing her analysis on such classic

5. See V. V. Ovechkin, *Izbrannoe povesti, rasskazy, ocherki* (Kursk: Kurskoe Khnizhnoe Izdatel'stvo, 1955); Galina Nikolaeva, "Povest' o direktore MTS i glavnom agronome," *Znamia*, no. 9 (September 1954), pp. 9–62, and "Zhatva," *Znamia*, no. 5 (May 1950), pp. 10–131, no. 6 (June 1950), pp. 28–104, and no. 7 (July 1950), pp. 7–96; Grigorii Medynskii, "Mar'ia," *Zvezda*, no. 3 (May 1949), pp. 3–31, no. 4 (April 1949), pp. 3–41, no. 5 (May 1949), pp. 3–72, and no. 6 (June 1949), pp. 21–85; Nikolai Virta, "Khleb nash nasushchnyi," *Zvezda*, no. 6 (1947), pp. 3–49.

6. Vera S. Dunham, "Comrade Chameleon: The Changing Image of the Party Official in Soviet Literature after Stalin" and "Rural Management," unpublished manuscripts.

and influential works as those by Valentin Ovechkin, Dunham highlights the contradictory behavior of local rural party leaders who, on the one hand, are " 'spineless culturists, hunters of sub-text, the timid purchasers of overinsurance,' " and on the other are often demobilized new party members who have a " 'surplus of initiative [and] replace everybody, know everything, do every-thing.' "[7] Under pressure to fulfill plans, these new party leaders are also urged to be sensitive and to respect the rights of peasants even while they suffer from depression, poor pay, and a sense of superfluousness.[8] As actual evidence suggests, the theoretical dic-tates of the party's new role were at odds with economic demands and the possibilities offered by local conditions. As a result, the self-assurance of local party representatives so typical of the early revolutionary or the builder of the new socialist society subsided to reveal the uncertainty of the new conservative administrator being pulled in several directions at once.

For the fictional and indeed the actual agricultural leaders, con-tradictory pressures were rooted in the official desire to increase the authority of economic leaders, expressed in the "big deal" and the emergent neopopulism of the postwar years.[9] What was to be the future of Soviet agriculture, given popular sentiments and a lack of expertise? Soviet fiction graphically captures the cross-pressures affecting the kolkhoz chairman. Neopopulism encour-ages him to represent peasant interests to higher party authorities, yet he must also represent the interests of those at the center in order to fulfill the plan. Whether the kolkhoz chairman chose to represent the peasant collective or higher party authorities or at-tempted to become a buffer between the two, he was almost certain to lose.[10] The high turnover rates found among kolkhoz chairmen, usually caused by their removal by local party representatives when they could not fulfill the plan, indicate the impossible nature of their jobs. Kolkhoz chairmen often served as scapegoats for local party organizations when plans went unfulfilled.[11] In the uncer-

7. V. V. Ovechkin, "Talent i iniziativa," *Novy mir,* no. 5 (1956), p. 14, cited in Dunham, "Comrade Chameleon," pp. 144–45.

8. Dunham, "Comrade Chameleon," p. 144.

9. See Vera S. Dunham, *In Stalin's Time* (New York: Cambridge University Press, 1976).

10. Dunham, "Rural Management," p. 17.

11. N. Sudarikov, "Berezhno otonit'sia i kadram presedatelei," *Sotsialistiche-skaia zakonnost',* no. 12 (December 1947), p. 6.

tain and suspicious postwar atmosphere, it is not surprising that the rural intelligentsia lost its moorings and was unable to cope with local problems.[12] To the extent that the fictional portraits are consistent with descriptive and statistical evidence, they provide a unique perspective on the dilemmas that confronted local party leaders and kolkhoz chairmen in the postwar years.

A detailed examination of local party organizations' actual activities in agriculture is hindered by the lack of direct access to party archival material. By focusing on two provinces, though, Leningrad and Rostov, we can piece together a detailed account of local party behavior. In Leningrad, a predominantly industrial region, we can see the difficulties faced by agricultural enterprises in the non-black-earth zone. Although agriculture was not central to the oblast's economic focus, it still served a critical function: it was expected after the war to provide the entire subsistence of the oblast's burgeoning urban industrial population.[13] Thus Leningrad Oblast was an important political and economic area in which agricultural production played a significant supporting role in industrial development.

The economy of Rostov Oblast, in contrast, was dominated by grain production. Much of Rostov's industrial production was devoted to agricultural machinery, although coal mining was also a prominent economic activity. Just as significant as Rostov's agriculture for the study of the party's functions is the critical role played by the Rostov party on the national political scene in redefining the roles of local rural party organizations. Throughout the 1940s, the local and national press closely examined the Rostov party in its efforts to assess rural party behavior.[14] Although the exact frequency of local party patterns of behavior found might vary by region and no national data exist to permit a systematic

12. Dunham, "Rural Management," p. 32.

13. *Zakon o piatiletnem plane vosstanovleniia i razvitiia narodnogo khoziaistva SSSR na 1946–1950 gg.*, in *Resheniia partii i pravitel'stva po khoziaist-vennym voprosam (1917–1967 gg.)*, vol. 3, *1941–1952 gody* (Moscow: Politicheskoi Literatury, 1968), pp. 246–319.

14. "O rabote Sal'skogo raikoma VKP(b) Rostovskoi oblasti" (Postanovlenie TsK VKP[b], August 17, 1946), *Partiinaia zhizn'*, no. 1–3 (November 1946), pp. 61–65; A. Kolosov and U. Zhukovin, eds., *Opyt Tselinskogo raikoma partii (Pis'ma o sel'skom raikome)* (Astrakhan: Volga, 1948).

assessment, the qualitative portrait that emerges seems to reflect party behavior throughout the country's agricultural areas.[15] Even the most prosperous regions had lagging kolkhozy whose poor performance triggered a pattern of crisis management. By focusing on Leningrad and Rostov oblasts, with a glance at other regional evidence, we can discern a distinctive pattern of local party behavior in agriculture.

Patterns of Party Behavior in Agriculture

Three central questions provide a focus for an inquiry into the behavior of rural party organizations in agriculture. First, which level of the local party hierarchy is responsible for the implementation of agricultural policy? Second, what types of activities and patterns of behavior are associated with various party organizations? Third, what are the defining characteristics of party leaders' relations with local economic leaders? The answers to these questions help us to understand the local party's actual role in the implementation of agricultural policy.

The Oblast Party Committee

Party obkoms devoted much of their attention to agricultural issues. In Leningrad and Rostov oblasts, the gorkoms of the provincial capitals assisted the obkoms by supervising urban raikoms and industries that were assigned to provide agricultural enterprises with machinery, technical expertise, or labor. While gorkoms in smaller cities exhibited greater involvement in agricultural matters, the central organ of authority within the province remained the obkom. As plenary reports and speeches by obkom secretaries make clear, the fulfillment of the agricultural plan dominated obkom agendas.[16]

15. This assessment is based on evidence in monographs and the national press. Newly incorporated areas in which collectivization was under way and those devoted exclusively to commercial crops in Central Asia may be exceptions.

16. For Leningrad, see "Resheniia iiul'skogo plenuma obkoma VKP(b) poboevomu pretvorit' v zhizn'," *Propaganda i agitatsiia*, no. 15 (August 1951), pp. 1–7; "Plenum Leningradskogo Obkoma VKP(b) ob itogakh vesennego seva i meropriiatiiakh po ukhoda za posevami i podgotovke k uborke urozhaia," *Propaganda*

Published accounts of obkom plenums and bureau meetings read like statistical summaries of agricultural plan fulfillment. The degree of attention devoted to plan fulfillment data runs counter to party theoreticians' conceptualization of the appropriate distribution of functions between the obkom and the oblast executive committee. The latter organization was, at least in theory, the appropriate organ to study the detailed results of policy execution. Yet the directives issued by the obkom to other organizations clearly indicate that the focal point for the assessment of policy results remained the obkom. The obkom frequently issued directives stating the specific goals to be fulfilled by various organizations, although not necessarily the means by which those goals were to be achieved.

In March 1947, for example, the Leningrad obkom asked Tikhvin Raikom to find means to deal with twenty-three lagging kolkhozy. The measures that had been taken were criticized as unrealistic, but no alternatives were suggested.[17] Directives of this type often went so far as to specify the time by which the recipient organizations were to submit reports to the obkom. The raikoms and raion executive committees of the soviet were the most frequent recipients of such directives. The centrality of the obkom in agriculture is reflected by both the range of organs subject to its demands and its role as a conduit for party as well as state directives within the oblast.[18] It was not only other party organs that received obkom directives; so did nonparty organs, such as raion soviets, and through them machine tractor stations and kolkhozy.[19]

The obkom bureau tended to rely on reports rather than actually to send its representatives out to localities. When it did occasionally send someone to a raion, the instructor was said to act "like a representative of an economic institution."[20] Of course, such

---

i *agitatsiia*, no. 12 (June 1946), pp. 30–37; *Leningradskaia pravda*, 1945–53. For Rostov, see D. I. Dubonosov, "Organizatorskaia i politicheskaia rabota kommunisticheskoi partii po vosstanovleniiu i razvitiiu narodogo khoziaistva v poslevoennyi period (1946–1950 gg.)," doctoral dissertation, Rostov-on-Don State Pedagogical Institute, 1972, pp. 654–68; *Molot*, 1946–52.

17. *Leningradskaia pravda*, March 4, 1947.

18. In this respect, the Rostov obkom also resembled area administration with special emphasis on economic issues.

19. *Leningradskaia pravda*, March 18, 1947.

20. Ibid., May 25, 1950.

behavior can be accounted for in part by the apparent inability of oblast agricultural administrations to provide adequate information. Rostov Oblast's agricultural administration was criticized for spending too much of its time preparing resolutions for the oblast soviet (608 in 1950) and the obkom (300 in 1950) in lieu of any actual involvement in agriculture.[21]

The major flow of directives, however, came from rural raikoms and the executive committees of raion soviets. Unlike the gorkoms' directives, which emphasized indirect control of industrial production through supervision and verification, those of rural organs emphasized results.

The obkom continued to issue demands for the improvement of political work and, echoing a dominant theme of the period, called for the strengthening of soviet and local party organs. Nonetheless, the fulfillment of the economic plan remained most important to obkoms. As V. M. Prokhov, secretary of Kingispennskii Raikom, noted, the Leningrad obkom "asks most about economic questions, and rarely about party work."[22] *Partiinaia zhizn'* made the same point in an article that held up the Orlov obkom as an example. In an eight-month period in 1946, the Orlov obkom was said to have adopted 183 resolutions, only 16 of them devoted to party work. A raikom secretary from Orlov Oblast noted that "we in the raions copied their practice and let party work go."[23]

This assessment of obkom functions is clearly supported by reports of the topics discussed at Leningrad and Rostov oblast plenums. Of the twenty-four obkom plenums in Leningrad Oblast held from March 1946 until Stalin's death, twenty-two dealt with agrarian issues, eleven with political agitation (primarily as applied to the countryside), and two with industrial questions. Rostov obkom plenums had almost exactly the same thematic breakdown.[24] Obkom plenum agendas reflect the cyclical nature

21. *Molot*, January 20, 1951.
22. Quoted in L. N. Kruglova, "Deiatel'nost' leningradskoi partiinoi organizatsii po ukrepleniiu raidov partii i marksistko-leninskomu proveshcheniiu kommunistov v pervoi poslevoennyi piatiletke (1946–1950 gg.)," candidate dissertation, Leningrad State University, 1971, p. 61.
23. "Rukovodstvo priemom v VKP(b) i vospitanie novykh chlenov partii: S plenumov TsK kompartii soiuznykh respublik, kraikomov i obkomov VKP(b)," *Partiinaia zhizn'*, no. 2 (November 1946), pp. 29–35.
24. During the same period, the Rostov obkom had 21 plenums on agriculture,

of agriculture itself—plowing, planting, harvesting—and only occasionally deal with topics of a more specialized nature. The party's leadership role and mass mobilization were discussed in this context.

The specific policy issues included on the obkom's agenda correspond to the major agricultural policies announced by the Central Committee. The major pronouncements of national significance for agriculture included a resolution to stop violations of charters of agricultural collectives in December 1946; the reformulation of the economic plan for agricultural recovery in 1947 in light of the 1946 drought; a resolution on livestock in July 1949; the amalgamation of the kolkhozy in September 1950; and the resolutions of the 19th Party Congress in September 1952. These issues dominated obkom agendas of the period. The remaining plenums were concerned with the assessment of plan fulfillment during agricultural campaigns. These discussions were narrow, focusing on the success or failure of efforts to fulfill the plan. The agendas of plenums convened outside of the planting or harvest periods were dominated by discussions of preparations for the coming season and of the need to construct storage facilities for agricultural produce and shelters for livestock.

From the mid-1940s through the early 1950s, the Central Committee focused national attention on Rostov in its examination of lower party and soviet organizations. The obkom's role proved to be of secondary interest to the Central Committee. From August 1946, when the Central Committee issued a resolution of Sal'skii Raikom (in the south of the oblast), until January 1952, when it issued the resolution "On the Work of Rostov Obkom VKP(b)," Rostov served as an example of what was to be criticized in local administrative and political practices.[25] The Central Committee noted that "one of the reasons for the serious deficiencies in the work of the Sal'skii Party Organization is the insufficient help given to the raion by the Rostov Obkom. With no supporting evidence the obkom reassures itself that Sal'skii is one of the better raions in fulfilling agrarian campaigns; it does not fathom what

11 on political issues and agita'tion, and 2 on industry (Dubonosov, "Organizatorskaia i politicheskaia rabota").

25. "Zadachi Rostovskoi oblastnoi partorganizatsii," *Partiinoe stroitel'stvo*, no. 12 (June 1945), pp. 26–27; "O rabote Sal'skogo raikoma," pp. 61–65; Kolosov and Zhukovin, *Opyt Tselinskogo raikoma partii; Molot*, January 25, 1952.

the raion organization actually does, nor does it reveal the mistakes and deficiencies in the raikom's leadership.''[26] This example was intended to pressure oblast party organizations not only to fulfill their economic plans in general but to pay particular attention to the problems of lagging districts and kolkhozy. It was in this context that obkoms were to become more deeply involved in the work of lower party and state organizations. Obkoms were to make sure that raikoms conformed to their new party role.[27] Thus Rostov provided the illustrative case by which the Central Committee showed specifically what it expected when it called for local party organizations to balance their economic activities with political organizational concerns.

In Leningrad, lower party and soviet organs became the focus of attention only when districts failed to attain their production goals. Indeed, in these cases the improper behavior of lower organs was frequently cited as the cause of agricultural failure. It is important in this context to distinguish between the political exhortations to greater political activity published by obkom officials in central party journals from directives issued at the time of plenums. Examination of the specific behavior of lower party and state organizations rarely led to calls for an increase in ideological work. Such assessments did frequently deplore a lack of clarity in the chain of command in the countryside, but the political emphasis found in the gorkom's exhortations to urban raikoms was absent.[28]

The obkom focused its attention on cadre policy as well as on plan fulfillment. Although the obkom appears rarely to have actually selected local cadres other than raikom secretaries, it nonetheless was concerned about the qualifications of rural leaders. This concern accounts for many of the topics classified as ideological at obkom plenums. The Central Committee's resolution on Sal'skii Raikom specifically called for the education and retraining of kolkhoz chairmen.[29] Leningrad obkom responded in 1946 by establishing training programs for 12,500 agricultural workers and

26. "O rabote Sal'skogo raikoma," p. 63.

27. See the statement by N. S. Patolichev, First secretary of the Rostov obkom, at the Fifth Rostov Party Conference, *Molot*, February 9, 1942.

28. E.g., *Leningradskaia pravda*, August 29, 1946, and the joint plenum of the Leningrad obkom and gorkom, reported in ibid., December 23, 1948.

29. "O rabote Sal'skogo raikoma," p. 65.

900 people engaged in work on agricultural machinery during 1946–47. The obkom specifically required the raikoms to formulate plans to train and retrain such personnel and to submit their plans to the obkom within ten days. Interest in these projects was renewed in response to the February Plenum of the Central Committee in 1947.[30]

Political work was often connected with personnel matters. The raikoms were to recruit the rural intelligentsia as party members and to use them in agitational work in the countryside, and they were encouraged to undertake the political instruction of young cadres.[31] The political efforts aimed at the countryside were more in the mode of political and cultural enlightenment than those confined more strictly to the mobilization of workers in pursuit of plan fulfillment. Given the paucity of primary party organizations in rural areas, a more general approach toward agricultural workers is understandable.

The postwar obkom, as typified by Leningrad and Rostov, can be viewed as much closer to what administrative theory would characterize as a line organization than to an organization that functioned as a critical external observer. To the extent that the obkom was the single regional organization to which economic and state organs directed their attention, it played a role similar to that of a prefect in area administration. The obkom's agricultural activities, as distinguished from its own and its gorkom counterparts' functions in industry, went beyond coordination. The obkom's interpretation of central economic plans actually specified local economic policies, rather than allowing economic and state institutions to do so. The obkom remained the major organ of agricultural supervision.

The obkom's role in industry was clearly differentiated from that of the gorkom in its delegation of authority to the raikom to implement policy. The obkom's directives to the raikom and raiispolkom (district executive committee) required the latter organs to play active roles in policy implementation. They were not merely to verify economic administration indirectly through other organs, but to assume direct line responsibility for policy execution. These demands included the formulation of local

30. *Leningradskaia pravda*, December 3, 1946, and March 18, 1947.
31. Ibid., August 5, 1950, reporting the June plenum of the Leningrad obkom.

plans and extensive authority over personnel decisions in the countryside.

Beneath the oblast level of agricultural administration, party, state, and economic organizations make up a network of authority rather more complex than that found in the industrial sector. The organs most important for the execution of agricultural policy include the raikom, the raiispolkom soviet (executive committee of the district council), the territorial party organization, the sel'soviet (village council), the rai'zemotdel (district land department), the machine tractor station, and primary party organizations at MTS's, sovkhozy, and kolkhozy. The multiplicity of these organizations reflects the regime's desire to construct a state /party system under geographic and demographic conditions that do not easily lend themselves to strict lines of authority. Indeed, the role of the new postwar party was more difficult to define in the agricultural sector than in the industrial sector.

Raion Party Committees

The center of authority in the countryside was the raikom. The functions of this party organization provoked major theoretical discussions during the postwar years. "In 1946," Pravda reported, "the Central Committee issued a resolution on the work of the Sal'skii Party Raikom. The Central Committee demanded the reconstruction of the work of rural raikoms, an end to the improper practices of excessive guidance in relation to soviet, economic, and kolkhoz organs, and the enlargement of the role of raikoms as organs of political leadership."[32] If rural economic and soviet organs were to be strengthened, the raikom would have to cede some of its leadership functions to them. The raikom was to supervise and verify their activities and to influence them through the selection and placement of personnel. Primary party organizations in the countryside were also to be strengthened by the rural raikom. These issues arose at the close of the war and continued to dominate central party discussions of raikom activities throughout the postwar period.

The raikom's official role was rarely realized. As early as 1945,

32. Pravda, June 1, 1948, cited in Kolosov and Zhukovin, Opyt Tselinskogo raikoma partii, p. 4.

an article in *Partiinoe stroitel'stvo* noted that "instead of increasing the authority of soviet organs and delegating responsibility to their leaders, the party committees frequently took upon their own shoulders matters that should have been studied by the executive committee and their departments. In rural raions, for example, the functions of party raikoms and raion agricultural departments are so confused that it is sometimes difficult to tell where one ends and the other begins."[33]

If this theme was frequently repeated, however, so was the theme of the raikom's central role in agricultural production: "The task of surmounting agricultural backwardness naturally ... belongs to the raion committee of the party, in whose hands are concentrated strands of incomparable influence over kolkhoz affairs";[34] "The party raikoms must assume the responsibility for the state and development of the kolkhozy. They must delve deeply into all details of kolkhoz life in the effort to strengthen each kolkhoz."[35]

The central party was conveying a dual message. Although the raikom was to become an organ of general political leadership consistent with the increasingly operational roles of other rural institutions, it was still to direct and intervene in the implementation of agricultural policy. Unlike the industrial raikom, which checked the results of other institutions' activities, the rural raikom implemented the demands of the central and obkom authorities. "In agriculture," a *Bol'shevik* commentator declared, "the party obkom influences the work of kolkhozy, machine tractor stations, and sovkhozy primarily through the actions of party raikoms in taking increased responsibility for the state of affairs."[36]

Several questions arise out of the charge placed upon the raikom. What were the actual functions of the raikom? Was it primarily a political organization involved in mobilization, or was this task secondary to its economic function? In either event, how

---

33. M. Domrachev, "Zametki o proverke ispolneniia," *Partiinoe stroitel'stvo*, no. 11 (1945), p. 41.

34. V. Lukianov, "Nekotorye voprosy partiinoi raboty v derevne," *Partiinaia zhizn'*, no. 1 (January 1947), p. 36.

35. "Za skoreishee vosstanovlenie i pod'em sel'skogo khoziaistva," *Bol'shevik*, no. 4 (February 1947), p. 9.

36. Lazar Slepov, *Mestnye partiinye organy* (Moscow: Vysshei Partiinoi Shkole pri TsK KPSS, 1954), p. 27.

did the raikom choose to carry out its obligations? And in what way was it related to lower party, state, and economic organizations in the countryside?

Rural raikoms were held responsible not only for the fulfillment of the agrarian plan (or the failure to fulfill it) but also for the organization and performance of personnel at kolkhozy, machine tractor stations, and other rural institutions. The nature of obkom demands suggests that rural raikoms were expected to focus their efforts on all elements of rural life, both material and organizational, on which fulfillment of the plan depended. No explanation for failure to fulfill the plan—lack of fertilizer, fodder, seed, personnel, machines, livestock shelters, or rain—was acceptable. Indeed, the obkom viewed such excuses as attempts to rationalize the raikom's own poor performance. Thus the nearly impossible demands made on the rural sector as a whole and the rural raikoms' responsibility for meeting those demands promoted their direct involvement in agricultural production.

The Central Committee, as we have seen, singled out Sal'skii Raikom in southern Rostov Oblast, as a classic case of behavior that had to be changed. Its resolution of August 1946 specified the behavior it hoped to transform: "Kolkhoz, sovkhoz, and MTS workers receive instructions from the raikom on all economic questions and as a rule turn only to it. The leading workers of the raiispolkom expect instructions from the raikom party on every matter, however minor. This practice leads to the substitution and deprivation of authority and to the lessening of soviet, economic, and agricultural organs' responsibility."[37] Such interventionist behavior was expected to stop.

The reports on raikom behavior and the agendas of raikom bureau meetings in Leningrad Oblast reinforce the image of an organization deeply involved in the details of economic policy. The December 1946 Leningrad obkom plenum criticized the rural raikoms for focusing on current problems rather than devoting themselves to political work. Nearly two years later, at the 1948 joint plenum of the Leningrad obkom and gorkom, the obkom secretary sounded the same theme: "Many of our raikoms, particularly rural ones, are still so wholly absorbed in decisions on a multitude of current matters that they fail to attend to the resolution of core,

37. "O rabote Sal'skogo raikoma," p. 62.

correctly supposing that anything to do with future prospects must be noted for them by the gorkom or obkom."[38]

Despite the constant criticisms, rural raikoms continued to be deeply involved in daily agricultural matters.[39] In Osvminskii Raion, in Leningrad Oblast, the raikom's deep involvement in economic management led to the accusation that the "raikom's agricultural department... duplicates the work of the raiispolkom's agricultural department and neglects its basic tasks—the selection, placement, and education of cadres."[40] Similar behavior by rural raikoms in Rostov Oblast was criticized throughout the 1940s and early 1950s. A special correspondent of *Pravda* noted that one raikom secretary in Rostov Oblast was actually known as the "raion director."[41]

The raikoms' apparent obsession with economic details was not matched by their attention to the affairs of other rural institutions. Though their political work was supposed to include agitation, propaganda, and the organization of political study groups for party and nonparty leaders, rural raikoms frequently ignored both the work and the leaders of other rural political organizations, especially primary party organizations, and continued to assign economic functions to political instructors. *Molot* described the experience of a rural raikom in Rostov Oblast: "The workers of the organization-instruction section of the raikom—the leader of the section and two instructors—spent the major part of their time fulfilling the responsibilities of plenipotentiaries in economic campaigns and were constantly to be found at one or another kolkhoz. Otherwise they were occupied for the most part with economic matters, duplicating the responsibilities of the kolkhoz chairman and MTS director, and *not in the least* concerned about encouraging the activity of party organizations."[42] To deal with such problems, the Central Committee reorganized local party organizations' apparatuses. The organizational-instructional departments of raikoms and gorkoms were abolished; now party, union, and komsomol departments were to supervise the work of lower party organizations.[43]

---

38. *Leningradskaia pravda*, December 18, 1946, and December 23, 1948.
39. See, e.g., ibid., August 13, 1952.
40. Ibid., August 6, 1952.
41. *Molot*, January 22, 1947; see also July 20 and September 24, 1948; June 7, 1952.
42. *Molot*, May 29, 1946; emphasis in original.
43. S. G. Mogilevskii, "Partiino-organizatsionnaia rabota na sele v gody che-

Rural raikoms attempted to comply with the central party's wishes by sending out political lecturers to organize and instruct workers, but their efforts remained superficial. G. Badaev, a Leningrad obkom secretary, criticized rural raikoms' political work: "Mass political work is carried out in the countryside from time to time; lectures and discussions are led in a routine and uninteresting manner, with no account taken of the kolkhozniki's wishes. The raikoms frequently send lecturers to the kolkhozy on the basis not of the matters that should be explained to kolkhozniki but of the subjects on which they have lecturers."[44] A lead editorial in Leningradskaia pravda of January 15, 1948, headed "A Higher Level of Mass Political Work in the Countryside!" criticized the Oiatskii raikom's practice of confining its work on agitation to the periods of soviet election campaigns. The editorial noted that "the Central Committee of the Party has called upon rural raikoms to provide lectures by instructors at least twice a month and external consultation for agitators at kolkhozy, sovkhozy, and machine tractor stations. The raikoms must regularly call meetings and seminars of primary party secretaries to exchange work experiences from the best agitation teams, the subjects of lectures and conversations among workers." This advice resulted in only an occasional foray into agitational work that was still characterized by a campaign style. Rural raikoms continued to be only superficially involved in mass political work and devoted little time to ideological issues or to contact with PPOs and territorial party organizations.

The education and training of rural leaders fell under the auspices of the raikom and raiispolkom soviet. Raikoms frequently found it easier to remove party and economic leaders than to establish study programs or take other steps to help them improve their performance. Undoubtedly this response was fostered by pressure from the center. The Central Committee asked the Rostov

---

tvertoi piatiletki (1946–1950 gg.)," candidate dissertation, Rostov State University, 1972, p. 142. Mogilevskii cites the November 1948 Central Committee resolution "Reorganizatsii apparata raikomov, gorkomov, okruzhkomov i ukomov."

44. G. Badaev, "O khode vypolneniia postanovleniia Soveta Ministrov Soiuza SSSR i TsK VKP(b) 'O merakh po likvidatsii narushenii Ustava sel'skokhoziaistvennoi arteli v kolkhozakh' i zadachakh partiinykh organizatsii po usileniiu rukovodstva kolkhozami," Propaganda i agitatsiia, no. 23–24 (December 1946), p. 16.

obkom to replace 900 kolkhoz chairmen with agricultural specialists during 1949–51.[45] The goal was for all kolkhoz chairmen
in Rostov to have agricultural or technical education and to have
completed at least a one-year agricultural course by the end of the
Fourth Five-Year Plan.[46] An effort was made to train kolkhoz
cadres, especially chairmen, in the late 1940s. Local schools were
established so that chairmen could remain at their posts while
raising their qualifications. These plans were acknowledged to be
unsuccessful. In Luzhskom Raion, Leningrad Oblast, for example,
only 20 to 30 percent of kolkhoz chairmen attended such schools.
The failure was attributed to the poor work of raion party organizations.[47] Many of the inadequacies of the raikom's ideological
work, including that in education, are closely related to its style
of leadership, a bureaucratic style that relied heavily on special
representatives to supervise the implementation of policy. These
factors influenced raikom behavior in cadre matters.

Perhaps the most important indirect means of influencing policy
available to the party lay in manipulation of personnel. To the
extent that raikoms could select and place cadre in other rural
institutions, they enjoyed a significant advantage over those organs—political, state, and economic. Although many officials
were on the nomenklatura of the obkom or theoretically were to
be elected by the cooperative, the raikom's recommendation
served as the definitive factor in their appointment or removal.
Directors and assistant directors of machine tractor stations and
other economic personnel came within the raikom's purview, but
the most significant position so affected was that of the kolkhoz
chairman. Strong economic institutions "require stable cadres at
their head," a writer in *Partiinaia zhizn'* pointed out.

> Nevertheless, many kolkhoz leaders in some raions are removed
> after almost every agricultural campaign. As soon as it becomes
> clear that the kolkhoz's affairs are going poorly in some line of

45. Mogilevskii ("Partiino-organizatsionnaia rabota") cites a Rostov obkom resolution of April 18, 1949, located in the Rostov Party Archives. The resolution
was not published in *Molot*.

46. *Molot*, July 17, 1949.

47. B. Nikolaev, "Vospitanie rukovodiashchikh sel'skikh kadrov-vazhneishaia
zadacha partiinykh organizatsii," *Propaganda i agitatsiia*, no. 1 (January 1950), p.
32.

work, the question of changing the chairman is brought up. As Comrade Grigor'ev discussed at the Leningrad obkom plenum, the Pushkin Kolkhoz, Gatchinskii Raion, removed seven chairmen in two years, but nothing changed. The kolkhoz is still one of the weaker ones in the raion.[48]

Such practices were unlikely to help efforts to improve the long-term performance of kolkhoz chairmen. Indeed, poor raikom work with kolkhoz cadres, especially with the chairman, was a primary cause of the high turnover rates among rural cadres. The average turnover rate was 30 to 40 percent, while in some raions in Leningrad Oblast it approached 60 percent.[49] Despite a decline in turnover rates at the end of the 1940s and the early 1950s, they remained substantial. Lagging kolkhozy and poorer agricultural areas were particularly affected by the high turnover rates resulting from raikom intervention.

The raikoms used plenipotentiaries to exercise control over kolkhoz and MTS cadre policy. The plenipotentiary's role will be scrutinized in detail later; here we may only note that, as the word implies, these special representatives were empowered to make independent decisions, and they often did so. It was not unusual for plenipotentiaries to remove kolkhoz chairmen, appoint replacements, and have the raiispolkom soviet and raikom simply confirm their decisions after the fact.[50]

Cadre policy was criticized even in regard to party personnel issues. Many rural raion party organizations neglected party recruitment, in part because of the Central Committee's demands that new party members be more carefully scrutinized.[51] Recruitment was particularly difficult in rural areas because of the party's lingering suspicion of kolkhozniki and the limited size of the

48. S. Zadionchenko, "O nedostatkakh v rabote Belorusskoi partorganizatsii," *Partiinaia zhizn'*, no. 2 (January 1947), p. 52. The citation refers to a kolkhoz in Leningrad Oblast.

49. "Organizatsionno-khoziaistvennoe ukreplenie kolkhozov v tsentr vnimaniia partiinykh organizatsii," *Partiinaia zhizn'*, no. 7 (April 1947), pp. 8–9.

50. Ibid., p. 9.

51. Postanovlenie Soveta Ministrov SSSR i TsK VKP(b), "O zadachakh partiinykh i sovetskikh organizatsii po dal'neishemu ukrepleniiu sostava predsedatel'ei i drugikh rukovodiashchikh rabotnikov kolkhozov " (June 9, 1950), in *KPSS v rezoliutsiiakh i resheniiakh s"ezdov, konferentsii i plenumov TsK*, vol. 6, 1941–1954, 8th ed. (Moscow: Politicheskoi Literatury, 1971), pp. 323–31.

primary target group, the rural intelligentsia. In Leningrad Oblast, *Partiinaia zhizn'* complained in 1947, "a number of party organizations at kolkhozy ... failed to accept even one kolkhoznik or agricultural specialist into the party in the last year."[52]

Overall, current agrarian issues dominated the raikoms' agendas. Although some attention was paid to ideological work, actual involvement in this area tended to be sporadic. Cadre policy provided an important lever by which the raikom could not only affect policy execution but, more important, shape its own relations with other rural organizations. Thus the rural raikom combined a dominant direct role in economic policy with an indirect political role. Rural raikoms' behavior on the whole was consistent with that depicted by Robert Miller:

> ... the raikom mode of Party control in the countryside consisted not so much of two different roles as two phases of a single role. Although the production responsibilities of the raikom were paramount, they certainly did not exhaust its range of functions. During much of the year, when production questions were less urgent, the raikom secretaries were content to employ the indirect methods of economic leadership seemingly favored by the Party, while turning their attention to other tasks, such as the building up of the village PPO's and strengthening the staffs and capabilities of the local administrative organs. Once the pressures began to mount at campaign time, however, the raikom had to shift gears, so to speak, and move to the second phase of its duties, the more or less direct management of agricultural affairs.[53]

The cyclical nature of agricultural work was reflected in raikom behavior. The raikom's direct economic functions were paramount. Rural raikoms' relations with PPOs remained superficial. Although the direct economic leadership provided by the raikom suggests a deep involvement in rural affairs, particularly at kolkhozy, such an impression is mistaken. The raikom's secretaries and departmental heads were rarely involved in on-site activities in the countryside; they were in fact so preoccupied with the

52. "Organizatsionno-khoziaistvennoe ukreplenie," p. 30.

53. Robert F. Miller, *100,000 Tractors* (Cambridge: Harvard University Press, 1970), p. 201.

preparation of reports for submission to the obkom that they were frequently criticized for "rampant bureaucratism." Only when economic disaster actually struck, as when a kolkhoz failed to reach its plan target, did the raikom bureau or first secretary actually become involved in its affairs. Rural raikoms participated in agricultural management primarily through their instructors and plenipotentiaries.

Raikom instructors were often portrayed as living links between the raion and primary party organizations. The model for the instructor's role bore only a faint resemblance to actual behavior. Ideally, the rural raikom instructor was to impart political and, if necessary agricultural knowledge to the young, inexperienced members of the komsomol, territorial, and primary party organizations. The instructor, according to Leningradskaia pravda, was to give "practical aid to the secretaries of party organizations in the establishment of a work plan, the involvement of Communists in active party work, the preparation and execution of party meetings, the setting up of the party economy, and the collection of membership dues."[54] The emphasis was on political guidance. Of course, the periods that required the greatest assistance corresponded to the planting and harvest seasons. At these times, efforts were to be made to mobilize and organize the rural population. In the quieter periods between campaigns, political instruction was deemed more appropriate.[55] The heavy reliance on instructors was explained as a temporary measure necessitated by the scarcity of rural PPOs. Although instructors did occasionally engage in political activities, most evidence points to a rather different role for them: they served as plenipotentiaries, with full powers to act for the raikom.

Most rural raikoms and raisoviets sent plenipotentiaries to kolkhozy and sel'soviets during the planting and harvest periods. Rural raikoms, according to A. M. Stepanov, used "instructors as 'state' plenipotentiaries to carry out economic campaigns at kolkhozy."[56] The raikom and raisoviet made these plenipotentiaries

54. Leningradskaia pravda, August 17, 1947.
55. E.g., Leningradskaia pravda, November 11, 1947.
56. A. M. Stepanov, "Partino-organizatsionnaia rabota kommunisticheskaia partii v gody chetvertoi piatiletki," candidate dissertation, Rostov-on-Don State University, 1971, pp. 60–61.

personally responsible for fulfilling planting and harvest plans.[57]
Their superior organizations showed little concern about what
they actually did. Many raikom secretaries, a party organ complained, "devoted insufficient attention to instructors.... There
were often instances when instructors were used as plenipotentiaries of the raikom to carry out various economic assignments."[58]

In effect, the plenipotentiary directly carried out economic policy with scant supervision. Raikom secretaries themselves rarely
left raion centers. Most of their efforts were devoted to issuing
directives, assessing the results of agricultural campaigns, and
preparing reports to be forwarded to the obkom. Thus the raikom
occupied an intermediate position in agricultural management,
leaving direct intervention to its plenipotentiaries. At times, however, the whole staff of the raion party was drafted into the role
of plenipotentiary. In Voznesenskii Raion, Leningrad Oblast, "all
of the raikom workers were distributed among the kolkhozy as
plenipotentiaries" in 1946, *Propaganda i agitatsiia* reported, and
they remained there from the beginning of planting till the harvest
was in.[59]

In 1947 the head of the organization-instruction department of
the Leningrad obkom, P. Vagin, described the raikom's use of
plenipotentiaries: "during the most critical time of the agricultural
campaign some raikoms did not rely on primary party organizations, underestimated their role, and acted by administrative
methods, consulting only with kolkhoz chairmen and sel'soviets.
The party raikoms usually located all their departments far away,
including the organization-instruction and propaganda and agitation departments, but sent instructors and heads of departments
to kolkhozy and sel'soviets as plenipotentiaries."[60]

Many Soviet writers conceded the usefulness of plenipotentiaries in the immediate postwar years, when qualified personnel
were scarce in rural areas. Stepanov cited Sal'skii Raion as a prime
example:

57. *Leningradskaia pravda*, May 14, 1947; *Molot*, November 24, 1946, and May
13, 1947.

58. V. Osnos, "O rabote instruktora sel'skogo raikoma partii," *Propaganda i
agitatsiia*, no. 9 (May 1947), p. 41.

59. Ibid.

60. *Leningradskaia pravda*, June 10, 1947.

In the first postwar years ..., the practice of drawing upon external instructors from gorkom and raikom party departments
was widespread. This practice helped to widen the party committee's circle of active members and increase its strength. External instructors provided considerable help to PPOs in raising
their level of work. Thus at the end of 1949 Sal'skii Raikom had
twenty-nine external instructors certified to its bureau [fourteen
to the organization department and fifteen to propaganda and
agitation]. External instructors brought prepared questions to the
bureau; supervised PPO work, party cell organizations, and party
groups; and rendered them practical help in investigating workers' complaints and formal requests.[61]

The plenipotentiaries had such a disruptive impact on both
party and economic organizations that the practice came under
increasingly severe criticism in the central party press. A *Pravda*
editorial described the consequences of the raikom's use of plenipotentiaries: "Never say that the raikom didn't work with [other
rural raion institutions] at all. ... It remembered them when it was
necessary to send plenipotentiaries during the sowing, harvesting,
and gathering of grain. They pushed aside the rural leaders; these
plenipotentiaries attempted to work as chairmen of sel'soviets and
kolkhozy and as the secretaries of primary party organizations,
and even as MTS directors."[62] Some plenipotentiaries stayed on
the kolkhozy throughout the growing season and took an active
part in their direction, with no noticeable assistance from the
raikom. Despite complaints in the press, the use of raikom instructors as state plenipotentiaries continued.

Instructors were chosen as plenipotentiaries on the basis of their
political reliability. Often they lacked any knowledge of agriculture.[63] Yet, as their major task was to see that the directives of
superior party or state organizations were carried out, they dis-

61. Stepanov, "Partino-organizatsionnaia rabota," p. 62. Stepanov cites the Rostov Oblast Party Archives. Note that by this date, the use of plenipotentiaries was
to have ceased.
62. *Pravda* May 22, 1948, quoted in Kolosov and Zhukovin, *Opyt Tselinskogo
raikoma partii*, p. 10.
63. *Leningradskaia pravda*, May 14, 1947. The Leningrad obkom published
criticism of Gatchinskii and Tikhvinskii raikoms for sending second-rank people
who lacked agricultural educations as plenipotentiaries. The same criticism appears in *Molot*, October 5, 1946, where the process of choosing plenipotentiaries
is described as "frivolous."

placed the people who were formally responsible for the execution of policy.

Not all plenipotentiaries, however, were sent for extended stays in the countryside during agricultural campaigns. Some were used more sporadically. The agricultural plan of Kirishinskii Raion, Leningrad Oblast, for example, was fulfilled by only 30 percent in 1950. Some of the raion's kolkhoz leaders were accused of taking an antigovernment path by attempting to withhold grain. Nonetheless, the raikom did not directly intervene. The local press reported that "the party raikom and raiispolkom soviet did not rely in their work on the party organization or the sel'soviets and did not enlarge their roles, but organized work only through the sending of plenipotentiaries as 'tolkachy. ' ... Nevertheless, these plenipotentiaries were at kolkhozy only for visits, turning up in the morning and gone by evening. There was no verification of their work. Such a practice gives rise only to irresponsibility."[64] Other accounts note that the number of kolkhozy for which plenipotentiaries and instructors were held responsible made it virtually impossible for them to exercise close supervision.[65]

The responsibilities thrust upon raikom instructors stimulated their transformation from external staff troubleshooters and political expeditors to active managers in place of line personnel. Their involvement usually conformed to that typically found in a campaign approach to policy implementation: intense participation of limited duration. While they were to assist rural party organizations in the supervision and verification of agricultural work, this aspect of their work was usually secondary and often neglected altogether. There is relatively little evidence of the involvement of raikoms and their instructors in the direction of mass political work at primary party organizations. Typically the instructors consulted with economic leaders. If the results were unsatisfactory, the instructors temporarily supplanted those leaders and often permanently removed them. Sophisticated questions of agrarian policy were usually beyond the ken of raikom representatives. When problems arose at the machine tractor station or

64. *Leningradskaia pravda*, October 6, 1950. The Rostov press also cites the brevity and superficiality of raikom plenipotentiaries' visits; see *Molot*, April 16, 1946.

65. *Leningradskaia pravda*, April 16, 1949.

between the kolkhozy and the MTS, the raikom and its representatives simply removed the MTS director.[66]

The pattern of relations among the various rural state, party,
and economic organizations was complex and frequently confused. Responsibilities were ill defined, often simply reflecting
informal practices. The primary culprit in this web of rural relations was the raikom. A party journal explained in 1951:

> A serious inadequacy in the work of many raion party organi-
> zations is their failure to balance party-political work with eco-
> nomic work. Some raikoms still displace their soviet and
> economic organs. As a result of such practices, the workers of
> the MTS, sovkhozy, and kolkhozy wait for pronouncements from
> the party raikom on all economic questions and as a rule turn
> only to the raikom. This practice leads to the deprivation and
> lowering of the responsibility of soviet and agrarian organs. In-
> dividual leaders of the raikom, tied up in administrative-eco-
> nomic matters, completely forget about the organization of party-
> political work at kolkhozy, MTS's, and sovkhozy. They ignore
> violations of the agricultural collective's charter and permit the
> incorrect distribution of party strength in the raion.[67]

Thus the raikom's preoccupation with economic administration
led to its violation of officially designated functions.

The raikom and raiispolkom soviet, both at the same administrative level, shared the responsibility for plan fulfillment and
personnel policy. The raisoviet (district council of workers' deputies) was more involved in the details of policy implementation.
Nevertheless, rural raisoviets and their agricultural departments
frequently avoided any real involvement in agriculture. Instead
of taking an active role in policy, Bol'shevik charged, the typical
agricultural department resembled a "planning and statistical
administration."[68]

By issuing specific directives and sending its instructors to participate in policy implementation, the raikom often obliterated

66. Ibid., June 19, 1952.

67. B. Nikolaev, "Po-bol'shevistski provesti uborku urozhaia i zagotovki
sel'skokhoziaistvennykh produktov," Propaganda i agitatsiia, no. 15 (August
1951), pp. 23–24.

68. M. Rodionov, "O rabote mestnykh sovetov deputatov trudiashchikhsia,"
Bol'shevik, no. 13 (July 1948), p. 12.

any meaningful division of responsibility between itself and state organizations. The raikom frequently duplicated the work of the raisoviet's agricultural department.[69] Such a case was criticized in *Leningradskaia pravda*: "the raikom [Mginskii Raion, Leningrad Oblast] often supplants soviet organs. Out of 118 questions that were discussed at the raikom bureau during the reporting period, 48 should have been decided by the executive committee of the raion soviet. The little details of economic and state organizations distracted the raikom from party-political work. The raikom gave little help to lagging kolkhozy."[70]

The picture that emerges from official accounts is of raisoviets that constantly sought advice or even formal directives from raikoms before acting. Such an arrangement undermined the autonomy of the state apparatus. V. I. Khliupin's comparison of the local soviet's formal role and rural raikoms' behavior suggests the confluence of their functions:

> The executive committees of local soviets gave primary emphasis to the organizational-economic strengthening of kolkhozy and the improvement of the group consisting of chairmen and other leading kolkhoz cadre, to the spreading of exemplary experience and its use in propaganda, and to monitoring the observance of agricultural collectives' charters. At their meetings, soviets reviewed such questions as the repair of agricultural machinery, the preparation for planting, the harvest, the storing of feed, the wintering of public livestock, and the mechanization and electrificaton of agricultural work.[71]

These were the very issues that occupied obkoms and rural raikoms. K. Khmelsevskii, secretary of Molotov (Saratov) Obkom, writing in the central party journal, *Partiinaia zhizn'*, portrayed the activities of the rural raikom:

> The decline of the soviet apparatus in the raion is not all due to the rural raikom party's work. The raikom begins to carry out

69. *Leningradskaia pravda*, August 6, 1952, and June 13, 1951.

70. Ibid., April 14, 1948. See also *Molot*, October 26, 1946.

71. V. I. Khliupin, "Rol' mestnykh Sovetov deputatov trudiashchikhsia v vosstanovlenii i razvitii promyshlennosti i sel'skogo khoziaistva v poslevoennyi period (1945–1953 gg.)," in *Iz istorii deiatel'nosti sovetov*, ed. S. F. Naida (Moscow: Mysl', 1966), p. 104.

the administrative-economic functions belonging to others and to stop studying questions of party-political work. The first secretary turns into the head of the raion agricultural department and a plenipotentiary of the ministry; the second becomes the head veterinarian; all the rest of the raikom workers are plenipotentiaries who settle for months at the village soviets and kolkhozy. Such a practice leads the raion party committee to lose its role as the leading nucleus of all raion organizations and turns it into an ordinary institution.[72]

At best, party raikoms and raiispolkom soviets duplicated each other; more frequently the raiispolkom soviet took its direction from the raikom.[73] Often the raikom simply displaced the raiispolkom soviet. Instead of strengthening the raisoviet, the raikom and its representatives undermined its independence.

The raikom was severely criticized for its administrative activities, since they weakened its political functions. Lower-level state and party organs were not really in a position to maintain their autonomy vis-à-vis raikoms and raiispolkom soviets. The members of village soviets and of territorial and kolkhoz party organizations tended to be few and poorly educated. The staffs of raion party and state organizations at the raion center had little contact with them; when information was needed or an agricultural campaign was at hand, the raikom and raisoviet sent their plenipotentiaries.

Territorial Party Organizations

Territorial party organizations were responsible for all enterprises and institutions within the jurisdictions of sel'soviets in which there were no primary party organizations.[74] Immediately

72. K. Khmelsevskii, "O sekretare sel'skogo raikoma partii," *Partiinaia zhizn'*, no. 11 (June 1947), p. 20.

73. B. Nikolaev, "Po-bol'shevistski," p. 23; *Molot*, January 27, 1948, and February 13, 1948.

74. P. Vorontsov, "Sel'skie teritorial'nye partiinye organizatsii," *Partiinaia zhizn'* no. 7 (April 1947), p. 16.

after the war, territorial party organizations were the primary local party organs. Many rural areas had too few party members to establish PPOs. Party members were usually sent to territorial party organizations in rural areas after they returned from the war. Despite wartime enrollments, party membership in these areas remained low.[75] Only after the amalgamation of kolkhozy in 1950 were most members of territorial party organizations reassigned to form primary party organizations.

Reliance on territorial party organizations intensified the party's problems in the countryside. Though these organizations had no formal right of *kontrol'* over the work of kolkhozy and machine tractor stations, party members were so scarce among the rural population that they were informally given responsibility for supervising kolkhoz work and reporting their findings to raion party organizations for necessary action.[76] In fact, however, the territorial party organizations were weak and met infrequently.

The territorial party organizations were severely criticized for their poor work in political agitation, presumably their most important task. As one secretary in Leningrad Oblast observed, "the agitation team of the Tervaeskii Territorial Party Organization Vyborg Raion, did not meet once after local soviet elections, and agitators worked with the population only occasionally."[77] Territorial party organizations in Leningrad Oblast were constantly criticized for their lack of leadership in agitation and their general avoidance of mass political work at kolkhozy. Such criticism was frequent in Rostov Oblast as well. Territorial party organizations not only were cited for poor agitation and infrequent meetings but were said to lack any influence over agricultural enterprises.[78]

The constant calls for increased political work were regularly ignored. At a meeting of the Konzerskii Territorial Party, Lenin-

75. See chap. 2.

76. N. Ignatov, "Ukrepeliat' pervichnye partorganizatsii v derevne," *Partiinaia zhizn'*, no. 5 (March 1947), p. 42; P. Vorontsov, "Sel'skie teritorial'nye partiinye organizatsii," p. 16.

77. G. Badaev, "Zadachi pervichnykh partiinykh organizatsiiakh v bor'be za vypol'nenie i perevypolnenie plana razvitiia sel'skogo khoziaistva v 1948 gody," *Propaganda i agitatsiia*, no. 7 (April 1948), p. 11.

78. *Molot*, July 6, 1952.

grad Oblast, one member complained, "Raion meetings turn into occasions for recriminations, and one doesn't hear a positive word at them. They don't believe in us lowly worker Communists, but inundate us with plenipotentiaries who decide everything without our participation."[79] Raikoms in Rostov Oblast often didn't even bother to hear territorial party organizations' reports.[80] The limited role that territorial party organizations played in agriculture is not particularly surprising in view of the fact that most of their members were drawn from the rural intelligentsia, and had never been involved in agriculture.

Primary Party Organizations

Primary party organizations at machine tractor stations and kolkhozy were weak. Few kolkhozy had such organizations during the immediate postwar years. Even after 1950, the size and level of sophistication of their membership were extraordinarily low. The MTS party organizations were sometimes called upon to participate in propaganda work at the kolkhoz. Officially, such activity was criticized as inappropriate. The MTS party organization was not to take upon itself the work of the raikom, particularly not its mass political work. If the kolkhoz's political work was inadequate, the MTS party was to inform the raikom.[81] The MTS party organization was responsible for the fulfillment of its own plan, but otherwise devoted little attention to agricultural production.[82]

The assistant director of the MTS in charge of political affairs (the *zampolit*) was not the head of the MTS's party organization. The functions of the assistant director and the MTS PPO were separate. As reinstituted after the war, the office of zampolit was formally attached to the PPO of the raikom apparatus, with responsibility for operational issues at the MTS. Instead of supervising the director of the MTS and verifying the station's activities, the assistant director often became an accessory to the MTS di-

79. *Leningradskaia pravda*, June 9, 1949.

80. *Molot*, July 6, 1952.

81. "Pis'ma zamestitelei direktorov MTS po politchasti," *Partiinaia zhizn'*, no. 13 (July 1947), p. 43.

82. F. Kuznetsov, ed., *Partiino-politicheskaia rabota v MTS* (Leningrad: Leningradskoe Gazetno-Zhurnal'noe Izdatel'stvo, 1954), p. 67.

rector, helping him make the station look good in the eyes of the higher party and state officials. In a sense, these activities helped the raikom, but they were hardly the sort of thing for which the position was created.[83] The emergence of the zampolit's new role was made possible in part by the lack of supervision by the raikom.

Although the raikom frequently examined the question of mechanization, it avoided direct contact with the zampolit and the MTS party organization, preferring to send its representatives to consult directly with the MTS director. The familiar pattern of displacement is seen once again. In Lomonosovskii Raion, *Leningradskaia pravda* explained, "raikom workers long ago took on part of the functions of the MTS director. Where and how this or that brigade worked, what sort of mechanization existed, what labor productivity was, what they were going to be doing tomorrow and the day after tomorrow—these things were better known by the raikom than by the MTS director."[84]

The raikom undoubtedly enhanced its knowledge of economic details by sending its plenipotentiaries to the site of production. Tikhvin Raion, Leningrad Oblast, sent two plenipotentiaries during the planting season, one to the farm, the other to the tractor brigade."[85] Once again the raikom was more involved in economic matters than with party-political and organizational work, which it relegated to the MTS party organization. In light of this preference, it is not surprising that some zampolity began to assume the responsibilities of MTS directors.[86]

An article in *Partiinaia zhizn'* noted that zampolity were occasionally used by the raikom as staff plenipotentiaries.[87] The zampolit in Lomonsovskii Raion in 1952, for example, was said to have spent most of his time on economic matters rather than among the people.[88] The avoidance of "work with people" in this period indicated the failure of the party's central policy, which emphasized the importance of political work with primary party organizations.

MTS party work was sporadic. The zampolit was either rela-

83. Miller, *100,000 Tractors*, pp. 278–79, 285–86.
84. *Leningradskaia pravda*, June 19, 1952.
85. Ibid., May 25, 1950.
86. *Molot*, July 2, 1946.
87. "Pis'ma zamestitelei direktorov MTS," p. 43.
88. *Leningradskaia pravda*, September 21, 1952.

tively inactive or began to assume a purely economic role at the behest of the raikom. The relations between the raikom and the MTS PPO were characteristically amorphous, except when the raikom chose to use the zampolit instead of a raikom apparatchik as a plenipotentiary to supplant the MTS director.

In theory a kolkhoz PPO was to play a major role in the supervision and verification of the kolkhoz's work, the political education of its members, and the mobilization of its work force. These organizations received strong central support for such activities, yet they were unable to carry out their assigned functions. Given low party saturation rates among the rural population and the background characteristics of many rural party members and even PPO secretaries, particularly those at kolkhozy, the tasks confronting the kolkhoz PPO were virtually impossible.

Until the 1950 kolkhoz amalgamation campaign, many kolkhozy relied on territorial party organizations for political guidance and on assistance from komsomol groups. When a kolkhoz had no party organization, komsomol members were expected to take on the responsibility of helping to get the kolkhoz's work done.[89] As we have seen, kolkhoz PPOs tended to be small and their members young and inexperienced. Indeed, the reassignment of territorial party members to establish kolkhoz PPOs often created organizations that existed in nothing but name.[90] If the kolkhoz PPO was to strengthen its position within the agrarian sector, constant assistance from other organizations, particularly the raikom, was essential.

The raikom sent plenipotentiaries to establish primary party organizations at kolkhozy, but once a PPO was established, the raikom representative rarely helped it to set up plans and organize its work.[91] Party literature during the postwar years consistently stressed the significance of rural PPOs, and just as consistently criticized the raikom for its inattention to them.[92] PPO secretaries thus operated from a position of weakness. "If the secretary knows that when he is right, the raikom will always support him, he will behave with more assurance," a speaker pointed out at the Len-

---

89. Nikolaev, "Po-bol'shevistski," p. 23.
90. *Molot*, April 17, 1948.
91. *Leningradskaia pravda*, June 30, 1946.
92. Badaev, "O khode," p. 15. This criticism continued to be made as long as Stalin lived. See *Leningradskaia pravda*, August 5, 1950, and August 5, 1952.

ingrad obkom plenum in 1946.[93] Young, inexperienced kolkhoz cadres were in particular need of such support. Raikoms were said to be unable to work with kolkhoz cadres because they didn't "respect" them.[94]

Indeed, raikom plenipotentiaries were generally thought to undermine the kolkhoz PPO rather than strengthen it. A typical expression of this view appeared in *Leningradskaia pravda* on June 20, 1947: "Some raikoms, instead of strengthening village PPOs in every way possible in order to enlarge their role in and responsibility for the implementation of agricultural work . . . , send plenipotentiaries to village soviets and kolkhozy, [a practice] that weakens their own leadership of PPOs in verifying that planting has been carried out at lagging kolkhozy to the point of taking the responsibility for planting away from them." At the joint plenum of the Leningrad obkom and gorkom in 1948, the raikoms were criticized for giving little aid to PPOs and for a bureaucratic leadership style.[95]

The raikom and its representatives typically consulted with kolkhoz chairmen and all but ignored the kolkhoz PPOs.[96] Not surprisingly, kolkhoz chairmen felt that they, too, could ignore the PPOs and look instead to the raikom and its representatives. As one chairman of an agricultural collective noted, "when the raikom secretary comes to the kolkhoz, he doesn't go to the party organization secretary but comes to me. So my opinion is more important to him than that of the leaders of the party organization. I am going to consult directly with the raikom party."[97] As with political matters, so with economic issues. Plenipotentiaries generally avoided the PPOs, and themselves took over the economic functions of the kolkhoz chairmen.[98]

The style of raikom involvement at the kolkhoz had important consequences for cadre policy. As the raikom representatives either came to direct agricultural campaigns or made short, superficial visits to gather statistics, the raikom had very little in-

93. "Kak dolzhen rabotat' sekretar' pervichnoi partiinoi organizatsii," *Partiinaia zhizn'*, no. 2 (January 1947), p. 52.

94. Zadionchenko, "O nedostatkakh," p. 52.

95. *Leningradskaia pravda*, December 23, 1948.

96. Ibid., September 1, 1949.

97. *Molot*, June 12, 1948.

98. *Leningradskaia pravda*, September 14, 1949.

depth knowledge about the communists at kolkhozy. Thus the raikom, which seldom hesitated to remove leaders from their posts, did little in the way of selecting party members for important posts in the countryside. This lack of concern was reflected in the low level of rural party recruitment.[99]

With the 1950 kolkhoz amalgamation campaign, the number of primary party organizations at kolkhozy increased. Earlier rationales used to justify the use of raikom plenipotentiaries were modified.[100] Evidence of the party's role in the countryside, however, suggests that raikoms continued to use instructors as plenipotentiaries in economic policy. Raikom instructors who ostensibly came to the kolkhoz to assist the PPOs' mass political work frequently devoted all their attention to current agricultural campaigns.[101]

Kolkhoz PPOs remained weak, lacking political and agricultural expertise and experience. Although the number of organizations had increased by 1953, many of their new members were not actually involved in kolkhoz work. Former members of territorial organizations were widely scattered throughout the newly enlarged kolkhozy. These conditions contributed to the inactivity of kolkhoz PPOs.

In light of the continued displacement of agricultural leaders by raikom representatives, the kolkhoz PPO could do little in the way of supervising policy implementation. The raikom remained at a distance from the actual activities involved in plan execution, relying on detailed reports of results. The weakness of the kolkhoz PPO reflected the party's weakness in the countryside. The Leningrad obkom plenum, in directing the raikoms to improve their leadership, indirectly spelled out the inadequacies that typically plagued kolkhoz PPOs and other local rural party organizations:

> The plenum of the oblast party committee demanded that the raikoms of the rural raions improve their leadership of kolkhoz

99. Nikolaev, "Vospitanie," p. 32.

100. *Leningradskaia pravda*, August 24, 1950. Oredezhskii Raion, for example, "had to use plenipotentiaries because only two kolkhozy in the raion had PPOs. Now the raikom instructors were to help party leaders establish a work plan, prepare and conduct meetings, and encourage the verification of the implementation of decisions."

101. Ibid., October 26, 1951; August 14 and 20, 1952.

primary party organizations; increase their responsibility for the state of kolkhoz affairs, with particular attention to strengthening work discipline and improving labor organization at kolkhozy; strengthen mass political work in the countryside, systematically explaining to kolkhozniki and agricultural workers the resolutions of the party and government and aspects of the international situation that affect our country; mobilize workers in the timely implementation of all agricultural work and the fulfillment of state obligations; and improve the leadership of komsomol organizations in the countryside, so that all komsomol organizations are genuine helpers of the party organizations in the struggle for further growth in the productivity of agriculture and in the development and productivity of livestock.[102]

Thus the Leningrad and Rostov oblast parties' behavior in the field of agriculture differed sharply from their theoretically prescribed roles. The party's mandated tasks in agriculture—political work and the verification of agricultural policy implementation—were never carried out. Far from functioning as an organization whose goals in agriculture, as in all else, were primarily political, the party assumed the role of a generalist whose authority was based on politics but who nevertheless continued to intervene directly in economic line management.

102. "Resheniia iiul'skogo plenuma obkoma," p. 3.

CHAPTER 7

The Reality behind the Monolith: Local Party Behavior in Industry and Agriculture

Party behavior in industry and agriculture became increasingly differentiated after the war. Although the party's role would eventually reflect the multiple cleavages found in Soviet society, in the immediate postwar era party behavior reflected its primary responsibility, economic reconstruction. To the extent that party behavior focused on political functions during the late 1940s, even those activities were aimed at supporting economic recovery, primarily through the mass mobilization of labor. Local party organizations' principal functions emerged during the implementation of postwar industrial and agrarian policy. Differences in levels of economic development, priorities, and political traditions associated with the industrial and agrarian sectors directly contributed to the party's divergent behavior. The party's distinctive role in each sector was associated with a different allocation of functions within the party apparatus and between the local party organizations and economic leaders. Party behavior as it developed after the war was strongly to influence its subsequent practices. This behavior was replicated through the postwar generation's long-time dominance of the party apparatus and the inability of the Soviet regime to provide effective incentives to restructure behavior.[1] Thus the patterns of party behavior that emerged in the early postwar years continue to shape the administration of economic policy.

The traditional differences associated with agriculture and industry in the Soviet economy, society, and polity were intensified by the effects of World War II. The war was particularly devastating to agriculture. The industrial infrastructure survived the war, in part because of industrial expansion in the Urals, while the collectivized agrarian sector lay in ruins, totally disorganized.[2]

The war's consequences for capital investment and labor were equally critical for the well-being of agricultural production. The severe labor shortages suffered by agriculture were exacerbated by organized recruitment of labor for industry.[3] Capital investment in the agrarian sector could not substitute for lost labor. Indeed, many of the agrarian sector's difficulties reflected its long-term undercapitalization. Even when agricultural investment rose after the war, the gap between the funds invested in agriculture and in industry continued to increase. The absolute level of postwar agricultural investment could not overcome the accumulated effects of the prewar and wartime policies, particularly at kolkhozy, which were to supply half of their own investment funds. Thus, as a result of the policy environment and the regime's political and economic preferences for industry, the problems confronted by agricultural leaders were of a different magnitude than those facing industrial leaders. These factors fostered distinctive styles of party leadership in the implementation of agricultural and industrial policy.

Distinctions in the party's behavior also developed in response to the difficulty of the goals set by the five-year plans. Although both sectors confronted a system of taut planning and overly am-

1. Seweryn Bialer, *Stalin's Successors: Leadership, Stability, and Change in the Soviet Union* (New York: Cambridge University Press, 1980), p. 101; Arthur L. Stinchcombe, *Constructing Social Theories* (New York: Harcourt, Brace & World, 1968), p. 105; Robert E. Blackwell, Jr., "Cadres Policy in the Brezhnev Era," *Problems of Communism* 28 (March–April 1979): 29–42.

2. Sanford R. Lieberman, "The Evacuation of Industry in the Soviet Union during World War II," *Soviet Studies* 35 (January 1983): 90–102.

3. See Cynthia S. Kaplan, "The Impact of World War II on the Party," in *The Impact of World War II on the Soviet Union*, ed. Susan J. Linz (Totowa, N.J.: Rowman & Allanheld, 1985); Sheila Fitzpatrick, "Postwar Soviet Society: The 'Return to Normalcy,' 1944–1953," in ibid.

bitious targets, the probability of meeting plan goals was much greater in industry than in agriculture. The Fourth and Fifth five-year plans made demands on agricultural production which could not be met with available material and labor. While the quotas set for industrial production were demanding, the task of meeting them was facilitated by the salvaging of evacuated materials and plants, reparations, and an industrial base that survived the war. In addition, industrial managers were able to adopt quasi-legal means of adjusting plan goals—changing the mix of production, for example—so that technically they fulfilled their quotas. As a result of these multiple differences, national industrial production recovered its prewar level by 1948, while agriculture barely reached its prewar level in 1952.

Beyond the influence of policy goals, input factors necessary for production, and the policy environment, the very nature of agricultural and industrial production affected administrative patterns. Industry's ability to standardize production provided at least a modicum of certainty; agriculture's natural scheme of production and its low level of economic development fostered uncertainty. In the absence of widespread and sophisticated mechanization and chemical fertilizers to counter the effects of the harsh climate and poor soil in many areas, agriculture was unable to limit uncertainty. Poor livestock production and a lack of fodder and seed plagued the collective farm as it confronted one of the worst droughts in history during 1946.

The political priority accorded the industrial sector by the powerful central ministries protected industrial leaders' authority. Industry's relatively progressive policies were supported by the work of scientific research institutes, while the agrarian sector labored under the political and scientific albatross of Lysenkoism. In sharp contrast to the protection given industrial leaders by the central organs, agricultural leaders depended on local party and state organs for their continuance in office. The high turnover rates among agricultural leaders reflect this disparity. The authority and relative autonomy enjoyed by industrial leaders in heavy and defense industries provide a stark contrast to the instability suffered by agricultural leaders.[4]

---

4. For discussions of industrial leaders' authority, see Jerry F. Hough, The Soviet Prefects (Cambridge: Harvard University Press, 1969); William J. Conyngham, The Modernization of Soviet Industrial Management (New York: Cambridge

Two additional factors critically shaped local party organizations' evolving behavior in policy implementation, one economic,
the other political. The fact that rural district party committees
specified agricultural plans, thereby determining individual farm
quotas, increased their authority over agricultural leaders. Decisions on industrial production mix at least de facto fell to the
factory director. Political policies that sought to promote labor
productivity and to supervise economic activities relied heavily
on primary party organizations. Clearly, the absence or merely
formal existence of PPOs in many rural areas produced a political
environment at the agricultural workplace far different from the
kind that prevailed in industry.

Given the stark differences between the sectors of the Soviet
economy after World War II, it is not surprising that the party's
informal behavior should vary by policy arena. Distinctive patterns of behavior reflect the division of intraparty functions and
the nature of local party relations with state and economic organizations. These distinctive patterns of local party behavior con-
travene the popular image of a monolithic party (see table 7.1).

Provincial and City Party Committees

The obkom was preoccupied with the fulfillment of the agrarian
plan. Although obkoms were responsible for overall postwar recovery, many of them, particularly in oblasts that contained capitals of union republics or major industrial cities, delegated
supervision over the industrial sector to gorkoms. Initially, even
party offices were shared between obkoms and gorkoms. The obkom remained, however, the superior party organ and retained
ultimate responsibility for plan fulfillment.

The Leningrad obkom was most concerned with the major factories under the jurisdiction of the central ministries. This concern
fostered consultation between the obkom first secretary and the
directors of major factories. Occasionally the obkom first secretary
did intervene in the administration of heavy industry. Reports in
the party press condemned such behavior as inappropriate. Ob-

University Press, 1982) and *Industrial Management in the Soviet Union* (Stanford:
Hoover Institution Press, 1973); Kendall E. Bailes, *Technology and Society under
Lenin and Stalin* (Princeton: Princeton University Press, 1978).

TABLE 7.1
Involvement of provincial, city, and district party committees in implementation of policy in agriculture and industry

Party committee	Agriculture	Industry
Province (obkom)	Direct involvement in economic policy; issues specific directives on policy implementation	Technically responsible, but delegates authority to gorkom
City (gorkom)	No involvement	Indirect supervision of policy; reviews statistics; some coordinating functions; staff administrative role; focus for exercise of party authority
District or borough (raikom)	Episodic involvement, directly supplanting economic leaders; line administrative role; focus for exercise of party authority	Engaged primarily in collecting statistics for written reports; some propaganda activities

kom involvement in the details of industrial production remained informal and was limited primarily to responsible secretaries. Most of the staffwork was delegated to the gorkom, which was involved in daily supervision. The partnership between the party and industrial management described by Vera Dunham was limited for the most part to gorkom personnel.[5]

In agriculture, in contrast, obkoms acted as active supervisory organs. The obkom issued numerous specific directives detailing the plan, in violation of the central party's preference for indirect management after the war. The obkoms of both Leningrad and Rostov supplanted the oblast soviets as the repositories of agricultural statistics and periodic reports on policy execution. The entire system of soviets was weakened by the war, not to be effectively rebuilt until 1954.[6] Although the Leningrad and Rostov obkoms were preoccupied with the examination of reports and directives specifying the nature of plan implementation, they did not become directly involved in carrying out the plan. Obkom directives were dispatched primarily to organs of the raion party, which was most directly responsible for implementing the agricultural plan.

Despite the obkom's preoccupation with the statistical assessment of agricultural results, it did manage to direct some of its attention to ideological matters. It had no choice, given the scarcity of party members in rural areas, the youth and lack of experience of the few to be found, and the fact that a large proportion of those few was not directly engaged in agriculture. Even the political elite in rural areas compared unfavorably with their urban counterparts: they tended to be less well educated.[7] All of these factors intensified the obkom's emphasis on cadre policy. To the extent that obkoms encouraged mass mobilization and political education, however, these tasks were to be executed by rural raikoms and raisoviets.

The role played by the gorkoms of republican capitals and major industrial cities was analogous to that of the obkom in agriculture.

5. Vera S. Dunham, *In Stalin's Time* (Cambridge: Cambridge University Press, 1976), is a remarkable study of party–middle-class relations based on Soviet fiction. Also see Hough, *Soviet Prefects*.

6. See Theodore H. Friedgut, *Political Participation in the USSR* (Princeton: Princeton University Press, 1979), pp. 156–62.

7. See chap. 5.

These gorkoms concentrated on policy evaluation, rarely inter-
vening in the production process. Although the differences between gorkoms' directives concerning agriculture and those
concerning industry seem slight at first, they had significant consequences for local party functions.[8] Gorkoms' directives concentrated on the effectiveness of the party's work in helping industrial
management to fulfill the plan; their demands focused on the
methods and style of party leadership. Specifically, they attempted
to promote methods of mass plan verification as a means of supervising economic administration. They were faced simultaneously with the necessity of fulfilling the plan and of devising an
indirect role for local party members. These directives correspond
to the partnership depicted by Dunham, in which the party committee was to strengthen the manager as an economic leader while
not losing sight of the importance of the party; they represent the
foundation on which Jerry Hough bases his depiction of obkom
first secretaries as prefects.[9] This is the image of a party that assists
but does not supplant other economic and state organs. The role
of the party in the industrial sector, if viewed as a partnership, provides the basis for the obkom secretary's coordinating
functions.

This new party–state partnership was easier to realize in the
industrial sector than in the agrarian. The strength of the central
industrial ministries may have inhibited the party from violating
its new postwar code of behavior. The effect of personnel qualifications also contributed to diversified behavior patterns. Despite
the superior backgrounds of urban party leaders, they could not
compete with the captains of heavy industry in managerial experience and technical expertise. Ultimately, it was not only the
gorkom's preference but the industrial policy environment that
dictated a less direct role for the party. Thus both formal and
informal factors limited the incentives for gross party interference
in industrial management.

Whatever the confluence of reasons, the gorkom and its staff
representatives were generally removed from local party activities

8. To avoid confusion, I will refer to the gorkom's role in industrial policy
implementation, although many obkoms may have played a similar role.

9. Dunham, *In Stalin's Time*; Hough, *Soviet Prefects*. It should be noted that
obkom first secretaries' roles were not limited to coordinating functions.

and the production process. Gorkom representatives visited raion party organizations and factories only when they had to collect information for presentations at the gorkom bureau or for a plenum. The gorkom itself was not involved in organizational work. The political work it prescribed was to be organized by the raion and implemented by the primary party organization. From this assessment of obkom and gorkom activities in industry and in agriculture emerges a similarity of style but an important difference in content.

Urban and Rural Raikoms and Primary Party Organizations

Party behavior most clearly diverges at the raion and primary party levels. The raikom received directives from both the obkom and the gorkom. The urban raikom's directives related primarily to the organization of political activities at the workplace. Its role was to provide leadership in the organization of mass plan verification and economic administration. Urban raikoms, however, frequently neglected these tasks. Party literature focused on their ability to serve as links with factory party committees and cell organizations. Raikom representatives could not issue directives to economic managers, but were encouraged to organize meetings and seminars at which suggestions could be voiced. These forums focused on promoting innovation and mobilizing workers. In a sense, the raikom was to help create the party management team at the local level. Dunham notes the regime's "ambivalence towards its favorite partner," the manager. "The regime wants the manager to be both effective and unobtrusive, strong and pliable, inventive and docile."[10] A fictional passage cited by Dunham captures the essence of the manager's role.

> The function of the party organizer is, as political teacher and organizer of the masses, to *assist* the manager. It is also the function of a party "eye." He controls the enterprise in a broad sense. Therefore, good party organizers are first of all modest and tactful in their relationship with the manager. Can you imagine how much more weighty and truthful *such* a party organizer

10. Dunham, *In Stalin's Time*, p. 171.

would seem if his principled stance, despite everything, led him to a *clash* with the manager?...By the way, the secretary of the district committee also speaks...with [the manager] in a tone which is wrong and false for a party leader communicating with the manager of the largest kind of plant. He talks "down," as if ordering him about, or lecturing him, or mocking him! This is not the proper style for party leadership.[11]

The raikom was charged with two primary tasks: to gather material on industrial performance for reports to superior party organs and to organize mass political work. Leningrad raikoms were often preoccupied by reports—the sort of office work associated with bureaucracy. The urban raikom representatives, for the most part instructors, gathered data from industrial leaders and paid little attention to lower-level party organizations.

These representatives were expected to report abnormalities in economic administration to their political superiors, but they were no match for the factory managers. When they focused on technical issues, they lacked the education and experience necessary to question the managers' economic decisions. This problem gave impetus to efforts to improve the qualifications of local party cadres, but such efforts could not shift the existing imbalance.

Raikom representatives were equally ill prepared politically. As many of the raikom apparatchiki had joined the party during the war, raikom staffs lacked sufficient political training and experience to do the jobs expected of them. Heads of raikom departments and raikom secretaries busied themselves with political work at primary and plant organizations, but their knowledge of local conditions was so superficial that they were ill-equipped to argue with directors of important factories, who had direct access to gorkoms, obkoms, and the central ministries. Even party representatives specifically charged with organizational work tended to ignore political work with PPOs. Many production-level party organizations in industry received little more than an occasional phone call or telegram, followed by weeks of silence.[12]

Thus the transformation of the party's role from its direct eco-

11. A. Fadeev, *Za tridtsat let*, quoted in ibid., p. 175.

12. See Cynthia S. Kaplan, "The Role of the Communist Party of the Soviet Union in the Implementation of Industrial and Agrarian Policy: Leningrad, 1946–1953," Ph.D. dissertation, Columbia University, 1981, chap. 5.

nomic and coordinating functions during the war to indirect political functions afterward was consonant with conditions in the
industrial sector and with the qualifications of its personnel.
Nonetheless, these factors did not ensure the party's successful
adaptation to the role of a political assistant to the local economic
elite. Frequently the new party role was either superficially executed or neglected. Primary party organizations in industry were
often left virtually unsupervised. While campaigns were organized
for the purpose of extending mass control over economic administration and socialist competition, the actual implementation of
these policies often went unverified. Even when factory party
committees did organize political activities, the ultimate achievement was often the organizational effort itself rather than economic results.

Party members at the factory level tended to be young and inexperienced. Such secretaries could hardly confront an industrial
manager on economic issues. When conflict arose, though they
technically had the right to check the factory's economic administration, they were in fact unable to demand that economic leaders change their methods or policies. Thus the party organization
at the factory had every incentive to support economic measures
that contributed to plan fulfillment but was relatively powerless
to challenge the manager. Secretaries of factory party committees
and cells were at an even greater disadvantage than raikom secretaries in their relations with industrial managers.

The political work of factory party organizations received virtually no guidance from higher party organizations. In this vacuum
the lower party formally carried out the political dictates of the
raikom with little concern for their effectiveness. Factory party
leaders, few of whom were politically sophisticated, were hard
put to organize and implement a program of political education,
although the factory environment was in no way hostile to the
party's presence. They were on even shakier ground if they attempted to become involved in technological matters. Their task
was to publicize progressive methods and to mobilize labor for
industrial production. They did not challenge economic line
officials. Local party leaders not only had to inspire often ill-
prepared young workers but also attempted to improve their working and living conditions. In these functions, the factory party
committee assisted industrial management.

The behavior of local party leaders in the urban industrial sector contrasts strikingly with that found in the rural sector. Here the "partnership" found in industry never developed. Raikom members often functioned as line personnel. Raion party organization secretaries and department heads conformed to a familiar pattern of sedentary existence at the raion center. The directives they received and those they issued, however, went beyond calls for improved political and educational work: they demanded plan fulfillment on a specified schedule. In its involvement in agriculture the raikom mimicked the campaign style of the obkom.

Perhaps the most important difference between industrial and rural raikoms lies in their relations with state and economic organizations. Though urban raikoms could play a somewhat more active role in local and cooperative industries, they tended to avoid involvement in raisoviet activities and could not compete with the economic leadership at large factories. Thus urban raikoms' activities remained relatively distinct from those of economic and state organs, in sharp contrast to the behavior of rural raikoms.

In the rural sector, economic, state, and lower party officials all looked to the raikom for instructions before committing themselves to any action. In large part because of the kinds of demands made on the raikom, its influence over cadre assignments, and rural conditions—scarcity of materials and labor, local hostility toward the center and progress, the generally low level of expertise among rural workers and leaders—the rural raikom was more directly involved in plan implementation than its urban counterpart.

The tendency of raikom secretaries or their representatives to become crisis managers was enhanced by the questionable qualifications of agricultural leaders. Agricultural leaders were young and inexperienced, lacking the practical and technical knowledge that promoted industrial managers into the central administrative role. If the superior party organizations were to hold the raikom responsible for the successful implementation of agrarian policy, it made little sense to restrict the rural party to the role of an assistant to state or economic leaders of dubious competence.

The problems of "command farming" and the inadequacy of rural labor strongly contributed to a continual crisis of production. Given this crisis atmosphere, the euphoria of peace encouraged some rural residents to expect that the collective agricultural system of the past would not be reinstated. These expectations were immediately quashed by a central policy that attacked violations of the agricultural collective's charter as a means of strengthening the kolkhoz. These factors were inextricably linked to the emergence of agricultural crisis management.

By the late 1940s and early 1950s, the lure of economies of scale strengthened the regime's determination to transform cooperative farms into state farms. Kolkhozniki greeted these changes with hostility. The local press reported Luddite attitudes among rural leaders. Accusations that peasants were withholding grain appeared in the local press. Thus the atmosphere in which policy was executed was far more hostile and uncertain in the countryside than in the city. Urban workers might complain of poor living conditions, but many already knew the abject poverty of the countryside. People in the countryside faced conditions worse than those they had experienced during the war. Needless to say, the poor state of agriculture and popular attitudes made dealing with a labor-intensive economic system extremely difficult.

The lines of authority between the raisoviet and the raikom were blurred. Although neither institution was actively involved in policy implementation, both focused on the details of execution. In Leningrad and Rostov oblasts, the raikom held the stronger position, at least in part because the obkom had supplanted the oblast soviet and because of the widely acknowledged incompetence of the oblast's agricultural administration. Though technically the raisoviet was held accountable for policy implementation, demands for plan fulfillment usually fell upon the raikom. The raikom responded, as we have seen, by emerging from its mounds of paperwork only long enough to appoint plenipotentiaries to see that the plan was fulfilled.

Until the 1950 kolkhoz amalgamation campaign, territorial party organizations were the most prevalent type of primary-level party organization in the countryside. As they lacked the right of control over kolkhozy and covered large geographical areas in which many people were not directly involved in agricultural production, they were able to exert only limited influence in the countryside.

The kolkhoz amalgamation campaign increased the number of primary party organizations at the expense of territorial party organizations. Kolkhoz PPOs remained relatively weak during the early postwar years. Initially their memberships were quite limited. Although kolkhoz PPOs enjoyed the right to supervise agricultural work, their economic functions were insubstantial, and rural raikoms treated them accordingly. Technically, raikom instructors, secretaries, and department heads were to assist kolkhoz PPOs in political work. In fact, however, visits for this purpose were rare. Yet when a raikom representative did arrive at a kolkhoz, his concern for plan fulfillment led him to consult with economic leaders and ignore party members and the PPO secretary.

Because of the overall weakness of the party in the countryside after the war, komsomol candidate party groups assumed some of the primary party organization's functions. Their members were drawn from the youngest and least experienced segment of the population. It was not until the end of the reconstruction period that most kolkhoz chairmen were even party members. Local compliance with raikom directives was thus difficult to ensure. It was simpler all around for plenipotentiaries to ignore the local groups and concentrate on the more important matter of executing the economic plan. Thus the general weakness of rural primary party organizations made them relatively ineffective political instruments, while their economic functions remained rudimentary at best.

The machine tractor station's assistant director for political affairs—the zampolit—was potentially involved in economic policy implementation. When the zampolit acted on behalf of the raikom, as he occasionally did, he often duplicated the role of the MTS director. Less frequently his behavior mirrored that of a raikom representative in the displacement of economic leaders.

Clearly the raikom and its representatives assumed the dominant role vis-à-vis lower-level party and nonparty organizations in agricultural crisis management. The raikom plenipotentiary was the most important person at the local level of policy implementation. Plenipotentiaries were sent to sel'soviets, territorial party organizations, machine tractor stations, and brigades as well as to kolkhozy. They enjoyed a degree of autonomy in the exercise of economic authority not found in the urban context. The gist of the rural raikom's message to its representatives was that they were to do what they must to ensure the desired results. Reports show that plenipotentiaries often removed kolkhoz chairmen at the least sign of malfeasance or difficulty in fulfilling the plan, a nearly constant state of affairs in many areas. The raikom supported these decisions. Thus rural raikoms and their special representatives exercised a greater degree of authority over personnel decisions than their urban counterparts. The industrial raikom could not really affect personnel decisions in large factories, certainly not the appointment of directors of all-union enterprises. The rural raikom appears to have adopted a rather cavalier attitude toward cadre changes. Its representatives showed no hesitancy about removing rural leaders. As a result, raikom representatives actually controlled the careers of many agricultural leaders, including those of kolkhoz chairmen. The extraordinarily high turnover rates among kolkhoz chairmen prevented many young rural leaders, recently home from the war, from gaining confidence in their own abilities. Ultimately, the agricultural leader was dependent upon the goodwill of the raion party organization and its representatives, while the industrial leader enjoyed an autonomous position.

The urban raikom's functions contrasted sharply with those of the rural raikoms. Although neither raikom participated in local work, to the extent that they were involved, the substantive natures of their activities differed. The urban raikom focused on political mobilization within the enterprise, while the rural raikom directed policy implementation. The primary activity of urban raikom representatives remained the gathering of data. Rural raikom representatives, by contrast, exercised general political and economic authority. Urban raikom representatives tended to exercise constant, if superficial, supervision, while rural representatives intermittently displaced state and economic cadres. These patterns of behavior were encouraged by the disparity between local raikom cadres' qualifications and those of their economic counterparts.

In the short run, active intervention by rural plenipotentiaries probably improved plan fulfillment. Ultimately, however, it undermined agricultural administrators' ability to establish the independent lines of authority necessary for long-term efficiency. Although rural raikom instructors often spoke of adopting progressive methods, they themselves lacked the background in agronomy necessary to judge the usefulness of new practices. The periodic intervention by people who lacked expertise contributed to the long-term weakness of the agrarian sector. This mode of leadership, in the context of poor agricultural conditions and the absence of the central support necessary to satisfy plan demands, left agriculture functioning in 1953 below the precollectivization level.

The party's vision of dual supervision was not realized during the immediate postwar years. Conditions necessary for the new arrangement, however, had begun to emerge in the industrial sector. As urban party representatives improved their technical qualifications, they gained the ability to function as assistants within the industrial process. The rural party, functioning within a totally devastated sector, had no one technically competent to rely upon. Indeed, there was no one with whom to form a partnership. Thus the inevitable crisis management encouraged the continuance of traditional practices associated with the party's old instrumental role. The distinctive role of local party organizations in economic crisis management is clearest at the raion level. As a result of the sector-specific demands of policy implementation, the functions of urban and rural party organizations diverged. The urban party increasingly assumed a political role associated with staff functions. The obkom first secretary's coordinating functions, typical of area administration, arose in the implementation of industrial policy. Both the functions of the urban industrial party and the focus of authority within the party (the obkom) distinguished it from its rural counterpart. The rural party was associated primarily with economic line administration. These activities fell primarily to rural raikoms. These distinctive patterns of party behavior in the implementation of economic policy reflect the respective policy environments, the level of expertise exhibited by economic leaders, and ultimately the basis on which local authority was to be exercised. Although the two sectors began to diverge before World War II, the emergence of expertise as the basis for authority in the industrial sector and the continued reliance on political authority in agriculture were intensified after the war. The patterns of party behavior that emerged then were solidified by the regime's efforts to construct a conservative administrative system in place of the revolutionary social and economic system of the prewar period. The ultimate impact of these behavioral patterns can be traced not merely to the continuity of the conditions that first encouraged them but to the staying power of the new generation of party cadres who brought them into being. Innocent of prewar patterns of behavior, they were to dominate the party apparatus for decades. The political and economic consequences of local party organizations' distinctive behavioral patterns exerted a strong influence on the Soviet political system as it encountered an increasingly complex economy and society.

CHAPTER 8

The Party in
a Complex Society

The party's behavior in the postwar agricultural sector responded to the interaction of the regime's formal policies and the factors that shaped their implementation. The background characteristics of party and state cadres, the policy environment, and the difficulties of fulfilling the agricultural plans led to a system of crisis management in which local party leaders assumed the central administrative role. The ability of raikoms and their plenipotentiaries to exercise the economic authority of line administrators in the rural sector can be traced to the low level of expertise and experience of agricultural leaders, the politically sensitive nature of the countryside, the paucity of scientifically sound agricultural knowledge in the wake of Lysenko, and the constant threat of policy failure. The position of rural party leaders was further enhanced by their control over local nomenklaturas. Thus political authority gained at the expense of expert authority at the very time when industrial managers were expanding their role in one-man management and urban party organizations were beginning to assume greater staff functions. As the party sought to assume a new, less direct role in policy implementation in the increasingly conservative postwar Stalinist system, its behavior in the agricultural sector exhibited many of the characteristics associated with its instrumental role during the construction of the Soviet system. Clearly the party's divergent patterns of behavior belie the image of a monolithic organization.

The discovery of differentiated party behavior and of the factors that produced it modifies our view of the party as a unified organization and helps us to see its difficulties in implementing later policy reforms as arising from the persistence of the behavior that developed after World War II. Ultimately, a focus on the persistence or modification of party behavior helps us to see how local party organizations adjust to changing circumstances—in particular, how party behavior has adapted to the increasing complexity of the Soviet economy and society.

Such issues are of particular relevance to agriculture. Has the post-Stalin party continued to intervene in the implementation of agricultural policy? What factors have reinforced its behavioral patterns? What effect has the regime's post-1965 agricultural policies had on the party's behavior? Two questions are of fundamental importance. First, what effect has local party behavior had on the regime's ability to carry out agricultural reforms? The second question brings our focus back to the initial theoretical reasons for examining local party behavior. What can we learn from the party's behavior in the agricultural sector about party–state relations and the potential impact of the emerging new political generation of Soviet leaders?

The Persistence of Party Behavior

Many of the factors present in the immediate postwar Soviet environment have changed in the years since then. What is the nature of these changes and how extensive are they? Do the relations we have established between those factors and the party's functions retain their significance? Has the party's bifurcated behavior in local policy implementation affected its functions during the years since Stalin's death?

After Khrushchev was removed as first secretary of the Communist Party of the Soviet Union, he was accused of being a harebrained schemer. Yet, if we exclude his activities in foreign affairs and view his efforts from the perspective of unequal economic development and informal party behavior, many of them, such as his attempts to restructure the economy and the party, appear quite rational. Khrushchev sought to deconcentrate economic authority in industry through the formation of sovnarkhozes, the regional economic structures that replaced the central ministries in 1957. Most of his attention in the economic sphere, however, was devoted to improving agriculture. Both his general policies and those directed specifically toward agriculture attempted to modify the factors that shape the party's organizational behavior.

Overall, Khrushchev's agrarian policies provided for a major increase in the capitalization of agriculture, its partial decentralization, an expansion of cultivated area (the Virgin Lands program), and an increase in procurement prices to provide incentives for farmers.[1] Until 1958 he sought success in agriculture by greatly increasing cultivated acreage; subsequent economic stagnation influenced him to adopt a capital-intensive agricultural policy during the 1960s.[2] The ambitious programs of the Khrushchev era, although ultimately unfulfilled, nevertheless improved the relative as well as the absolute position of the agrarian sector. These achievements altered the agrarian environment.

Khrushchev also sought to raise the level of expertise among state agricultural personnel. Campaigns sent cadres with higher and specialized education into the countryside.[3] Although an increasing proportion of kolkhoz chairmen boasted higher education, of greater significance was the proliferation of graduates of specialized secondary schools among them (see table 8.1). With the sending of recent graduates of institutions of higher education and urban cadres to the countryside and a decline in the number of kolkhozy, the percentage of kolkhoz chairmen who relied solely on practical experience dropped from 82 percent in 1953 to 64 percent in 1957.[4] By 1960 fully 55.6 percent had attained either higher or specialized secondary education.[5]

1. David M. Schoonover, "Soviet Agricultural Policies," in Soviet Economy in a Time of Change (Washington, D.C.: Government Printing Office, 1979), p. 94.

2. Martin McCauley, Khrushchev and the Development of Soviet Agriculture (New York: Holmes & Meier, 1976), pp. 107–46.

3. A. N. Karamelev, "Dvizhenie tridtsatitysiachnikov i ukreplenie kolkhozov," Voprosy istorii KPSS, no. 1 (1962), pp. 115–26; A. P. Tiurina, "Ukreplenie kolkhozov i MTS kadrami rukovoditelei i spetsialitov (1951–1958 gg.)," in Razvitie sel'skogo khoziaistva SSSR v poslevoennye gody (1946–1970 gg.), ed. I. M. Volkov (Moscow: Nauka, 1972).

4. Tiurina, "Ukreplenie kadrami rukovoditelei," pp. 239, 252.

5. Sel'skoe khoziaistvo SSSR (Moscow: Statistika, 1971), p. 459.

TABLE 8.1
Educational attainment of kolkhoz chairmen, USSR, 1955–1977 (percent)

Year	Higher education	Specialized secondary education	Other
1955	3.7%	25.6%	70.7%
1957	7.4	28.6	64.0
1960	15.5	40.1	44.4
1965	22.1	45.2	32.7
1970	38.2	42.7	19.1
1977[a]	57.0	35.0	8.0

[a]Data are for the RSFSR. Educational levels of kolkhoz chairmen are slightly lower in the RSFSR than in the USSR as a whole.

Sources: A. P. Tiurina,"Ukreplenie kolkhozov i MTS kadrami rukovoditelei i spetsialistov (1946–1958 gg.)," in *Razvitie sel'skogo khoziaistva SSSR v poslevoennye gody (1946–1970 gg.)*, ed. I. M. Volkov (Moscow: Nauka, 1972), pp. 250, 252; *Sel'skoe khoziaistvo SSSR* (Moscow: Statistika, 1971), p. 459; *Narodnoe khoziaistvo RSFSR za 60 let* (Moscow: Statistika, 1977), p. 168.

The steady decline in the number of kolkhozy and the influx of outside cadres into the countryside had two additional consequences: party membership among kolkhoz chairmen, which had begun to increase significantly after the kolkhoz amalgamation campaign of the early 1950s, exceeded 90 percent by the end of the decade,[6] and the turnover rate among kolkhoz chairmen declined. In 1956, 29.7 percent of kolkhoz chairmen had held their positions for less than a year; by 1959 that figure had dropped to 4.6 percent. As urban cadres left after three to five years in the countryside, however, the turnover rate began to rise again. By 1961 it may have been even higher than the 24 percent of kolkhoz chairmen in Bashkiria with less than one year tenure and the 33 percent with one to three years' tenure, as many unsuccessful kolkhozy were merged with more productive ones or transformed into sovkhozy; the practice of limiting data on kolkhoz chairmen to their tenure in office masks their actual rate of removal.[7] The return to relatively high turnover rates prevented incumbents from establishing stable authority relations locally and acquiring knowledge of local conditions.

How did the kolkhoz chairman's improved qualifications com-

6. Tiurina, "Ukreplenie kadrami rukovoditelei," p. 25.
7. Ibid., p. 254; Jerry F. Hough, "The Changing Nature of the Kolkhoz Chairman," in *The Soviet Rural Community*, ed. James R. Millar (Urbana: University of Illinois Press, 1971), pp. 113, 117.

pare with those of his party counterpart, the rural raikom secretary? Educational levels of rural raikom party secretaries continued to exceed those of kolkhoz chairmen during the Khrushchev era. In 1958 more than 85 percent of all rural raikom secretaries had had at least some higher education.[8] This level of expertise maintained the party's relative advantage over kolkhoz chairmen. During the Khrushchev period, however, the local party organization renewed its efforts to increase the expertise of agricultural leaders.[9] The improvement in the qualifications of rural personnel allowed the party to place greater reliance on indirect elements of control while maintaining its ultimate authority.

Data providing direct evidence of job tenure among rural raikom secretaries are unavailable. It is known that provincial secretaries appointed by Khrushchev enjoyed a high survival rate.[10] District-level turnover rates, however, may be higher because of structural changes.[11] Yet the most important secretaries may have retained their authoritative positions. Eighty percent of the rural raikom secretaries in Chkalovsk Oblast in 1956, for example, had had at least some higher education and had engaged in leading party work for substantial periods of time.[12]

Did the achievements of Khrushchev's policies—increased capitalization of agriculture, higher levels of education among kolkhoz chairmen and rural raikom secretaries, and an increase in party membership among kolkhoz chairmen—change the party's role, or did the party's advantages and ingrained patterns of behavior keep it on its familiar path? Local party behavior during the Khrushchev years resembled that of the immediate postwar years. As Khrushchev noted in his first foray into agrarian policy after Stalin's death, at the September 1953 Central Committee Plenum, the party held local leaders personally accountable for

8. P. N. Sharova, "Ukreplenie sel'skikh partiinykh organizatsii v 1950–1960 gg." in Razvitie sel'skogo khoziaistva, ed. Volkov, p. 276.

9. Barbara Ann Chotiner, "The Role of the Apparatchiks in Agriculture since Stalin," paper presented at the Annual Meeting of the American Association for the Advancement of Slavic Studies, New Haven, Conn., 1979, p. 27.

10. Jerry F. Hough and Merle Fainsod, How the Soviet Union Is Governed, rev. and enl. ed. (Cambridge: Harvard University Press, 1979), pp. 119–201.

11. I. E. Zelenin, Obshchestvenno-politicheskaia zhizn' sovetskoi derevni (Moscow: Nauka, 1978), p. 65.

12. Kommunist, no. 10 (1956), p. 103, and no. 15 (1956), p. 61, cited in Zelenin, Obshchestvenno-politicheskaia zhizn', p. 68.

the results achieved by the state agricultural agencies they supervised.[13] Later policies encouraged active intervention by the local party in the administration of agriculture.

At the November 1962 Central Committee Plenum, Khrushchev restructured the Communist Party to correspond to the functional division of labor between industry and agriculture. This functional division recognized the informal patterns of behavior that had developed within organizations involved in the two economic sectors. Rural raikoms were abolished in favor of territorial administration of kolkhoz and sovkhoz production. The higher priority accorded the agrarian sector did not diminish the role of local party cadres, but, on the contrary, seems to have encouraged even greater participation. The party remained the repository of final authority in the agrarian sector.[14]

If the changes of the Khrushchev years were a rational means of approaching the problems of agricultural administration and informal party behavior, why were they ultimately rejected? Or were they rejected? Leonid Brezhnev's agricultural policy not only continued the emphasis introduced by Khrushchev but extended many of his agrarian initiatives.[15] Beginning with the March 1965 Central Committee Plenum, Brezhnev fundamentally altered the Soviet economic model. Agriculture assumed a position of top priority, as indicated by the fact that 27 percent of capital investment went to the sector in 1976.[16] When support industries are included, according to David Carey, investment "exceeded 34 percent of gross investment in the entire economy."[17] Monetary incentives and social policies also have sought to increase agricultural productivity and to reverse the outward migration of both skilled and unskilled workers.[18]

The agrarian policies of the 1960s and 1970s stressed the spe-

13. Chotiner, "Role of the Apparatchiks," p. 6.

14. Ibid., pp. 8, 9, 24; McCauley, Khrushchev, pp. 111–13, 116.

15. Thane Gustafson, Reform in Soviet Politics (New York: Cambridge University Press, 1981), p. 115.

16. Schoonover, "Soviet Agricultural Policies," p. 93.

17. David W. Carey, "Soviet Agriculture: Recent Performance and Future Plans," in Soviet Economy in a New Perspective (Washington, D.C.: Government Printing Office, 1976), pp. 586–87.

18. James R. Millar, "Post-Stalin Agriculture and Its Future," in The Soviet Union since Stalin, ed. Stephen F. Cohen, Alexander Rabinowitch, and Robert Sharlet (Bloomington: Indiana University Press, 1980), pp. 145–50.

cialization of agricultural production and its mechanization, both trends begun earlier.[19] Brezhnev also experimented with structural changes, such as interfarm associations and agroindustrial complexes that permitted greater local autonomy.[20] These policies were expensive during a period of growing economic stringency in the Soviet Union. Although absolute levels of agricultural production rose, the low rate of factor productivity in capital investment in agriculture led to only moderate increases in investment after 1974; indeed, an increase to only approximately 31 percent of total capital investment (from 27 percent) was proclaimed as part of Brezhnev's food program in 1982.[21] The major features of the Brezhnev food program constituted the core of the agricultural policies adopted under Iurii Andropov and Nikolai Chernenko.[22]

In tandem with these changes in the policy environment since 1965, the regime has attempted to create a pool of professionally competent agricultural leaders who can exercise greater authority in policy implementation. Indeed, where expertise is concerned, the 1970s may be seen as the equivalent for agriculture of the 1930s for industry. Given the critical relationship between local party leaders and local agricultural leaders, the latter's qualifications are of fundamental importance to the continuity of local party involvement in agricultural policy implementation.

Soviet personnel policies over the last two decades have sought to enhance the position of agricultural leaders in policy imple-

19. Schoonover, "Soviet Agricultural Policies," p. 107.

20. Arcadius Kahan, "The Problems of the 'Agrarian-Industrial Complexes' in the Soviet Union," in Economic Development in the Soviet Union and Eastern Europe, ed. Zbigniew M. Fallenbuchl (New York: Praeger, 1976), 2:205–22; Robert Miller, "The Politics of Policy Implementation in the USSR: Soviet Policies on Agricultural Integration under Brezhnev," Soviet Studies 32 (1980): 171–94; Valentin Litvin, "Agro-Industrial Complexes: Recent Structural Reform in the Rural Economy of the USSR," in The Soviet Rural Economy, ed. Robert C. Stuart (Totowa, N.J.: Rowman & Allanheld, 1984), pp. 258–72.

21. "Prodovol'stvennaia programma SSSR na period do 1990 goda i mery po ee realizatsii: Materialy maiskogo Plenuma TsK KPSS 1982 gody," Partiinaia zhizn', no. 12 (1982); D. Gale Johnson and Karen McConnell Brooks, Prospects for Soviet Agriculture in the 1980s (Bloomington: Indiana University Press, 1983), pp. 25–28, 92–99.

22. At, for example, the April 1983 special meeting for leading local party and state agricultural officials and the Central Committee plenums of November 1982, June 1983, and October 1984.

mentation. Agricultural production's increased complexity, along with the need for greater efficiency necessitated by an intensive approach to development, places a premium on flexibility, which in turn heightens the sector's need for technically competent local leaders. Soviet policy makers no longer ignore the detrimental effects of centralized planning on agricultural production. K. M. Bogoliubov wrote in 1983: "In our country the distinctive and extraordinary variety of production and of natural and climatic conditions can no longer permit the use of a single model. Here it is fundamentally necessary to be independent in making decisions.... This is why it is important that new administrative organs, together with party organizations, free kolkhozy and sovkhozy from bureaucratic administration and petty oversight."[23]

Among such new administrative organs are district agroindustrial association councils (RAPO councils), which exercise coordinating and many decision-making functions once officially associated with the district agricultural administration but usually carried out by raikoms and gorkoms. These local party organs are specifically prohibited from displacing members of RAPO councils and from taking upon themselves functions under the latter's competence.[24]

The roles of agricultural specialists have been expanded. An increasing number of such specialists, Bogoliubov writes, are now working in soviet and economic organs. "They, and not workers of the party apparatus, are called upon to decide questions related to their areas of competence."[25] Indeed, a major portion of the May 1982 production program was devoted to the "further

23. K. M. Bogoliubov, "KPSS o sovershenstvovanii upravleniia agropromyshlennym kompleksom," *Voprosy istorii KPSS*, no. 2 (1983), p. 23. See also F. Ivanov, "Organizatsiia raboty," *Partiinaia zhizn'* 22 (November 1982): 33; *Pravda*, January 27, 1984.

24. G. Usmanov, "Partiinoe rukovodstvo organami upravleniia APK," *Kadry sel'skogo khoziaistva*, no. 1 (January–February 1984), pp. 49–56. RAPO councils are (1) to ensure the balanced development of agroindustrial complexes; (2) to improve service to kolkhozy, sovkhozy, and other production enterprises and to strengthen and ensure their technical material bases; (3) to improve the rural living standard and social structure; (4) to ensure rural economic ties; and (5) to make agricultural institutions self-sufficient and increase labor productivity (I. Ushachev, "Sistema upravleniia agropromyshlennym kompleksom," *Ekonomika sel'skogo khoziaistva*, no. 5 [May 1983], p. 44).

25. K. M. Bogoliubov, "Kóntrol' i proverku ispolneniia uroven' novykh trebovanii partii," *Kadry sel'skogo khoziaistva*, no. 3 (May–June 1983), p. 25.

strengthening of kolkhoz and sovkhoz leading cadres and specialists [and] the increase of their roles and responsibility in the
development of agricultural production."[26] Andropov forcefully
restated this theme at a special meeting of leading local party and
state agricultural officials in April 1983 and at the Central Committee plenums of November 1982 and June 1983.

Although calls for increased autonomy for professionals and an
end to local party intervention are all too familiar, recent Soviet
policies have introduced measures that may finally bring these
goals within reach. These policies seek to improve the quality of
agricultural schools by strengthening their curricula, to found new
educational institutions, to provide students with greater practical
experience, and to make more stipends available to rural students.[27] Other measures seek to make matriculation easier for students who choose "deficient" professions, such as agriculture—
especially in the non-black-earth zone, the north, Siberia, and the
Far East[28]—by eliminating entrance examinations and the need to

26. "Prodovol'stvennaia programma," pp. 78–83; "O dal'neishem ukreplenii
kolkhozov i sovkhozov rukovodiashchimi kadrami i spetsialistami, povyshenii ikh
roli i otvetstvennosti v razvitii sel'skokhoziaistvennogo proizvodstva" (Postanovlenie TsK KPSS i Soveta Ministrov SSSR, May 24, 1982), in *Leninskaia agrarnaia politika KPSS: Sbornik vazhneishikh dokumentov (avgust 1978 g.–avgust
1982 g.)* (Moscow: Politicheskoi Literatury, 1983), pp. 147–54.

27. See, for example, "O rabote sel'skokhoziaistvennykh organov po perepodgotovke i povyshenii kvalifikatsii rukovodshchikh kadrov i spetsialistov kolkhozov i sovkhozov" (Postanovlenie TsK KPSS, August 6, 1974), in *Voprosy
organizatsionno-partiinoi raboty KPSS: Sbornik dokumentov,* 3d enl. ed. (Moscow:
Politcheskoi Literatury, 1981), pp. 557–61; "O merakh po rasshireniiu seti srednikh
sel'skikh professional'no-technicheskikh uchilishch i po ulucheniiu ikh raboty"
(Postanovlenie TsK KPSS i Soveta Ministrov SSSR, January 28, 1975), in *Leninskaia agrarnaia politika KPSS: Sbornik vazhneishikh dokumentov (mart 1965 g.–
iiul' 1978 g.)* (Moscow: Politicheskoi Literatury, 1978), pp. 414–17; "O sostoianii
i merakh po dal'neishemu sovershenstvovanie podgotovki spetsialistov s vyshim
k srednim sel'skokhoziaistvennym obrazovaniem" (Prikaz Ministerstva vysshego
i srednego spetsial'nogo obrazovaniia SSSR, January 31, 1980, no. 93), *Biulleten'
Ministerstva vysshego i srednogo spetsial'nogo obrazovaniia SSSR,* no. 4 (April
1980), pp. 11–14.

28. "O provedenii eksperimenta po priemu v srednie spetsial'nye uchebnye
zavedeniia na ostrodefitsitnye spetsial'nosti bez vstupitel'nykh ekzamenov v 1982
g." (Prikaz Ministerstva vysshego i srednogo spetsial'nogo obrazovaniia SSSR,
March 17, 1982, no. 331), *Biulleten' MViSSO SSSR,* no. 6 (June 1982), pp. 5–11,
and "O rasshirenii eksperimenta po priemu v srednie spetsial'nye uchebnye zavedeniia na ostrodefitsitnye spetsial'nosti bez vstupitel'nykh ekzamenov v 1983

document practical work experience. The scope of these experiments increased through the 1970s and early 1980s to include twenty oblasts and six autonomous republics.

Despite lowered admission standards at agricultural schools, professional standards are to be maintained through the periodic certification of specialists every three to five years.[29] The measures to improve the quality of specialized secondary education and to broaden the social base of students at both the specialized secondary and higher educational institutions are part of the overall strategy of rural development. They are further strengthened by the 1984 educational reforms announced at the December 1983 Central Committee Plenum.[30]

The increased emphasis on professionalism evident in general agricultural personnel policy is reflected in efforts to improve the qualifications and effectiveness of leading cadres. In 1975, a Higher School for Agricultural Administration was established on the grounds of the Timiriasev Agricultural Academy in Moscow. The resolution that established the school also called for the founding of a professional journal, *Kadry sel'skogo khoziaistva* (Agricultural personnel), to share the experience of educational institutions and scientific establishments in training agricultural workers and to publish "methodological material, lectures, and articles that would be helpful in organizing, retraining, and improving the qualifications of leading cadres and economic specialists, kolkhozniki, and sovkhoz workers."[31] Originally sponsored by the Ministry of Agriculture, the journal has been issued by the Central Committee of the CPSU since 1980.[32]

Efforts to increase the variety and sophistication of training programs reflect agricultural production's growing complexity and reliance on expertise. Both RAPOs and normless brigades require

---

g." (March 5, 1983, no. 308), *Biulleten' MViSSO SSSR*, no. 5 (May 1983), pp. 15–19.

29. "O vvedenii attestatsii rukovodiashchikh, inzhenerno-tekhnicheskikh rabotnikov i drugikh spetsialistov predpriiatii i organizatsii promyshlennosti, stroitel'stva, sel'skogo khoziaistva, transporta i sviasi" (Postanovlenie Soveta Ministrov SSSR, July 26, 1973), in *Resheniia partii i pravitel'stva po khoziaistvennym voprosam (1972–1973 gg.)* (Moscow: Politicheskoi Literatury, 1974), 9:557.

30. "Proekt TsK KPSS: Osnovnye napravleniia reformy obshcheobrazovatel'noi i professional'noi shkoly," *Sel'skaia zhizn'*, January 4, 1984.

31. "O rabote sel'skokhoziaistvennykh organov," p. 560.

32. See *Kadry sel'skogo khoziaistva*, no. 6 (1979) and no. 2 (1980).

highly skilled rural leaders.[33] Traditional rural leaders—kolkhoz chairmen and sovkhoz directors—make up 54 percent of the membership of district agroindustrial association councils, the administrative organs of RAPOs, which are responsible for coordinating production within the district.[34] Although RAPO councils are to play a central role in agricultural administration, their formation and assumption of new duties is relatively slow.[35] Owing to formation of new administrative units and the increased sophistication of large-scale production, the qualifications of middle-level cadres, such as brigade leaders and the heads of livestock firms, have received greater attention.[36] Overall, agricultural change since the 1970s has produced a more highly differentiated set of roles, placing a premium on rural leaders' technical knowledge and skills.

Soviet policy has also sought to increase stability among agricultural personnel. With lengthier tenures, agricultural leaders are more likely to establish informal ties with rural personnel and to gain a clearer understanding of local conditions. The stability of agricultural personnel is enhanced by the training of rural workers, who are more likely than urban "volunteers" to remain in the countryside. If successful, these personnel policies should in-

33. Normless brigades are assigned plots of land on which they decide what is to be grown and receive profits from the sale of their produce to the state, with no fixed quotas. See "O dal'neishem uluchshenii ekonomicheskogo obrazovaniia i vospitaniia trudiashchikhsia" (Postanovlenie TsK KPSS, Soveta Ministrov SSSR, VTs SPS i TsK VLKSM, June 17, 1982), Leninskaia agrarnaia politika (avgust 1978 g.–avgust 1982 g.), pp. 710–14.

34. K. M. Bogoliubov, "Prodovol'stvennia programma SSSR—novyi etap sovremennoi agrarnoi politik partii," Kommunist, no. 13 (September 1983), p. 43. RAPO councils represent a deconcentration of authority from district party committees to economic cadres. To some extent they may limit the decentralization of authority to kolkhoz chairmen and sovkhoz directors, as Everett Jacobs has argued in "Soviet Agricultural Management and Planning and the 1982 Administrative Reforms," in Soviet Rural Economy, ed. Stuart, p. 287. Although I disagree with Jacobs' contention that this arrangement represents a centralization of authority, it is true that the entire council does delegate its authority to a smaller body of perhaps seven individuals, usually from the RAPO itself. Nonetheless, authority remains officially in the hands of the council and the enterprises that belong to the RAPO, which remain legal entities.

35. Sel'skaia zhizn', December 27, 1983.

36. "O rabote Altaiskogo Kraikoma KPSS po povysheniiu roli spetsialistov v razvitii kolkhoznogo i sovkhoznogo proizvodstva" (Postanovlenie TsK KPSS, July 11, 1974), in Voprosy organizatsionno-partiinoi raboty KPSS, pp. 537–45.

TABLE 8.2

Number of kolkhoz and sovkhoz personnel with higher and secondary
education, 1965–1980 (per thousand)

	1965	1970	1977	1980
Kolkhoz personnel	12	23	41	51
Sovkhoz personnel	27	41	68	75

Sources: A. M. Emel'ianov, *Kompleksnaia programma razvitiia sel'skogo khoziaistvo v deistvii*, 2d ed. (Moscow: Ekonomika, 1980), p. 263; *Narodnoe khoziaistvo SSSR v 1980 g.* (Moscow: Finansy i Statistika, 1981), pp. 282, 283.

crease the professionalism of agricultural leaders and enhance
their ability to carry out their responsibilities successfully. The
agricultural sector's growing sophistication and its leaders' improved capacity to meet plan targets in turn make them more
plausible as partners of local party leaders rather than adversaries
to be displaced during crises of production.

To what extent are today's agricultural leaders actually better
qualified than their predecessors? Table 8.2 shows a substantial
improvement in agricultural workers' education. The average
number of agricultural experts per kolkhoz and sovkhoz has increased markedly since 1965.[37] Nonetheless, most agricultural experts still have only specialized secondary education.[38]

One of the most significant achievements of the post-1965 policies has been the increase in education among kolkhoz chairmen
and sovkhoz directors. The educational gap that separated them
was substantially narrowed by the late 1970s, as table 8.3 indicates.[39] In 1965, 91.8 percent of sovkhoz directors were agricultural specialists with higher and specialized secondary educations, compared to 67.3 percent of kolkhoz chairmen. In 1982,
the respective figures were 99.0 and 96.7 percent.[40] Educational

37. A. M. Emel'ianov, *Kompleksnaia programma razvitiia sel'skogo khoziaistvo v deistvii*, 2d ed. (Moscow: Ekonomika, 1980), p. 263.

38. *Narodnoe khoziaistvo SSSR v 1980 g.*, pp. 254, 270, 283; V. Gaevskaia, "Analiz chislennosti i sostova rukovodiashchikh rabotnikov na sel'skokhoziaistvennykh predpriiatiiakh," *Vestnik statistiki*, 2d ser., no. 6 (1983), pp. 14–15.

39. *Narodnoe khoziaistvo SSSR v 1980 g.*, pp. 254–55, 270–72. Sovkhoz directors were better qualified than kolkhoz chairmen because of the regime's preference for the sovkhoz as the politically more progressive form of agricultural production and the sector's smaller size until 1975.

40. *Sel'skoe khoziaistvo SSSR* (Moscow: Statistika, 1971), pp. 459, 462; *Narodnoe khoziaistvo SSSR, 1922–1982*, (Moscow: Finansy i Statistika, 1982), pp. 318, 320.

TABLE 8.3

Educational attainment of sovkhoz directors and kolkhoz chairmen, 1965–1982 (percent)

	1965	1970	1975	1980	1982
Sovkhoz directors					
Higher education	57.1%	68.7%	78.6%	86.2%	88.1%
Specialized second- ary education	34.7	26.8	19.1	12.6	10.9
Practical experience only	8.2	4.5	2.3	1.2	1.0
Kolkhoz chairmen					
Higher education	22.1	38.2	57.0	71.4	75.8
Specialized second- ary education	45.2	42.7	33.9	24.6	20.9
Practical experience only	32.7	19.1	9.1	4.0	3.3

Source: V. Gaevskaia, "Analiz chislennosti i sostava rukovodiashchikh rabotnikov na sel'skokhoziaistvennykh predpriiatiiakh," Vestnik statistiki, 2d ser., no. 6 (1983), p. 16.

levels of kolkhoz chairmen and sovkhoz directors in the union republics did not vary significantly from the national averages by 1980.[41] Among all sovkhoz directors and kolkhoz chairmen in 1983, 43 and 48 percent respectively were agronomists, 26 and 16 percent zoological technicians, 18 and 16 percent engineers and technicians, and 7 and 8 percent economists.[42] Clearly, the level of expertise among agricultural leaders had improved dramatically since 1965.

The recent formation of agroindustrial associations and complexes has added new types of rural administrative positions that require professional personnel. Of the 4,376 leaders of agroindustrial enterprises in 1982, 97.1 percent had higher and specialized secondary education.[43] Among RAPO council chairmen, Bogoliubov tells us, "72.5 percent are agronomists, zoological technicians, and veterinarians; 6.3 percent are economists; 19.1 percent are engineers; and 2.1 percent are agricultural specialists of other kinds. More than two-thirds of the council chairmen have

41. Data are from the annual volumes of Narodnoe khoziaistvo SSSR (Moscow: Finansy i Statistika, 1965, 1969, 1974, 1980, 1982) for the years 1966, 1970, 1975, 1980, and 1982. Provincial data are incomplete.

42. Gaevskaia, "Analiz," pp. 15–16.

43. Narodnoe khoziaistvo SSSR, 1922–1982, p. 320.

had more than ten years' tenure in direct agricultural work."[44] By the end of the 1970s, then, the educational levels of the major figures in local agricultural production had risen significantly.

Since the mid-1970s, efforts to improve the qualifications of agricultural leaders have been extended to middle-level cadres, such as brigade leaders. By 1982 their qualifications had markedly improved, as table 8.4 shows. Among the leaders of kolkhoz and sovkhoz production brigades who had higher and specialized secondary education, 40 percent were agronomists, 35 percent zoological technicians, veterinarians, and veterinary technicians, and 10 percent engineers and technicians in 1983.[45] The qualifications of middle-level cadres have grown in importance as they assume greater responsibility within a more complex agricultural system.

Although national data demonstrate a substantial improvement in the qualifications of middle-level cadres, significant regional variation was found. Regional variation may serve as an indirect indicator of scattered but not insignificant pockets of continuity. To the extent that such areas may be the very targets of reformist policies, they provide an interesting glimpse of local resistance to change. In Lithuania, Belorussia, Georgia, Estonia, and Moldavia; Krasnodar, Stavropol', and Altai Krai; Mordovsk and Kabardino-Balkarsk Autonomous Republics; and Moscow, Leningrad, Lipetsk, and Rostov oblasts, the percentage of specialists among middle-level leaders varied from 62 to 78 percent. In Central Asia, parts of the non-black-earth zone, and Siberia, only 26 to 38 percent were so classified.[46] Thus efforts to improve the qualifications

44. Bogoliubov, "Prodovol'stvennia programma SSSR," p. 43.

45. Gaevskaia, "Analiz," p. 18.

46. "Povyshat' kachestvo rukovoditelei srednego zvena," *Kadry sel'skogo khoziaistva*, no. 5 (1982), p. 82. Data are for 1982. In 1974 those areas of the RSFSR with the greatest need for additional agricultural experts, according to Soviet analysts, did produce the largest percentage of graduates with specialized secondary agricultural education. A significant problem existed, however, in transforming graduates into professionals. From 1967 to 1974, for example, agricultural technical institutions in the RSFSR graduated approximately 260,000 specialists, but the number of agricultural specialists with secondary specialized education increased by only 36,000 (A. D. Gladkii, I. D. Kishko, and M. M. Marusin, "K voprosy ob obespechennosti sela kadrami srednego zvena," in *Problemy sotsial'no-ekonomicheskogo razvitiia sela v usloviiakh zrelogo sotsializma*, ed. V. G. Ignatov [Rostov-on-Don: Rostov Pedagogical Institute, 1975], pp. 101, 105). See also N. Stepanov, "Podgotovka spetsialistov dlia nechernozemnoi zoni RSFSR," *Kadry sel'skogo khoziaistva*, no. 3 (1976), pp. 14–18.

TABLE 8.4
Educational attainment of middle-level sovkhoz and kolkhoz cadres, 1965–1982 (percent)

	Sovkhozy				Kolkhozy			
	1965	1970	1977	1982	1965	1970	1977	1982
Heads of field brigades								
Higher education	3%	4%	6%	8%	1%	2%	4%	7%
Secondary specialized education	19	22	33	39	9	16	31	41
Practical experience only	78	74	61	53	90	82	65	52
Heads of livestock brigades								
Higher education	2	2	5	9	1	2	3	6
Specialized secondary education	16	19	31	41	10	16	31	48
Practical experience only	82	79	64	50	89	82	66	46

Source: V. Gaevskaia, "Analiz chislennosti i sostava rukovodiashchikh rabotnikov na sel'skokhoziaistvennykh predpriiatiiakh," Vestnik statistiki, 2d ser., no. 6 (1983), p. 18.

of middle-level leaders had more mixed results than national averages indicate. Significantly, the results were the most disappointing in areas that were the focus of intensive efforts to improve agricultural production.

Turnover rates also affect the professional capacities of agricultural leaders. The high turnover rates found among new appointees are frequently attributed to youth and lack of previous job experience.[47] The replacement of young leaders who fail to meet production targets still prevents them from gaining the experience and knowledge of local conditions which might have brought them success another year. Numerous reports cite the impatience of local party organizations with young agricultural leaders, and the practice of dismissing unsuccessful leaders before they have had a chance to improve has been criticized within the Moscow Party organization.[48] Although such action is counterproductive in the long run, local parties have continued to exercise their informal authority over local leaders, even when the leaders in question are formally on the nomenklatura of the provincial party organization. The local party's intimate involvement in personnel policy clearly reflects the continuation of behavior that originated during the late Stalin era.

A recent mechanism created to stem cadre instability is the use of rural cadre reserves. The reserve system, by which local party organizations can indirectly exercise authority over personnel appointments, is meant to provide valuable experience for young specialists and to give the people who make appointments an opportunity to become familiar with potential appointees. The raikom normally recommends agricultural specialists for membership in the reserve group at the oblast level. These reserve positions serve as a pool of candidates for future leadership. By the late 1970s and early 1980s, 70 to 80 percent of newly appointed cadres came from such reserves.[49]

47. For example, I. Voskresenskaia, "Opyt altaiskoi shkoly upravleniia," *Kadry sel'skogo khoziaistva*, no. 5 (1977), p. 89; M. Gapurov, "Pravil'naia rasstanovka kadrov—reshaiushchee uslovia uspekha proizvodstva," *Kadry sel'skogo khoziaistva*, no. 3 (1977), p. 36.

48. M. Voropaev, "Rabota s kadrami-pervostepennaia zadacha partiinykh organizatsii," *Partiinaia zhizn'*, no. 4 (February 1981), p. 25; "XXIV Moskovskaia gorodskaia partiinaia konferentsiia," ibid., p. 48.

49. *Sel'skaia zhizn'*, November 13, 1981; V. V. Shcherbitskii, "Podbor i vos-

Cadre reserves increase the raikom's formal influence over the nomenklatura, since certification is required for all responsible positions.[50] Raikoms also continue to exercise their informal influence over the appointment of directors and heads of associations even though they remain on the nomenklatura of the obkom.[51] The rural raikom's recommendation to the obkom or the oblast commission on cadre questions is usually decisive.[52] Chief specialists and middle-level cadres are on the nomenklatura of the raikom or gorkom.[53] The establishment in 1983 of special agricultural departments at all gorkoms and raikoms in rural areas also strengthens their influence over personnel decisions.[54] Local party organizations' control over agricultural appointments without the countervailing influence of strong central ministries maintains a mechanism by which traditional patterns of behavior are replicated.

To what extent have such policies succeeded in increasing stability among agricultural leaders? In April 1982, 40 percent of all sovkhoz directors had been working at the same farms for more than five years; in 1965, only 24 percent had had five years' tenure. Among kolkhoz chairmen in 1970, 52 percent had tenure of more than five years, 15 percent three to five years, 20 percent one to three years, and 13 percent less than a year. These figures represent a substantial improvement over the high turnover rates of the 1960s. By 1982, however, kolkhoz chairmen with five years of tenure dropped to 45 percent; the 37 percent who had less than

pitanie kadrov povyshenie otvetstvennosti rukovoditelei," *Partiinaia zhizn'*, no. 15 (August 1981), p. 16; G. Orlov, "Printsipy kadrovoi politiki KPSS," *Kadry sel'skogo khoziaistva*, no. 1 (1978), p. 12.

50. Formal oblast and raion committees were established to improve the preparation and selection of agricultural leaders and specialists. See M. Shatalov, "Iz opyta kadrovoi raboty," *Kadry sel'skogo khozaizistva*, no. 5 (1979), pp. 85–86; "Kratkie soobshcheniia," *Kadry sel'skogo khoziaistva*, no. 3 (1979), p. 68; N. Vostrikov, "Peresheshchenie rabotnikov v interesakh dela," *Kadry sel'skogo khoziaistva*, no. 6 (1979), p. 24.

51. G. Burdenkov, "Stabil'nost' kadrov vazhnoe uslovie uspekha v rabote," *Kadry sel'skogo khoziaistva*, no. 2 (1978), p. 36.

52. M. Shatalov, "Iz opyta kadrovoi raboty," p. 85.

53. Burdenkov, "Stabil'nost'," p. 38.

54. N. I. Konotop, "Iz opyta raboty sel'skokhoziaistvennykh otdelov gorkomov, raikomov KPSS," *Voprosy istorii KPSS*, no. 6 (1983), p. 5.

three years included 33 percent with less than one year.[55] The Soviets consider these turnover rates too high.[56]

Turnover rates, too, varied by region. Data for relatively well-off rural areas distinguish them from regions that suffer from perennial problems of production, typical target areas for party intervention.[57] L. Florent'ev, minister of agriculture of the RSFSR, complained of high turnover rates among agricultural experts at kolkhozy and sovkhozy in the Russian oblasts of Novgorod, Kaluga, Kostromsk, Orlovsk, Tul', Iaroslavl, Kursk, Tambov, and Tomsk; and in the Mari and Tuvin republics, "fewer than half of those sent from agricultural and technical institutes are still at work."[58] High turnover rates found among agricultural specialists in middle-level positions at kolkhozy and sovkhozy in the non-black-earth zone, Central Asia, and Siberia have persisted.[59]

Soviet attempts to increase stability among agricultural professionals are in tension with measures aimed at raising educational levels. Certainly a portion of the turnover rate among rural leaders is attributable to the replacement of older, more poorly educated cadres by younger, better- educated ones, the upward mobility of those with better education, and some horizontal movement among the elite, as when an economic administrator is transferred to the party or soviet hierarchy.[60]

55. Gaevskaia, "Analiz," p. 16; *Sel'skoe khoziaistvo SSSR* (Moscow: Statistika, 1971), p. 460.

56. *Pravda*, May 29, 1982; "Otvetstvennost' kadrov za pretvorenie v zhizn' reshenii iiun'skogo plenuma TsK KPSS," *Kadry sel'skogo khoziaistva*, no. 5 (September–October 1983), p. 22.

57. Published data on turnover rates are rarely broken down by region. Twenty to 26% of sovkhoz directors in Georgia, Azerbaidzhan, and Turkmenistan had less than one year of job tenure (Gaevskaia, "Analiz," p. 16). High turnover rates were also found among kolkhoz chairmen in less prosperous areas, especially in the non-black-earth zone and parts of Belorussia. See, for example, *Kadry sel'skogo khoziaistva*, no. 5 (1981) and no. 5 (1983); *Sel'skaia zhizn'*, January 30, 1981.

58. L. Florent'ev, "Kak vypolniaiutsia resheniia XXVI s"ezda KPSS na kadrovym voprosam," *Kadry sel'skogo khoziaistva*, no. 3 (1980), p. 11.

59. "Povyshat' kachestva," p. 82.

60. According to D. M. Kukin, "each year approximately 11 percent of kolkhoz chairmen and sovkhoz directors out of the total number changed are appointed to more responsible positions; 33 percent resign for family reasons, illness, or retirement on pension, and 23 percent for other reasons.... Approximately 25 percent of the leaders are let go because they could not meet the demands of their work or had compromised themselves. Among middle-link cadres this percentage

Soviet agricultural policies since the death of Stalin have improved the conditions of production through increased capitalization and have partially succeeded in improving the qualifications of rural leaders. Much of this change, however, has come only within the last decade—perhaps too recently to permit us to judge its ultimate effects. Nonetheless, it is noteworthy that in poorer agricultural areas, those that would benefit most from additional expertise, high turnover rates and low levels of education persist among agricultural leaders. Thus available evidence indicates that measures intended to improve the quality of agricultural cadres and to lengthen their job tenure appear to have succeeded with the significant exception of poorer and less economically developed regions of the USSR—the foci of the new intensive agricultural programs.

Professional Autonomy and Local Party Leaders

Agricultural leaders' improved qualifications are not automatically translated into greater professional autonomy. For the pattern of rural crisis management to be broken, the factors that encourage local party members to displace economic leaders must also change. Thus, as official policy redefines these roles by granting greater authority to local economic leaders, the qualifications of agricultural and party leaders and the presence of an older generation that encourages the replication of earlier behavior grow in importance. Indeed, it is the relative qualifications of agricultural and party leaders and the presence of younger party personnel that facilitate a break with the past, thereby increasing the probability that agricultural leaders may in fact exercise greater professional autonomy.

Efforts to increase the responsibility of agricultural leaders often lead to deconcentration rather than decentralization of authority; frequently authority comes to be lodged in the hands of local economic leaders. None of these changes, however, does away with the ambiguity between agricultural leaders' authority and

---

is significantly higher" (*Voprosy raboty KPSS s kadrami na sovremennom etape* [Moscow: Mysl', 1976]).

that enjoyed by the local party.[61] Such ambiguity may, however, be consistent with a system of dual administration in which co-operation between state and party leaders produces mutual benefits. Do the relative qualifications of agricultural and party leaders facilitate such a system of dual administration in agriculture?

Secretaries of obkoms, kraikoms, and the central committees of union republics, the potential arbiters between local officials and between local and central officials, have long enjoyed high levels of education, which have reinforced their positions vis-à-vis local agricultural leaders. As early as 1957, 86.8 percent had higher education. This figure rose to 97.6 percent in 1967 and to 99.9 percent in 1981.[62] Three-quarters of these party secretaries had engineering/technical, economic, or agricultural educations.[63] These qualifications are far superior to those of local agricultural leaders (see table 8.3).

A more appropriate basis on which to assess the creation of a system of dual administration is a comparison of the qualifications of kolkhoz chairmen and sovkhoz directors with those of gorkom and raikom secretaries, as the latter party officials are more deeply involved in the implementation of agricultural and rural policies. The educational superiority of local party secretaries is apparent when table 8.3 is compared with table 8.5.[64]

On a national basis, data continue to document the superiority of party officials' qualifications. As we saw earlier in the case of agricultural leaders, however, attention must be paid to regional variations. Although regional data are limited, two cases, each representative of a particular functional mix in an oblast economy, provide a basis for analysis. One represents a mixed industrial-agricultural economy, the other a region targeted for agricultural

61. Jacobs, "Soviet Agricultural Management"; Miller, "Agricultural Integration under Brezhnev," pp. 171–94; I. Ushachev, "Sistema upravleniia agro-promysh-lennym kompleksom," *Ekonomika sel'skogo khoziaistva*, no. 5 (May 1983), p. 44; V. S. Nechiporenko, *Partiinye organizatsii mezhkhoziaistvennykh i agropromysh-lennykh formirovanii* (Moscow: Mysl', 1981).

62. "KPSS v tsifrakh," *Partiinaia zhizn'*, no. 21 (November 1977), p. 40; *Spravochnik partiinogo rabotnika* (Moscow: Politicheskoi Literatury, 1981), 21:501.

63. *Materialy XXVI s"ezda KPSS* (Moscow: Politicheskoi Literatury, 1981), pp. 71–72.

64. Heads of RAPOs and RAPO councils are probably better educated than local party secretaries, but data on the holders of these recently created positions are not yet available.

TABLE 8.5
Educational attainment of raikom, gorkom, and okruzhkom secretaries, 1967–
1981 (percent)

Year	Higher education	Incomplete higher education	Secondary education
1967	91.1%	6.3%	2.6%
1977	99.3	0.6	0.1
1981	99.7	0.2	0.1

Sources: "KPSS v tsifrakh (K 60-i godovshchie Velikoi Oktiabr'skoi sotsialisticheskoi re-
voliutsii)," *Partiinaia zhizn'*, no. 21 (November 1977), p. 40, and "KPSS v tsifrakh," *Partiinaia
zhizn'*, no. 14 (July 1981), p. 25.

development. Though in the early 1970s their qualifications varied
in the two regions, agricultural leaders in both Rostov Oblast, the
relatively successful agricultural area, and Kalinin Oblast, a poorer
area in the non-black-earth zone, were disadvantaged vis-à-vis
local party leaders as measured by education (see table 8.6). The
disparity in qualifications, however, was greater in the less productive area.

By 1975, all raikom and gorkom secretaries in Kalinin Oblast

TABLE 8.6
Educational attainment of gorkom and raikom secretaries, sovkhoz directors,
and kolkhoz chairmen, Rostov and Kalinin oblasts, 1971 (percent)

	Higher education	Specialized secondary education	Other
Rostov Oblast			
Gorkom and raikom secretaries	98.5%	n.a.	n.a.
Sovkhoz directors	85.3	14.3%	0.4%
Kolkhoz chairmen	66.9	30.3	2.8
Kalinin Oblast			
Gorkom and raikom secretaries[a]	93.5[b]	6.5	0.0
Sovkhoz directors	37.3	52.4	10.3
Kolkhoz chairmen	15.1	47.4	37.5

Sources: *Bloknot agitatora (spetsial'nyi vypusk)*, March 1971, p. 120, cited in P. V. Bar-
gugov, *Ocherkii istorii partiinykh organizatsii Dona, 1921–1971*, chast'2 (Rostov-on-Don: Rostovskoe Knizhnoe Izdatel'stvo, 1973), p. 693; *Narodnoe khoziaistvo Rostovskoi oblast'*
(Rostov-on-Don: Rostovskoe Otdelenie Izdatel'stvo Statistiki, 1971), pp. 145–46; *Kalininskaia
oblastnaia organizatsiia KPSS v tsifrakh* (Moscow: Moskovskii Rabochii, 1979), p. 112; *Kalininskaia oblast' za gody vos'moi piatiletki 1966–1970 v tsifrakh* (Vologda: Statistiki, 1971),
p. 186.
[a]Data are for 1970.
[b]Includes incomplete higher education.

had higher (96.8 percent) or incomplete higher (3.2 percent) education.[65] Only 25 percent of kolkhoz and sovkhoz leaders had higher education and 50 percent had attended specialized secondary schools.[66] In Rostov Oblast, 99.5 percent of the gorkom, raikom, and PPO secretaries had higher education and 0.48 percent incomplete higher education.[67] Data for the agricultural leaders of Rostov Oblast are unavailable, but data for the RSFSR suggest that agricultural leaders are unlikely to have reached an educational level equivalent to that of their party leaders in either Kalinin or Rostov oblast until the end of the 1970s.[68]

As agricultural leaders become experts, the local party leaders' education grows in importance. Local party leaders' fields of expertise are more difficult to ascertain than their educational attainment. Though two-thirds of gorkom and raikom party secretaries were said to have engineering/technical, economic, or agricultural educations, E. Z. Razumov, assistant chief of the Central Committee's department of party organization work, deplored the lack of agricultural education among rural raikom members.[69] The first secretary of the Communist Party of Estonia, K. Vaino, for example, noted that while all gorkom and raikom secretaries have higher education, half are economic specialists and three-quarters have political educations; only a third of rural raikom instructors have specialized agricultural educations.[70]

A second factor influencing agricultural leaders' functions, especially the curtailment of the party's role in rural crisis management, is the replacement of older political cadres by the younger political generation. Both the turnover rate and the preponderance

65. *Kalininskaia oblastnaia organizatsiia KPSS v tsifrakh* (Moscow: Moskovskii Rabochii, 1979), p. 112.

66. N. Korytkov, "Podbor i vospitanie rukovoditelei," *Kadry sel'skogo khoziaistva*, no. 5 (1975), p. 39.

67. *Rostovskaia oblastnaia organizatsiia KPSS v tsifrakh, 1917–1975* (Rostov-on-Don: Rostovskoe Knizhnoe Izdatel'stvo, 1976), p. 134.

68. Only RSFSR data are available; see *Narodnoe khoziaistvo RSFSR za 60 let* (Moscow: Statistika, 1977), pp. 168–69.

69. E. Z. Razumov, "XXVI s"ezdu KPSS i nekotorye voprosy kadrovoi politiki," *Voprosy istorii KPSS*, no. 8 (1981), pp. 8–9.

70. K. Vaino, "Podbor rasstanovka i vospitanie rukovodiashchikh kadrov," *Partiinaia zhizn'*, no. 10 (May 1980), p. 22. An earlier article on Riazan Oblast provides a somewhat different view: half of all gorkom and raikom secretaries were said to have agricultural education (N. Priezhev, "Obkom i sel'skie raikomy," *Partiinaia zhizn'*, no. 12 [June 1968], p. 9).

of younger cadres represent a break with the past which should facilitate the formation of new behavioral patterns. When Brezhnev assumed office, he made a point of not removing party cadres from their positions. Consequently, the party apparatus remained in place until the mid-1970s, when older party officials began to retire.[71] During the Andropov era, turnover rates among local party secretaries had stabilized at an annual average of no more than 11 percent among obkom secretaries and 15 percent among gorkom and raikom secretaries.[72] At the December 1983 Central Committee Plenum, approximately 20 percent of all obkom first secretaries were replaced. Thus the emergence of the younger political generation in local party positions since the mid-1970s provides a potential break with past behavior, facilitating the growth of agricultural leaders' professional autonomy.

On balance, the agricultural and rural policies begun by Brezhnev and followed by his successors improved the conditions of policy implementation through investment and social policies and set more reasonable goals, thereby reducing the factors that foster crisis management. The increased complexity of agricultural production heightened its reliance on scientific expertise, making political methods less desirable and more costly. By the late 1970s, agricultural leaders could match the educational qualifications of their local party cohorts. Indeed, many agricultural leaders with specialized agricultural educations may now be more knowledgeable than their local party counterparts. Thus, if the regime no longer prefers a system of rural administration that relies on political authority, local party leaders now have agricultural partners with whom they could form management teams in a system of dual administration.

Significant exceptions to this assessment, however, are found in the non-black-earth zone and other areas that have been the focus of post-1965 agricultural policy. Difficulties in improving agricultural leaders' educational qualifications and tenure rates reflect problems of policy implementation and exogenous factors

71. Seweryn Bialer, *Stalin's Successors* (New York: Cambridge University Press, 1980), pp. 109–112; Jerry F. Hough, "Changes in Soviet Elite Composition," in *Russia at the Crossroads*, ed. Seweryn Bialer and Thane Gustafson (Boston: George Allen & Unwin, 1982), pp. 57–60.

72. E. Z. Razumov, "XXVI s"ezdu KPSS i nekotorye voprosy kadrovoi politiki," *Voprosy istorii KPSS*, no. 8 (1981), p. 16.

related to migration and continued interference by local party organizations. Soviet accounts suggest that the high turnover rates among agricultural leaders in these areas result from their continued displacement by local party leaders. Thus, in the regions that confront the greatest difficulties in meeting economic targets, the traditional pattern of party crisis management appears to persist. This is an important finding, as these are the very areas in which reform requires long-term commitment. Such a long-range perspective necessitates policy supervision by highly trained and stable cadres who can adapt to local conditions rather than the short-run solutions offered by party intervention, which favor immediate results at the expense of the long-term interests of the agrarian sector. Perhaps, given the fact that personnel changes among both agricultural and party cadres reached significant proportions only at the end of the 1970s and beginning of the 1980s, any judgment in regard to the issue of professional autonomy is premature. Nonetheless, in those areas that pose the greatest challenge to the creation of a system of dual administration, the exercise of political authority at the expense of agricultural expertise appears to persist.

Party–State Relations after Brezhnev

The evident durability of the behavioral patterns that developed after World War II have hindered the regime's attempts to transform the system of agricultural administration. Recent changes suggest, however, that local party organizations have begun to adapt to the new, more complex conditions of agricultural production which emphasize expertise. Just as the postwar party attempted to define a new indirect role for itself in the late Stalin era, current party members are in the midst of a great divide marking the possible maturation of the party in an advanced industrial society. The new political generation that assumed the reigns of the Soviet political system at the accession of Mikhail Gorbachev is the heir to the Brezhnev generation, itself the first cohort to have specialized education. Yet the older generation, while adopting standards of economic rationality, nonetheless remained the product of a party apparatus that produced political generalists. Clearly, the Brezhnev generation became a transition leadership, edging away from the ideological, revolutionary traditions of the past towards a technical professionalism.

Two factors are likely to play a significant role in defining the nature of the post-Brezhnev political generation. Educational backgrounds and career patterns are crucial elements in the shaping of the new generation of Soviet leaders. It is increasingly evident that the people who rose to positions of authority by the end of the 1970s not only are better educated than their predecessors but are the products of specialized career ladders. Almost 70 percent of the post-Stalin generation, Bialer notes, "have been employed throughout their careers in only one province...and in only one type of job geared to the profile of their provinces."[73] This pattern reflects a cleavage among the elite based on localism and functional specialization within the party apparatus.[74] The segment of the party that assumes responsibility for agriculture, like those in other specialized policy arenas, seems increasingly to consist of experts who move into and out of political positions. The increase in horizontal mobility between the party and state apparatuses portends not only the adoption of expert standards but a decline in state/party distinctions and a rise in cleavages within the party apparatus itself. Such a development might lead to a closer association between party leaders and experts outside the party apparatus. At the same time, as an unanticipated consequence, cleavages within the party are likely to be mirrored by cleavages among outside experts, thereby intensifying intraparty/intrastate policy debates. In such circumstances political discussion moves beyond a simple competition for personal power or a competition between the party and other institutions in the Soviet Union to the policy arena. Such a development, in an economy and society of growing complexity, certainly portends a decline

73. Bialer, *Stalin's Successors*, p. 121.

74. Robert E. Blackwell, Jr., "Elite Recruitment and Functional Change: An Analysis of the Soviet Obkom Elite, 1950–1968," *Journal of Politics* 34 (February 1972): 124–52, and "Cadres Policy in the Brezhnev Era," *Problems of Communism* 28 (1979): 29–42; Grey Hodnett, *Leadership in the Soviet National Republics: A Quantitative Study of Recruitment Policy* (Oaksville, Ont.: Mosaic, 1978); T. H. Rigby, "The Soviet Regional Leadership: The Brezhnev Generation," *Slavic Review* 37 (1978): 1–24; Joel C. Moses, "Functional Career Specialization in Soviet Regional Elite Recruitment," in *Leadership Selection and Patron–Client Relations in the USSR and Yugoslavia*, ed. T. H. Rigby and Bohdan Harasymiw (Boston: George Allen & Unwin, 1983), pp. 15–61.

in the automous power wielded by the party, but it need not indicate the decline of the individual party/state professionals whose authority is based not only on political power but on expertise. This analysis calls into question the widely held notion of individual party members as clinging tenaciously to their politically based authority out of personal self-interest. The very assumption that party and state leaders must base their authority primarily on political power seems questionable from this perspective.

A second, perhaps less positive consequence of this image of the Soviet political system is its implications for the regime's ability to make difficult choices, all of which entail high opportunity costs. A party in which authority is based on expertise is implicitly a party that adapts to change—perhaps to the detriment of its organizational interests. The internalization of diversified interests suggests an incremental approach to policy formation. Obviously, such an approach is in no way unusual for a relatively advanced society. Yet the problems the USSR confronts may require more than an ability to muddle through. Herein lies the danger. A multiplicity of interests internalized by the broad political leadership could lead to a situation of immobility as crosscutting cleavages prevent decisions from being made. Thus the immobility characteristic of the late Brezhnev period and evident during the Andropov and Chernenko years may continue despite the intentions of Gorbachev and his colleagues of a new political generation.

There is no reason to assume, however, that either extreme will be realized. Indeed, the increase in horizontal mobility between positions of political and expert authority may encourage a greater sensitivity to the needs of society when policies are formulated. An informal mechanism that permits increased flexibility and exchange of information may arise. Certainly, none of us can foresee the future. We can, however, look at the informal patterns of behavior behind the formal structures and assess their import. The party's postwar behavior in agriculture demonstrates the permeability of political organizations to influences from a variety of sources, the relative rigidity of behavioral patterns, and their long-term consequences for reformist efforts. Behind what from afar appears to be a monolithic facade pulses a complex and dynamic political system.

Selected Bibliography

Abramov, V. A. "Organizatsionno-partiinaia rabota KPSS v gody chetvertoi piatiletki." *Voprosy istorii KPSS*, no. 3 (1973), pp. 55–65.

Agafonenkov, E. F. "Podgotovka i perepodgotovka partiinykh i sovetskikh kadrov (1946–1950 gg.)." *Voprosy istorii KPSS*, no. 11 (1970), pp. 101–9.

Armstrong, John A. "Party Bifurcation and Elite Interests." *Soviet Studies* 17 (April 1966): 417–30.

Arutiunian, Iu. V. *Mekhanizatory sel'skogo khoziaistva SSSR v 1929–1957 gg.* Moscow: Nauka, 1959.

——. *Sovetskoe krest'ianstvo v gody Velikoi Otechestvennoi voiny.* 2d ed. Moscow: Nauka, 1970.

Azrael, Jeremy R. *Managerial Power and Soviet Politics.* Cambridge: Harvard University Press, 1966.

Bailes, Kendall E. *Technology and Society under Lenin and Stalin.* Princeton: Princeton University Press, 1978.

Bakhsiev, D. *Partiinoe stroitel'stvo v usloviiakh pobedy sotsializma v SSSR (1934–1941 gody).* Moscow: Politicheskoi Literatury, 1954.

Baradulina, T. I. "Povyshenie ideino teoreticheskogo urovnia kommunistov v raionakh o svobozhdennykh ot fashistskoi okkupatsii." In *Deiatel'nost' KPSS v pervye gody posle Velikoi Otechestvennoi voiny,* ed. L. V. Shivikov. Moscow: Akademiia Obshchestvennykh Nauk pri TsK KPSS, 1978.

Barchugov, P. V., ed. *Ocheri istorii partiinykh organizatsii Dona, 1921–1971.* Chast' 2. Rostov-on-Don: Rostovskoe Knizhnoe Izdatel'stvo, 1973.

Beisembaev, S. B., and P. M. Pakmurnyi. *Kommunisticheskaia partiia*

Kazakhstana v dokumentakh i tsifrakh. Alma Ata: Kazakhskoe Gosudarstvennoe Izdatel'stvo, 1960.

Berliner, Joseph S. Factory and Manager in the USSR. Cambridge: Harvard University Press, 1957.

Bialer, Seweryn. Stalin's Successors: Leadership, Stability, and Change
in the Soviet Union. New York: Cambridge University Press, 1980.

Biulleten' Ministerstva vysshego i srednogo spetsial'nogo obrazovaniia
SSSR. 1975–1985.

Blackwell, Robert E., Jr. "Elite Recruitment and Functional Change: An
Analysis of the Soviet Obkom Elite, 1950–1968." Journal of Politics 34
(February 1972): 124–52.

———. "Cadres Policy in the Brezhnev Era." Problems of Communism 28
(March–April 1979): 29–42.

Blau, Peter M. "Decentralization in Bureaucracies." In Power in Organizations, ed. Mayer N. Zald. Nashville: Vanderbilt University Press,
1970.

Bogdenko, M. L. Sovkhozy SSSR, 1951–1958. Moscow: Nauka, 1972.

———and I. E. Zelenin. Sovkhozy SSSR. Moscow: Nauka, 1976.

Bogoliubov, K. M. "KPSS o sovershenstvovanii upravleniia agropromyshlennym kompleksom." Voprosy istorii KPSS, no. 2 (1983), pp. 17–
38.

Bol'shevik. 1945–1952.

Brzezinski, Zbigniew, and Samuel Huntington. Political Power USA/
USSR. New York: Viking, 1965.

Carey, David W. "Soviet Agriculture: Recent Performance and Future
Plans." Soviet Economy in a New Perspective. Washington, D.C.: Government Printing Office, 1976.

Chigrinov, G. A. "Meropriiatiia partii po razvitiiu sel'skokhoziaistvennogo proizvodstva v predvoennye gody." Voprosy istorii KPSS, no. 1
(1962), pp. 127–41.

Chistiakov, V. B. "Deiatel'nost' partii po podgotovke spetsialistov
sel'skogo khoziaistva i rukovodiashchikh kadrov kolhozov RSFSR v
pervy poslevoennye gody (1946–1950 gg.)." Abstract, candidate dissertation, G. V. Plekhanov Institute of Economics, Moscow, 1976.

Chotiner, Barbara Ann. "The Role of the Apparatchiks in Agriculture
since Stalin." Paper presented at the Annual Meeting of the American
Association for the Advancement of Slavic Studies, New Haven, Conn.,
1979.

Cohen, Stephen F. Bukharin and the Bolshevik Revolution. New York:
Knopf, 1973.

Conyngham, William J. Industrial Management in the Soviet Union. Stanford: Hoover Institution Press, 1973.

———.The Modernization of Soviet Industrial Management. New York:
Cambridge University Press, 1982.

Danilov, P. P. "Bor'ba kommunisticheskoi partii sovetskogo soiuza za vypolenenie chetvertogo piatiletnego plana v oblasti promyshlennosti." Candidate dissertation, Leningrad State University, 1972.

Denisov, Iu. P. "Kadry predsedatelei kolkhozov v 1950–1968 gg." *Istorii SSSR* 15 (1971): 38–57.

Deputaty Verkhovnogo Soveta SSSR. Moscow: Izdatel'stvo Izvestiia, 1959, 1962, 1966.

Directory of Soviet Officials. Washington, D.C.: Government Printing Office, 1955.

Direktivy KPSS i Sovetskogo pravitel'stva po khoziaistvennym voprosam. Vol. 3, *1946–1952 gody.* Moscow: Politicheskoi Literatury, 1958.

Dmitriev, S. S., et al., eds. *Leningradskaia organizatsiia KPSS v tsifrakh, 1917–1973.* Leningrad: Lenizdat, 1974.

Dolgov, V. S. "Razukrupnenie kolkhozov v pervye poslevoennye gody (1945–1950 gg.)." In *Problemy otechestvennoi istorii*, chast' 2, ed. A. M. Anfimov. Moscow: Institut Istorii SSSR, 1973.

Donchenko, V. N. "Demobilizatsiia sovetskoi armii i reshenie problemy kadrov v pervye poslevoennye gody." *Istoriia SSSR*, no. 3 (May–June 1970), pp. 96–102.

———. "Perestroika riadov VKP(b) v period perekhoda SSSR ot voiny k miru (1945–1948 gody)." Candidate dissertation, Moscow State University, 1972.

Dubonosov, D. I. "Osveshchenie v istoriko-partiinoi literature deiatel'-nosti KPSS po vosstanovleniiu i razvitiiu narodnogo khoziaistva (1945–1950 gg.)." In *Nekotorye voprosy partiinogo i sovetskogo stroitel'stva*, ed. V. I. Ivanov et al. Rostov-on-Don: Rostov Pedagogical Institute, 1969.

———. *Deiatel'nost' kommunisticheskoi partii po vosstanovleniiu i razvitiiu sel'skogo khoziaistva (1945–1950 gg.).* Rostov-on-Don: Rostov Pedagogical Institute, 1970.

———. "Organizatorskaia i politicheskaia rabota kommunisticheskoi partii po vosstanovleniiu i razvitiiu narodogo khoziaistva v poslevoennyi period (1946–1950 gg.)." Doctoral dissertation, Rostov Pedagogical Institute, 1972.

Dunham, Vera S. "Comrade Chameleon: The Changing Image of the Party Official in Soviet Literature after Stalin." Unpublished manuscript, n.p., n.d.

———. *In Stalin's Time.* New York: Cambridge University Press, 1976.

———. "Rural Management." Unpublished manuscript, n.p., n.d.

Dunmore, Timothy. *The Stalinist Command Economy: The Soviet State Apparatus and Economic Policy, 1945–53.* New York: St. Martin's Press, 1980.

Egrova, A. V., ed. *Kalininskaia oblastnaia organizatsiia KPSS v tsifrakh, 1917–1977 gg.* Moscow: Moskovskii Rabochii, 1979.

Ekonomika sel'skogo khoziaistva. 1982–1985.

Emel'ianov, A. M. *Kompleksnaia programma razvitiia sel'skogo khoziaistvo v deistvii.* 2d ed. Moscow: Ekonomika, 1980.

Fainsod, Merle. *Smolensk under Soviet Rule*. New York: Vintage, 1958.
——. *How Russia Is Ruled*. Rev. and enl. ed. Cambridge: Harvard University Press, 1967.
Fischer, George. *The Soviet System and Modern Society*. New York: Atherton, 1968.
Fitzpatrick, Sheila. "Postwar Soviet Society: The 'Return to Normalcy,' 1944–1953." In *The Impact of World War II on the Soviet Union*, ed. Susan J. Linz. Totowa, N.J.: Rowman & Allanheld, 1985.
Fried, Robert. *The Italian Prefects: A Study in Administrative Politics*. New Haven: Yale University Press, 1963.
Frolov, D. F. *Edinstvo tyla i fronta*. Saratov: Saratovskoe Knizhnoe Izdatel'stvo, 1961.
Gaevskaia, V. "Analiz chislennosti i sostava rukovodiashchikh rabotnikov na sel'skokhoziaistvennykh predpriiatiiakh." *Vestnik statistiki*, 2d ser., no. 6 (1983), pp. 14–18.
Gladkii, A. D., I. D. Kishko, and M. M. Marusin. "K voprosy ob obespechennosti sela kadrami srednego zvena." In *Problemy sotsial'no-ekonomicheskogo razvitiia sela v usloviiakh zrelogo sotsializma*, ed. V. G. Ignatov. Rostov-on-Don: Rostov Pedagogical Institute, 1975.
Granick, David. *Management of the Industrial Firm in the USSR*. New York: Columbia University Press, 1954.
Grishchin, N. Ia., et al. *Obshchestvenno-politicheskaia zhizn' sovetskoi sibirskoi derevni*. Novosibirsk: Nauka, 1974.
Gustafson, Thane. *Reform in Soviet Politics*. New York: Cambridge University Press, 1981.
Gutin, M. L. "Vosstanovlenie partiinykh organizatsii na osvobozhdennoi territorii v gody Velikoi Otechestvennoi voiny." *Voprosy istorii KPSS*, no. 7 (1974), p. 82.
Hahn, Werner C. *Postwar Soviet Politics*. Ithaca: Cornell University Press, 1982.
Hall, Richard H. *Organizations: Structure and Process*. 2d ed. Englewood Cliffs, N.J.: Prentice-Hall, 1977.
Hodnett, Grey. *Leadership in the Soviet National Republics: A Quantitative Study of Recruitment Policy*. Oaksville, Ont.: Mosaic, 1978.
Hough, Jerry F. "The Soviet Concept of the Relationship between the Lower Party Organs and the State Administration." *Slavic Review* 24 (June 1965): 215–40.
——. *The Soviet Prefects*. Cambridge: Harvard University Press, 1969.
——. "The Changing Nature of the Kolkhoz Chairman." In *The Soviet Rural Community*, ed. James R. Millar. Urbana: University of Illinois Press, 1971.
——. "Changes in Soviet Elite Composition." In *Russia at the Crossroads*, ed. Seweryn Bialer and Thane Gustafson. Boston: George Allen & Unwin, 1982.
Huntington, Samuel P. "Social and Institutional Dynamics of One-Party

Systems." In *Authoritarian Politics in Modern Society*, ed. Samuel P. Huntington and Clement C. Moore. New York: Basic Books, 1970.

Iarobkov, V. V. "Partiino-politicheskaia rabota v zheleznodorozhnykh voiskakh v iiune-avguste 1944 g." In *Iz istorii partiinykh organizatsii severo-zapada RSFSR (1941–1945 gg.)*, ed. N. N. Shushkin et al. Petrozavodsk: Petrozavodsk State University, 1976.

Istoriia Velikoi Otechestvennoi voiny Sovetskogo Soiuza, 1941–1945. Vol. 5. Moscow: Voennoe Izdatel'stvo Ministerstva Oborony Soiuza SSR, 1963.

Ivanov, N. S. "Chislennost' i sostav krest'ianstva tsentral'nykh oblastei nechernozemnoi zony RSFSR (1951–1958 gg.)." In *Problemy istorii sovetskogo krest'ianstva*, ed. M. P. Kim. Moscow: Nauka, 1981.

Jacobs, Everett. "Soviet Agricultural Management and Planning and the 1982 Administrative Reforms." In *The Soviet Rural Economy*, ed. Robert C. Stuart. Totowa, N.J.: Rowman & Allanheld, 1984.

Johnson, D. Gale, and Karen McConnell Brooks. *Prospects for Soviet Agriculture in the 1980s*. Bloomington: Indiana University Press, 1983.

Joravsky, David. *The Lysenko Affair*. Cambridge: Harvard University Press, 1970.

Kadry sel'skogo khoziaistva. 1975–1985.

Kahan, Arcadius. "The Problems of the 'Agrarian Industrial Complexes' in the Soviet Union." In *Economic Development in the Soviet Union and Eastern Europe*, ed. Zbigniew M. Fallenbuchl, vol. 2. New York: Praeger, 1976.

Kalininskaia oblastnaia organizatsiia KPSS v tsifrakh. Moscow: Moskovskii Rabochii, 1979.

Kaplan, Cynthia S. "The Role of the Communist Party of the Soviet Union in the Implementation of Industrial and Agrarian Policy: Leningrad, 1946–1953." Ph.D. dissertation, Columbia University, 1981.

———. "The Communist Party of the Soviet Union and Local Policy Implementation." *Journal of Politics* 45 (1983): 2–27.

———. "The Impact of World War II on the Party." In *The Impact of World War II on the Soviet Union*, ed. Susan J. Linz. Totowa, N.J.: Rowman & Allanheld, 1985.

Karamelev, A. N. "Dvizhenie tridtsatitysiachnikov i ukreplenie kolkhozov." *Voprosy istorii KPSS*, no. 1 (1962), pp. 115–26.

Khavin, A. F. "Novyi moguchii pod'em tiazheloi promyshlennosti SSSR v 1946–1950 gg." *Istoriia SSSR*, no. 1 (1963), pp. 22–47.

Khliupin, V. I. "Rol' mestnykh Sovetov deputatov trudiashchikhsia v vosstanovlenii i razvitii promyshlennosti i sel'skogo khoziaistva v poslevoennyi period (1945–1953 gg.)." In *Iz istorii deiatel'nosti sovetov*, ed. S. F. Naida. Moscow: Mysl', 1966.

Khlusov, M. I. and S. Seniavskii. "Industrial'nye kadry SSSR v 1946–1955 godakh." *Voprosy istorii*, no. 10 (1965), pp. 29–45.

———. *Razvitie sovetskoi industrii, 1946–1958*. Moscow: Nauka, 1977.

Khristoforov, N. V., ed. *Penzenskaia partiinaia organizatsiia v gody Velikoi Otechestvennoi voiny (1941–1945 gg.).* Saratov: Privolzhskoe Knizhnoe Izdatel'stvo, 1964.

Kolosov, A., and U. Zhukovin, eds. *Opyt Tselinskogo raikoma partii (Pis'ma o sel'skom raikome).* Astrakhan: Volga, 1948.

Kommunist. 1965–1985.

Konotop, N. I. "Iz opyta raboty sel'skokhoziaistvennykh otdelov gorkomov, raikomov KPSS." *Voprosy istorii KPSS,* no. 6 (1983), pp. 3–15.

KPSS v rezoliutsiiakh i resheniiakh s"ezdov, konferentsii i plenumov TsK. Vol. 6, 1941–1954. 8th ed. Moscow: Politicheskoi Literatury, 1971.

"KPSS v tsifrakh." *Kommunist,* no. 15 (October 1967), pp. 89–103.

"KPSS v tsifrakh." *Partiinaia zhizn',* no. 14 (July 1973), pp. 9–26.

"KPSS v tsifrakh." *Partiinaia zhizn',* no. 21 (November 1977), pp. 20–43.

Krasnov, A. V., et al., eds. *Bor'ba partii i rabochego klassa za vosstanovlenie i razvitie narodnogo khoziaistva SSSR (1943–1950 gg.).* Moscow: Mysl', 1978.

Krasnov, N. A. *Partiinye mobilizatsii na front v gody Velikoi Otechestvennoi voinu.* Moscow: Izdatel'stvo Moskovskogo Universiteta, 1978.

Kriulenko, I. M., et al., eds. *Rostovskaia oblastnaia organizatsiia KPSS v tsifrakh, 1917–1975.* Rostov-on-Don: Rostovskoe Knizhnoe Izdatel'stvo, 1976.

Kruglova, L. N. "Deiatel'nost' leningradskoi partiinoi organizatsii po ukrepleniiu raidov partii i marksistko-leninskomy proveshcheniiu kommunistov v pervoi poslevoennyi piatiletke (1946–1950 gg.)." Candidate dissertation, Leningrad State University, 1971.

Kurbatova, P. I. *Smolenskaia partiinaia organizatsiia v gody Velikoi Otechestvennoi voiny.* Smolensk: Smolenskoe Knizhnoe Izdatel'stvo, 1958.

Kurtynin, M. S. *Pokoleniia udarnikov.* Leningrad: Leninzdat, 1963.

Kutuzov, V. A. "Nekotorye voprosy partiinogo stroitel'stva v Leningradskoi organizatsii v pervye poslevoennye gody (1946–1948 gg.)." *Uchenie zapiski 1* (Institut istorii partii Leningradskogo Obkoma KPSS) (1970).

Laird, Roy D. "Khrushchev's Administrative Reforms in Agriculture: An Appraisal." In *Soviet and East European Agriculture,* ed. Jerzy F. Karcz. Berkeley: University of California Press, 1967.

———. "The Politics of Soviet Agriculture." In *Soviet Agricultural and Peasant Affairs,* ed. Roy D. Laird. Lawrence: University of Kansas Press, 1968.

Leningrad: Entsiklopedicheskii sprovochnik. Moscow and Leningrad: Bol'shaia Sovetskaia Entsiklopediia, 1957.

Leningradskaia pravda. 1946–1953.

Leningradtsy—geroi sotsialisticheskogo truda. Leningrad: Lenizdat, 1967.

Leninskaia agrarnaia politika KPSS: Sbornik vazhneishikh dokumentov (mart 1965 g.–iiul' 1978 g.). Moscow: Politicheskoi Literatury, 1978.

Leninskaia agrarnaia politika KPSS: Sbornik vazhneishikh dokumentov (avgust 1978 g.–avgust 1982 g.). Moscow: Politicheskoi Literatury, 1983.

Lewin, Moshe. *Russian Peasants and Soviet Power.* Trans. Irene Nove with assistance of John Biggart. Evanston: Northwestern University Press, 1968.

Lieberman, Sanford R. "The Evacuation of Industry in the Soviet Union during World War II." *Soviet Studies* 35 (January 1983): 90–102.

Litvin, Valentin. "Agro-Industrial Complexes: Recent Structural Reform in the Rural Economy of the USSR." In *The Soviet Rural Economy,* ed. Robert C. Stuart. Totowa, N.J.: Rowman & Allanheld, 1984.

Lokshin, E. Iu. *Promyshlennost' SSSR: Ocherk istorii, 1940–1963.* Moscow: Mysl', 1964.

McCauley, Martin. *Khrushchev and the Development of Soviet Agriculture.* New York: Holmes & Meier, 1976.

Manning, Roberta. "The Collective Farm Peasantry and the Local Administration: Peasant Letters of Complaint in Belyi Raion in 1937." Paper presented at the National Seminar for the Study of Russian Society in the Twentieth Century, Philadelphia, n.d.

Materialy XXVI s"ezda KPSS. Moscow: Politicheskoi Literatury, 1981.

Medvedev, Zhores A. *The Rise and Fall of T. D. Lysenko.* Trans. I. Michael Lerner. Garden City, N.Y.: Anchor, Doubleday, 1971.

Medynskii, Grigorii. "Mar'ia." Zvezda, no. 3 (March 1949), pp. 3–31; no. 4 (April 1949), pp. 3–41; no. 5 (May 1949), pp. 3–72; no. 6 (June 1949), pp. 21–85.

Merton, Robert K. *Social Theory and Social Structure.* Enl. ed. New York: Free Press, 1968.

Meyer, Alfred. *The Soviet Political System.* New York: Random House, 1965.

Millar, James R. "Mass Collectivization and the Contribution of Soviet Agriculture to the First Five-Year Plan," *Slavic Review* 31 (1974): 750–66.

———. "Post-Stalin Agriculture and Its Future." In *The Soviet Union since Stalin,* ed. Stephen F. Cohen, Alexander Rabinowitch, and Robert Sharlet. Bloomington: Indiana University Press, 1980.

———. *The ABCs of Soviet Socialism.* Urbana: University of Illinois Press, 1981.

Miller, Robert F. *100,000 Tractors.* Cambridge: Harvard University Press, 1970.

———. "The Politics of Policy Implementation in the USSR: Soviet Politics on Agricultural Integration under Brezhnev." *Soviet Studies* 32 (1980): 171–94.

Mitrofanova, A. V. *Rabochii klass SSSR v gody Velikoi Otechestvennoi voiny.* Moscow: Nauka, 1971.

Mogilevskii, S. G. "Partiino-organizatsionnaia rabota na sele v gody che-
tvertoi piatiletki (1946–1950 gg.) (Na materialakh partiinykh organi-
zatsii Rostovskoi oblasti, Krasnodarskogo i Stavropol'skogo kraev)."
Candidate dissertation, Rostov State University, 1972.
Molot. 1946–1952.
Moore, Barrington, Jr. *Terror and Progress USSR.* New York: Harper
Torchbooks, 1954.
Narodnoe khoziaistvo RSFSR za 60 let. Moscow: Statistika, 1977.
Narodnoe khoziaistvo SSSR. Moscow: Finansy i Statistika, 1965, 1969,
1974, 1980, 1982.
Narodnoe khoziaistvo SSSR, 1922–1982. Moscow: Finansy i Statistika,
1982.
Narodnoe khoziaistvo SSSR v 1959 godu. Moscow: Gosudarstvennoe Sta-
tisticheskoe Izdatel'stvo, 1960.
Narodnoe khoziaistvo SSSR v 1960 godu. St. ezhegodnik. Moscow: Gos-
statizdat, 1961.
Narodnoe khoziaistvo SSSR v 1980 g. Moscow: Finansy i Statistika, 1981.
Naumova, A. G. *Permskaia partiinaia organizatsiia v gody Velikoi Ote-
chestvennoi voiny (1941–1945 gg.)* Perm: Permskoe Knizhnoe Izdatel'-
stvo, 1960.
Nechiporenko, V. S. *Partiinye organizatsii mezhkhoziaistvennykh i agro-
promyshlennykh formirovanii.* Moscow: Mysl', 1981.
Nikolaeva, Galina. "Zhatva." *Znamia,* no. 5 (May 1950), pp. 10–131; no.
6 (June 1950), pp. 28–104; no. 7 (July 1950), pp. 7–96.
——. "Povest' o direktore MTS i glavnom agronome." *Znamia,* no. 9
(September 1954), pp. 9–62.
Nove, Alec. *An Economic History of the USSR.* Baltimore: Penguin, 1969.
——and James R. Millar. "Was Stalin Really Necessary? A Debate on
Collectivization." *Problems of Communism* 25 (July–August 1976): 49–
66.
Ocherki istorii Iaroslavskoi organizatsii KPSS. Iaroslavl: Verkhne-Volzh-
skoe Knizhnoe Izdatel'stvo, 1967.
Ocherki istorii Kuibyshevskoi organizatsii KPSS. Kuibyshev: Kuibyshev-
skoe Knizhnoe Izdatel'stvo, 1967.
Ocherki istorii Moskovskoi organizatsii KPSS (1883–1965 gg.). Moscow:
Moskovskii Rabochii, 1966.
Ovechkin, V. V. *Izbrannoe povesti, rasskazy, ocherki.* Kursk: Kurskoe
Khnizhnoe Izdatel'stvo, 1955.
Partiinaia zhizn'. 1946–1948, 1980–1985.
Partiinoe stroitel'stvo. 1942–1946.
Petrov, Iu. P. *Partiinoe stroitel'stvo v sovetskoi armii i flote (1918–1961
gg.).* Moscow: Voennoe Izdatel'stvo Ministerstva Oborony SSSR, 1964.
Pravda. 1945–1953.
Prikhod'ko, Iu. A. *Vosstanovlenie industrii, 1942–50.* Moscow: Mysl',
1973.

"Prodovol'stvennaia programma SSSR na period do 1990 goda i mery po ee realizatsii: Materialy maiskogo Plenuma TsK KPSS, 1982 goda." *Partiinaia zhizn'*, no. 12 (1982).

Propaganda i agitatsiia. 1946–1953.

Razumov, E. Z. "XXVI s"ezdu KPSS i nekotorye voprosy kadrovoi politiki." *Voprosy istorii KPSS*, no. 8 (1981), pp. 3–19.

Resheniia partii i pravitel'stva po khoziaistvennym voprosam (1917– 1967 gg.). Vol. 2, *1929–1940 gody.* Moscow: Politicheskoi Literatury, 1967.

Resheniia partii i pravitel'stva po khoziaistvennym voprosam (1917– 1967 gg.). Vol. 3, *1941–1952 gody.* Moscow: Politicheskoi Literatury, 1968.

Rezvanov, V. M., ed. *Organizatorskaia i politicheskaia rabota partii na sele: Mezhdu XIX i XXI s"ezdami KPSS.* Rostov-on-Don: Izdatel'stvo Rostovskogo Universiteta, 1966.

Rigby, T. H. *Communist Party Membership in the U.S.S.R., 1917–1967.* Princeton: Princeton University Press, 1968.

———. "Politics in the Mono-Organizational Society." In *Authoritarian Politics in Communist Europe*, ed. Andrew C. Janos. Berkeley: Institute of International Studies, University of California, 1976.

———. "The Soviet Regional Leadership: The Brezhnev Generation." *Slavic Review* 37 (1978): 1–24.

Rostovskaia oblastnaia organizatsiia KPSS v tsifrakh, 1917–1975. Rostov-on-Don: Rostovskoe Knizhnoe Izdatel'stvo, 1976.

Saburov, M. Z. "Directives of the 19th Party Congress for the Fifth Five-Year Plan of Development in the USSR, 1951–1955." *Pravda*, October 12, 1952. Reprinted in *Current Digest of Soviet Policies*, ed. Leo Gruliow, vol. 1. New York: Praeger, 1953.

Schoonover, David M. "Soviet Agricultural Policies." In *Soviet Economy in a Time of Change.* Washington, D.C.: Government Printing Office, 1979.

Sel'skaia zhizn'. 1981–1986.

Sel'skoe khoziaistvo SSSR: St. sb. Moscow: Gosstatizdat, 1960.

Sel'skoe khoziaistvo SSSR: St. sb. Moscow: Statistika, 1971.

Seniavskii, S. L. "Rabochii klass SSSR." *Voprosy istorii*, no. 2 (1969), pp. 3–18.

Sharova, P. N. "Ukreplenie sel'skikh partiinykh organizatsii v 1950–1960 gg." In *Razvitie sel'skogo khoziaistva SSSR v poslevoennye gody (1946–1970 gg.)*, ed. I. M. Volkov. Moscow: Nauka, 1972.

Shatik, V. K. "Deiatel'nost' KPB po ukrepleniiu sostava predsedatelei kolkhozov respubliki v piatoi piatiletke (1950–1955 gg.)." In *Deiatel'- nost' kompartii Belorusii v period sotsialisticheskogo kommunisticheskogo stroitel'stva*, ed. V. M. Sikorskii, Minsk: BGU, 1969.

Shushkin, N. N. *Vo imia pobedy.* Petrozavodsk: Kareliia, 1970.

Siniazhnikov, M. L., ed. *Ocherki istorii Kostromskoi organizatsii KPSS.* Iaroslavl: Vernkhna-Volzhskoe Knizhnoe Izdatel'stvo, 1967.

Slepov, L. "Stalinskaia programma pod'ema partiino-politicheskoi raboty (K piatnadtsatiletiiu doklada I. V. Stalina na febral'sko-martovskom Plenume TsK VKP[b] v 1937 godu)." *Bol'shevik*, no. 3 (February 1952), pp. 21–34.

———. *Mestnye partiinye organy*. Moscow: Vysshei Partiinoi Shkole pri TsK KPSS, 1954.

Smirnov, A. V. "Rabochie kadry tiazhelogo mashinostroeniia SSSR v 1946–1958 gg." *Istoricheskie zapiski* 71 (1962): 3–24.

Sonin, M. Ia. *Vosproizvodstvo rabochei sily v SSSR i balans truda*. Moscow: Gosplanizdat, 1959.

Spravochnik partiinogo rabotnika. Vol. 21. Moscow: Politicheskoi Literatury, 1981.

Stalin, I. V. "Ekonomicheskie problemy sotsializma v SSSR." In *Works of Joseph Stalin*, vol. 3, *1946–1953*, ed. Robert H. McNeal. Stanford: Hoover Institute on War, Revolution, and Peace, 1967.

Stepanov, A. M. "Partiino-organizatsionnaia rabota kommunisticheskoi partii v gody chetvertoi piatiletki." Candidate dissertation, Rostov State University, 1971.

Stepanov, S. V. *Za krutoi pod'em sel'skogo khoziaistva: Iz opyta raboty partiinykh organizatsii Leningradskoi oblasti (1953–1960gg.)*. Leningrad: Lenizdat, 1961.

Stinchcombe, Arthur L. *Constructing Social Theories*. New York: Harcourt, Brace & World, 1968.

Strana sovetov za 50 let: Sbornik statisticheskikh materialov. Moscow: Statistika, 1967.

Stremilov, V. V. "Leningradskaia partiinaia organizatsiia v period blokady goroda (1941–1943 gg.)." *Voprosy istorii KPSS*, no. 5 (1959), pp. 101–21.

Sudarikov, N. "Berezhno otonit'sia i kadram presedatelei." *Sotsialisticheskaia zakonnost'*, no. 12 (December 1947), pp. 4–6.

Tiazhel'nikov, E. M., ed. *Ocherki istorii Cheliabinskoi oblastnoi partiinoi organizatsii*. Cheliabinsk: Iuzhno-Ural'skoe Knizhnoe Izdatel'stvo, 1967.

Tiurina, A. P. "Ukreplenie kolkhozov i MTS kadrami rukovoditelei i spetsialistov (1946–1958 gg.)." In *Razvitie sel'skogo khoziaistva SSSR v poslevoennye gody (1946–1970 gg.)*, ed. I. M. Volkov. Moscow: Nauka, 1972.

———. *Formirovanie kadrov spetsialistov i organizatorov kolkhoznogo proizvodstva, 1946–1958 gg*. Moscow: Nauka, 1973.

Trud v SSSR. Moscow: Statistika, 1968.

Tucker, Robert C. "On Revolutionary Mass-Movement Regimes." In *The Soviet Political Mind*, ed. Robert C. Tucker. Rev. ed. New York: Norton, 1971.

Ul'ianov, L. N. *Trudovoi podvig rabochego klassa i krest'ianstvo Sibiri, 1945–1953 gg*. Tomsk: Izdatel'stvo Tomskogo Universiteta, 1979.

Utenkov, A. Ia. Bor'ba KPSS za vosstanovlenie narodnogo khoziaistva i dal'neishee razvitie sotsialisticheskogo obschchestva, 1946–1955 gg. Moscow: Izdatel'stvo Vysshaia Shkola, 1974.

Vasil'ev, Iu. A. Sibirskii arsenal, 1941–1945. Sverdlovsk: Sredne Ural'skoe Knizhnoe Izdatel'stvo, 1965.

Verbitskaia, O. M. "Izmeneniia chislennosti sostava kolkhoznogo krest'ianstva RSFSR v pervye poslevoennye gody (1946–1950)." Istoriia SSSR, no. 5 (September–October 1980), pp. 124–38.

———. "Izmenenie chislennost' kolkhoznogo krest'ianstva RSFSR v gody chetvertoi piatiletki." In Problemy istorii sovetskogo krest'ianstva: Sb. st., ed. M. P. Kim. Moscow: Nauka, 1981.

Vinogradov, I. I. Politotdely MTS i sovkhozov v gody Velikoi Otechestvennoi voiny (1941–1943 gg.). Leningrad: Izdatel'stvo Leningradskogo Universiteta, 1976.

Virta, Nikolai. "Khleb nash nasushchnyi." Zvezda, no. 6 (1947), pp. 3–49.

Volkov, I. M. "Kolkhoznaia derevnia v pervyi poslevoennyi god." Voprosy istorii, no. 1 (1966), pp. 15–32.

———. "Ukreplenie material'no-tekhnicheskoi bazy sel'sko-khoziaistva v pervye poslevoennye gody (1946–1950)." Vestnik Moskovskogo Universiteta, no. 6 (1968), pp. 3–13.

———. "Kolkhoznoe krest'ianstvo SSSR v pervye poslevoennye gody (1946–1950 gg.)." Voprosy istorii, no. 6 (1970), pp. 3–19.

———. Trudovoi podvig sovetskogo krest'ianstva v poslevoennye gody: Kolkhozy SSSR v 1946–1950 godakh. Moscow: Mysl', 1972.

———. et al., eds. Sovetskaia derevnia v pervye poslevoennye gody, 1946–1950. Moscow: Nauka, 1978.

Voprosy organizatsionno-partiinoi raboty KPSS: Sbornik dokumentov. 3d enl. ed. Moscow: Politcheskoi Literatury, 1981.

XVIII s"ezd vsesoiuznyi kommunisticheskoi partii (b), 10–12 marta 1939 g.: Stenograficheskii otchet. Moscow: Politicheskoi Literatury, 1939.

Vosstanovlenie narodnogo khoziaistva SSSR razvitie sotsialisticheskoi. Vol. 6 of Istoriia sotsialisticheskoi ekonomiki SSSR. Moscow: Nauka, 1980.

Voznesensky, Nikolai A. The Economy of the USSR during World War II. Washington, D.C.: Public Affairs Press, 1948.

Vyltsan, M. A. Sovetskaia derevnia nakanune Velikoi Otechestvennoi voiny. Moscow: Politizdat, 1970.

———. Vosstanovlenie i razvitie material'no tekhnicheskoi baza kolkhoznogo stroia (1945–1958). Moscow: Mysl', 1976.

———. Zavershaiushchii etap sozdaniia kolkhoznogo stroia (1935–1937 gg.). Moscow: Nauka, 1978.

Vysshee obrazovanie v SSSR Stat. sb. Moscow: Gosstatizdat TsSU SSSR, 1961.

Zaleski, Eugene. Planning for Economic Growth in the Soviet Union,

1918–1932. Trans. and ed. Marie-Christine MacAndrew and G. Warren Nutter. Chapel Hill: University of North Carolina Press, 1971.

———. *Stalinist Planning for Economic Growth, 1933–1952.* Trans. and ed. Marie-Christine MacAndrew and John H. Moore. Chapel Hill: University of North Carolina Press, 1980.

Zelenin, I. E. *Sovkhozy SSSR, 1941–1950.* Moscow: Nauka, 1969.

———. *Obshchestvenno-politicheskaia zhizn' sovetskoi derevni, 1946–1958 gg.* Moscow: Nauka, 1978.

Zelenkov, I. A. "Deiatel'nost' Moskovskoi partiinoi organizatsii po vosstanovlenniiu i razvitiiu sotsialisticheskogo narodnogo khoziaistva (1945–1952 gg.)." Candidate dissertation, Akademiia Obshchestvennykh Nauk pri TsK KPSS, 1965.

Index